# FASHION STUDIES

**Dress, Body, Culture**

**Series Editor: Joanne B. Eicher,** *Regents' Professor, University of Minnesota*

Advisory Board:

Books in this provocative series seek to articulate the connections between culture and dress, which is defined here in its broadest possible sense as any modification or supplement to the body. Interdisciplinary in approach, the series highlights the dialogue between identity and dress, cosmetics, coiffure and body alterations as manifested in practices as varied as plastic surgery, tattooing, and ritual scarification. The series aims, in particular, to analyze the meaning of dress in relation to popular culture and gender issues and will include works grounded in anthropology, sociology, history, art history, literature, and folklore.

ISSN: 1360-466X

*Previously published in the Series*

**Helen Bradley Foster,** *"New Raiments of Self": African American Clothing in the Antebellum South*
**Claudine Griggs,** *S/he: Changing Sex and Changing Clothes*
**Michaele Thurgood Haynes,** *Dressing Up Debutantes: Pageantry and Glitz in Texas*
**Anne Brydon and Sandra Niessen,** *Consuming Fashion: Adorning the Transnational Body*
**Dani Cavallaro and Alexandra Warwick,** *Fashioning the Frame: Boundaries, Dress and the Body*
**Judith Perani and Norma H. Wolff,** *Cloth, Dress and Art Patronage in Africa*
**Linda B. Arthur,** *Religion, Dress and the Body*
**Paul Jobling,** *Fashion Spreads: Word and Image in Fashion Photography*
**Fadwa El Guindi,** *Veil: Modesty, Privacy and Resistance*
**Thomas S. Abler,** *Hinterland Warriors and Military Dress: European Empires and Exotic Uniforms*
**Linda Welters,** *Folk Dress in Europe and Anatolia: Beliefs about Protection and Fertility*

# FASHION STUDIES

Research Methods, Sites and Practices

Edited by
**Heike Jenss**

Bloomsbury Academic
An imprint of Bloomsbury Publishing Plc

B L O O M S B U R Y
LONDON · OXFORD · NEW YORK · NEW DELHI · SYDNEY

**Bloomsbury Academic**

An imprint of Bloomsbury Publishing Plc

50 Bedford Square
London
WC1B 3DP
UK

1385 Broadway
New York
NY 10018
USA

**www.bloomsbury.com**

**BLOOMSBURY and the Diana logo are trademarks of
Bloomsbury Publishing Plc**

First published 2016

© Heike Jenss, 2016

**British Library Cataloguing-in-Publication Data**
A catalogue record for this book is available from the British Library.

ISBN: HB: 978-1-4725-8317-8
PB: 978-1-4725-8316-1
ePDF: 978-1-4725-8318-5
ePub: 978-1-4725-8319-2

**Library of Congress Cataloging-in-Publication Data**
Names: Jenss, Heike author.
Title: Fashion studies: research methods, sites, and practices / Heike Jenss.
Description: London; New York : Bloomsbury Academic, an imprint of
Bloomsbury Publishing, Plc, [2016] | Series: Dress, body, culture |
Includes bibliographical references and index.
Identifiers: LCCN 2015025893| ISBN 9781472583178 (hardback) |
ISBN 9781472583161 (pbk.) | ISBN 9781472583185 (ePDF) |
ISBN 9781472583192 (ePub)
Subjects: LCSH: Fashion–Social aspects. | Clothing and dress–Social aspects. |
Fashion–Research. | Clothing and dress–Research.
Classification: LCC GT525 .J46 2016 | DDC 391–dc23
LC record available at http://lccn.loc.gov/2015025893

Typeset by Deanta Global Publishing Services, Chennai, India
Printed and bound in Great Britain

# CONTENTS

# LIST OF ILLUSTRATIONS

## Tables

## Figures

# NOTES ON CONTRIBUTORS

**Christopher Breward** is the principal, Edinburgh College of Art and the vice principal, Creative Industries & Performing Arts at the University of Edinburgh. He has published widely on the cultural history of fashion, fashion and its relationship to masculinities, and fashion in a metropolitan context. Prior to his tenure at the University of Edinburgh, Christopher Breward was the head of research at the Victoria and Albert Museum, London where he cocurated exhibitions on London fashion in the 1960s and on design in postwar Britain. He is a trustee of the National Museums of Scotland, a governor of the Pasold Research Fund, an honorary fellow of the Royal College of Art, an honorary research fellow of the Victoria and Albert Museum, and a fellow of the Royal Society of Arts.

**Cheryl Buckley** is a professor in design history at Brighton University. Her research deals with the history of design in the twentieth century including fashion, ceramics, interiors, and architecture. Her publications include *Designing Modern Britain* (Reaktion 2007). She has written about fashion over many years, including: "De-humanised Females and Amazonians: Fashioning the Female Body in *Home Chat*, 1914–1918" in *Gender and History*; "On the Margins: Theorising the History and Significance of Making and Designing Clothes at Home" in the *Journal Of Design History*; and with Hilary Fawcett *Fashioning the Feminine, Representation and Women's Fashion from the fin de siècle to the Present Day* (I. B. Tauris 2002). She is currently cowriting a book with Hazel Clark on *Fashion and Everyday Life* (Bloomsbury).

**Hazel Clark** is a professor of design studies and fashion studies, and Research Chair of Fashion at Parsons School of Design, The New School. There, she initiated the curriculum in design studies and fashion studies, including the MA Fashion Studies that commenced in fall 2010. Her publications include the coedited books *Old Clothes, New Looks: Second-Hand Fashion* (Berg 2005); *The Fabric of Cultures: Fashion, Identity, and Globalization* (Routledge 2009); *Design Studies: A Reader* (Berg 2009). Her research interests include design, fashion, and cultural identity, with a particular interest in New York and East Asia; a current project, with Cheryl Buckley, focuses on fashion and everyday life in New York and London, ca. 1890–2010.

**Joanne B. Eicher**, Regents Professor Emerita, Department of Design, Housing and Apparel, University of Minnesota, specializes in cultural aspects of dress, with her primary field of research in West Africa, specifically Nigeria. As well as editor in chief for *The Encyclopedia of World Dress and Fashion*, she is the editor of the series *Dress, Body, Culture*, and *Fashion and Dress Research* (both Bloomsbury), and the associate editor of *Scribner's Encyclopedia of Clothing and Fashion* (2005). She is a coauthor of *The Visible Self* (2014, 4e), the editor of *Dress and Ethnicity* (2005), the coeditor of *Fashion Foundations: Early Writings on Dress* (2003), *Dress and Gender* (1992), *Dress and Identity* (1995), *Beads and Beadmakers* (1998) and author of *Mother, Daughter, Sister, Bride: Rituals of Womanhood* (2005), with Lisa Ling.

**Francesca Granata** is an assistant professor and director of the MA Fashion Studies program in the School of Art and Design History and Theory at Parsons School of Design, The New School. She is founder and editor of the nonprofit journal *Fashion Projects: On Art, Fashion, and Visual Culture* (fashionprojects.org). She holds a PhD from Central Saint Martins, University of the Arts London. Her research centers on the twentieth-century and contemporary visual and material culture, with a focus on fashion history and theory, gender and performance studies. She has published in *Fashion Theory, Fashion Practice,* and in the *Journal of Design History.* Her monograph *Experimental Fashion: Carnival, Performance Art, and the Grotesque Body* is forthcoming with I. B. Tauris in 2016.

**Denise Nicole Green** is an assistant professor in the Department of Fiber Science and Apparel Design and director of the Cornell Costume and Textile Collection at Cornell University. She received a PhD in sociocultural anthropology from the University of British Columbia, where she was also part of the Ethnographic Film Unit. Her ongoing ethnographic research focuses on Nuu-chah-nulth First Nations' textiles, identity, and aboriginal title to traditional territories on Vancouver Island, British Columbia, Canada. Prior to this, she earned a master of science in textiles from the University of California at Davis and a bachelor of science with honors in apparel design from Cornell University. Her research uses ethnography, video production, archival methods and curatorial practice to explore production of fashion, textiles, and visual design.

**Heike Jenss** is an assistant professor at Parsons School of Design, The New School. Located in the School of Art and Design History and Theory, she worked on the development of fashion studies at undergraduate and graduate levels and was the founding director of Parsons' MA Fashion Studies program (2009–2012). Jenss received her PhD in cultural anthropology of textiles from TU Dortmund University. Her research on themes including fashion and identity, vintage and secondhand consumption, memory and nostalgia is published in *Critical Studies in Fashion and Beauty*, *Fashion Theory*, *Design Studies: A Reader* (Berg 2009), *Berg Encyclopedia of World Dress and Fashion*, and in her books *Sixties Dress Only! Mode und Konsum in der Retro-Szene der Mods* (Campus 2007) and *Fashioning Memory: Vintage Style and Youth Culture* (Bloomsbury 2015).

**Susan B. Kaiser** is a professor of women and gender studies and textiles and clothing, and interim dean of humanities, arts, and cultural studies at the University of California at Davis. Her research and teaching bridge fashion studies and feminist cultural studies, with current interests in shifting articulations of masculinities; fashion and space/place; and possibilities for critical fashion studies through popular and political cultural discourses. She is the author of *The Social Psychology of Clothing* (1997) and *Fashion and Cultural Studies* (2012), and of about 100 articles and book chapters in the fields of textile/fashion studies, sociology, gender studies, cultural studies, popular culture, and consumer behavior. She is a fellow and past president of the International Textile and Apparel Association.

**Brent Luvaas** is an associate professor of anthropology at Drexel University. His work, on the global circulation of fashion and aesthetics, has appeared in *Cultural Anthropology*, *Visual Anthropology Review*, *Fashion Theory*, *Fashion Practice*, *Clothing Cultures*, *Asian Music*, and *The International Journal of Cultural Studies*, among other publications. His first book, *DIY Style: Fashion, Music, and Global Digital Cultures*, was published by Berg in 2012. His latest book, on street style photography and blogging, will be released by Bloomsbury in 2016. Follow the progress of his street style project at www.urbanfieldnotes.com.

**Todd E. Nicewonger** is a postdoctoral research fellow in LETStudio, an interdisciplinary research initiative in the learning sciences at the University of Gothenburg. He received his doctorate in applied anthropology from Columbia University, Teachers College, and was previously a postdoctoral fellow in fashion studies at Parsons School of Design, The New School. His research is focused generally on the anthropology of design, and specifically on the ethnographic study of making in educational and professional work settings. This includes his ongoing research on fashion design pedagogy and two new projects on sustainable architecture and experimental ethnography. In this work, he employs ethnographic and other qualitative methods, including techniques borrowed from art and design for modeling and studying the embodied practices of cultural producers.

**Christina H. Moon** is an assistant professor in the School of Art and Design History and Theory at Parsons School of Design, The New School and was the director of Parsons' Masters of Arts program in fashion studies from 2012 to 2015. She holds a PhD in anthropology from Yale University. She writes on design and labor worlds across Asia and the Americas, fashion and material culture, social memory, the ephemeral and the everyday, and ways of knowing and representing in ethnographic practice. She is currently working on a book on fast fashion with the photographer Lauren Lancaster. Her most recent publications can be found in *The Baffler, Pacific Standard Magazine, Critical Studies in Fashion and Beauty*, and *Speculation, Now: Essays and Artwork*.

**Stephanie Sadre-Orafai** is an assistant professor of anthropology and codirector of the Critical Visions Certificate Program at the University of Cincinnati. Her research focuses on transformations in contemporary US racial thinking and visual culture by ethnographically examining emerging forms of expertise, cultural and institutional practices of type production, and the intersection of race, language, and visual practices in aesthetic industries. Her essays on casting, model development, and fashion reality television have appeared in edited volumes, including *Fashion as Photograph* (I. B. Tauris 2008), *Images in Time* (Wunderkammer 2011), *Fashioning Models* (Bloomsbury 2012), and *Fashioning Crime* (I. B. Tauris 2015). She is currently working on her first book, which examines how modeling and casting agents create new articulations of mediation, visibility, and difference.

**Otto von Busch** is an associate professor for integrated design in the School of Design Strategies, Parsons School of Design, The New School in New York. Previously, he has taught at Konstfack University College of Arts, Craft and Design in Stockholm. He received his PhD from the University of Gothenburg and has a background in arts, craft, fashion design, and theory. In his research, writing and practice he explores how design and craft can be reverse engineered, hacked, and shared among many participants as a form of civic engagement, building community capabilities through collaborative craft and social activism. Publications include contributions to *Fashion Practice: The Journal of Design, Creative Practice and Industry, Craft Research*, and *Textile: The Journal of Cloth and Culture*.

**Sophie Woodward** is a lecturer in sociology at the University of Manchester and carries out research in material culture, clothing, and everyday fashion practices and feminist theory. She is the author of *Why Women Wear What They Wear* (Berg 2007), *Why Feminism Matters* (with K. Woodward, Palgrave Macmillan 2009) and *Blue Jeans: The Art of the Ordinary* (with D. Miller, University of California Press 2012); she is cofounder of the Global Denim Project and coeditor of the book *Global Denim* (Bloomsbury 2010). She is currently carrying out research into "dormant things"—things people keep in the home but are not currently using (http://projects.socialsciences.manchester.ac.uk/dormant-things).

# ACKNOWLEDGMENTS

This book has been some time in the making. The seeds were planted with the *Locating Fashion/Studies* symposium organized in 2010 alongside the commencement of the MA Fashion Studies program at Parsons School of Design, The New School. I want to express my gratitude to the scholars who participated in this initial conversation about fashion and research sites and practices, including: Christopher Breward, Cheryl Buckley, Hazel Clark, Joanne Eicher, Shelley Fox, Pascale Gatzen, Francesca Granata, Susan B. Kaiser, Christina H. Moon, Todd Nicewonger, Alexandra Palmer, Stephanie Sadre-Orafai, Valerie Steele, Otto von Busch, and Sophie Woodward. I am deeply indebted to each of the contributors to this book for their openness throughout this project, and for making thinking about fashion and research methods so engaging with their reflective and inspiring chapters.

Without the unique experience and opportunity to develop and direct the MA Fashion Studies program at Parsons, I would likely not have come to embark on this book. For the collegial and productive collaboration throughout the years and support and friendship I want to thank Hazel Clark, Research Chair of Fashion, and former dean of the School of Art and Design History and Theory, who deserves special recognition here for her work at Parsons, and for her initiative and commitment to the development of critical fashion studies as part of the school's curricular mission. I also extend my thanks to the friends and colleagues at Parsons and The New School who have shaped the MA Fashion Studies program and its scholarly community since its inception: Christina Moon, Hazel Clark, Francesca Granata, Elizabeth Morano, Rachel Lifter, Todd Nicewonger. Additionally, I wish to thank Pascale Gatzen, Marilyn Cohen, Jeffrey Lieber, David Brody, Shelley Fox, Ethan Robey, and Sarah Lawrence, dean of the School of Art and Design History and Theory, who has been an important source of advice and support. Thanks also to Rebecca Nison, Jennifer McHugh, Scott Amen, Courtney Malenius, and John Haffner Layden.

I am grateful for the generous funding I received from Parsons School of Design that enabled the organization of the *Locating Fashion/Studies* symposium and also the invaluable support of research assistants. My special thanks to Stephanie E. Herold, for her thoughtful and diligent work in helping me complete this book, including feedback on contents, proofreading, the organization of images, and many last-minute tasks around the finalization of the manuscript. My thanks go also to my former research assistants Leilah Vevaina, Corrinne Crewe, and Laura Snelgrove, who were involved in the organization of the symposium and who helped with preliminary research. For her creativity and work on the book cover design, I want to thank Cayla O'Connell.

For their considerate comments and scholarly advice at various stages of this book project I thank Rachel Lifter, Hazel Clark, Susan B. Kaiser, and Carol Tulloch, as well as the anonymous reviewers at Bloomsbury, whose comments helped shape this book. Anna Wright receives my special thanks for her excitement for and tireless belief in this book project, since I first approached her with the idea, and for her constructive comments and professional guidance. Further thanks to Joanne B. Eicher and Kathryn Earle for encouraging me to pursue this book, and especially to Hannah Crump and Ariadne Godwin for all their support, patience and for helping me to ensure that this book made the deadline.

# FOREWORD

## Christopher Breward

At the time of writing (spring 2015), the practice and culture of fashion received one of those periodic frontal attacks from an industry insider. Lidewij Edelkoort, the most celebrated proponent of trend forecasting, has engineered optimum exposure for her own brand through the publication of her manifesto "Anti_Fashion [*sic*]: Ten Reasons Why the Fashion System Is Obsolete." A call to arms, her document critiques the educational model in which—as she sees it—fashion students across the world are encouraged to believe in the delusional mirage of star designers, the catwalk show, and the luxury brand. It berates the narcissistic cult of celebrity that places individualism above community. It bemoans the loss of skill and an understanding of the value of craft that has destroyed the European textile industry, and regrets the exploitation of labor and natural resources in low-wage regions. It challenges a consumerist understanding of value, where low price and ephemeral modishness trump quality and pleasure. It ridicules the limited imaginations and historical amnesia of creatives within the industry. It dismisses the timidity and defensiveness of both the corporate face of fashion and its media reflection, damning standards of journalism and the pervasiveness of press relations. And finally, it welcomes the emergence of the new, informed antifashion consumer (increasingly, according to Edelkoort, men rather than women), emboldened by alternative networks, excited by independence and driven to seek uniqueness.

Setting aside the question of complicity (the polished messages of trend forecasters are perhaps at the root of many of these problems, and glossy consultancy has provided a dubious sheen for several global corporations whose practices put powerful industrial nations to shame), "Anti_Fashion" nevertheless captures the spirit of our times and suggests that the concept of fashion, as it has existed for the past two decades, is ripe for reconstruction. Many of its points are hard to disagree with, though any historian of fashion worth their salt would argue that such debates are not new, and that anxieties around the moral worth of fashion culture, or the ethical implications of sweated labor and global trade, are as old as the first presentation of clothes designed for form as much as for function, for extrinsic as much as for intrinsic value. That said, Edelkoort certainly gives us something to chew on, and shows us why an informed and critical apparatus for the study of historical and contemporary fashion is more important now than ever.

"Anti_Fashion" also provokes reflection on the manner in which fashion discourse has changed since the turn of the twenty-first century. While innovation and standards have seemingly atrophied in the world of fashion business, critique and commentary have blossomed in academia, cultural institutions and in the free university that constitutes the blogosphere or the worldwide web. Edelkoort (herself onetime director of the Design Academy in Eindhoven) may despair of teaching in some fashion design schools, but there is no cause to lament the vibrancy of analysis that continues to open up in the humanities and social sciences, in exhibition spaces and galleries, and indeed in many forward-thinking practice-based fashion and textile college departments for whom research and social, economic, political, technical, and aesthetic contexts are primary concerns.

So, in recognition that this is the age of the manifesto (and its debased internet form the "listicle"), and as a foreword to the excellent primer for understanding twenty-first-century fashion through critical modes of research that this volume is, it seems apposite to identify ten points for the promotion, not of an "Anti_Fashion" position, but of an informed understanding of fashion's role in historical and contemporary cultures. Manifestos are perhaps the tools of revolutionaries and dictators. They are difficult to live up to. Aphorisms have a gentler philosophical function, and it is in the latter spirit that I offer these up, inspired here by the many different sites, materials, and practices of fashion that the work in this book exemplifies:

*Fashion is made manifest in material forms. It demands study in the same way that ancient artifacts are made meaningful by archaeologists: through careful excavation.*

*Fashion has a tendency to construct its own canons. Like every cultural form these should be documented and then subjected to debate and challenge. Art historians are expert creators and destroyers of these canons, as surely as modernism follows romanticism. Like art historians, fashion scholars need to look and question.*

*Fashion is not necessarily spectacular (though it often conforms to the theory of the society of the spectacle), it can also be demotic, ordinary, mundane, routine and humble. It is the stuff of the ethnographer and the anthropologist.*

*Fashion moves in space and time. It shares in the complexity of physics and mathematics, making patterns and networks, forming mazes and constellations. Through its forms we have an opportunity to re-unite art and science and to heal the rift of the two cultures.*

*Fashion is gossip. Never underestimate the power of gossip. Semiologists are driven into ecstasies of supposition by its whispers.*

*Fashion can be about confirmation, of self and others. But it is also about anxiety, ambiguity and worry. As an aid to understanding psychological complexities it is unsurpassed.*

*Fashion studies has always thrived, as many disciplines do, by positioning itself between borders and at the periphery. Its apparent lack of respectability provided energy. Now there are many journals and conferences to serve its purposes. They give more space for multiple points of view, but the field must strive to avoid co-option and exhaustion.*

*Fashion is intensely personal, in the same way that poetry is intensely personal. It is a medium through which personal stories can be told, memories re-lived and futures foretold.*

*Fashion is so all-encompassing and encyclopedic in its terrain that it seems tailor-made for the era of big-data. The old antiquarians used it to map national customs and habits. We have the tools to put it to the service of as yet unimagined projects, of even greater scope and impact.*

*Fashion does not define. It is instead a term that demands definition.*

That final aphorism is the property of Hazel Clark, who uttered it at the *Locating Fashion/Studies* conference organized by Heike Jenss at Parsons School of Design, The New School in 2010. Many of the scholars whose work is presented in this book first came together then and their work offers an insightful series of definitions that can set out the terrain for fashion studies in the future. Ranging across the consideration of fashion and dress as material culture and everyday artifact, as embodied and located practice, and as a form of intellectual and scholarly endeavor, the following chapters present a number of exemplary case studies that will aid students of this vibrant subject, as they hone their understanding of fashion's multiple layers of meaning. Research, reflection, and good scholarship take time to perfect. Indeed, in that searching for quality and insight, for a version of "slow fashion," perhaps we can find some common ground with Edelkoort's demands for deeper engagement. Whatever our motivations, I hope you will find this book to be as inspiring and as useful a tool, for the exploration of fashion and the methods necessary for its study, as I did. I hope it will provoke many more aphorisms and encourage the next generation of fashion scholars to do good work.

# INTRODUCTION LOCATING FASHION/ STUDIES: RESEARCH METHODS, SITES AND PRACTICES

## Heike Jenss

Foregrounding methodological reflection on the exploration of fashion through material culture, ethnography, and the mixing of sources and methods through selected case studies, this book offers nuanced insights into how interdisciplinary scholars approach and make sense of fashion in its multifaceted appearances. Focusing on both fashion and its research as situated practices, this book moves from a discussion of fashion collecting in museums in London and New York to the study of fashion and dress in people's everyday lives. It includes ethnographic explorations of fashion conducted through working in the global garment industry, working in model casting agencies, making a street style blog, and observing the creative process in a fashion design school. And it offers examples of the bridging of theory and practice in fashion research, demonstrating the tailoring and fitting of methodological approaches to suit research interests as varied as the design collections of Martin Margiela in the 1990s, the fashioning of masculinities in early twenty-first-century America, or the practice-based exploration of fashion as a site of conflict. Through these wide-ranging examples, the chapters in this book illuminate together underexamined sites of fashion, including the "backstage" practices of the cultural production of fashion, as well as the possibilities and challenges that are part of the interpretive, intersubjective, and interdisciplinary practice of doing fashion research.

In recent decades the study of fashion has expanded across academic disciplines into a thriving field of scholarly investigation and is becoming further institutionalized through the founding of new courses and research concentrations at universities internationally, fostering the critical analysis of fashion in its varied and complex material and visual manifestations. In light of the rising interdisciplinary and global scope of fashion and fashion studies, there is a growing need to discuss research methods and practices that aid students and scholars in exploring the wide-ranging and multilayered forms, experiences, and meaning dimensions of fashion—from the intimate, corporeal sensations of making an appearance with the wearing of fashion and clothes, to the designing, making, mediation, or distribution of fashion in objects, images, and imaginaries.

Facing the wide scope of fashion as a global industry and as matter, practice, and dynamics that shape and change bodies and identities, figuring out one's method/s in the conducting of fashion research is anything but a straightforward process. In the context of fashion studies, this seems to be even more so the case since the field has evolved without a defined "methodological canon," as traditionally part of longer existing university disciplines, such as anthropology or art history, which along with numerous other disciplines and fields feed into research and knowledge formation in fashion studies. The *Oxford English Dictionary* (2015) implies the significance of method in the formation and identification of academic fields and disciplines, by defining "method" as a "special form of procedure or characteristic set of procedures employed . . . in an intellectual discipline or field of study as a mode of investigation and inquiry." Following such a definition, method—or more specifically the development and use of "characteristic" methods—can be understood as part of the principles, beliefs, and concepts that underlie academic disciplines or fields. As procedures, or modes of doing research, which are intertwined with ontological assumptions about the world, methods form an integral part of the constitution and learning of disciplinary and professional practices, knowledges and "positions." However, the briefness and abstractness of such a dictionary definition does not reflect much of the actual interdisciplinary and intersubjective dynamics of research and methodological practices, particularly as they have emerged in scholarly work over the last decades, which have led to the development of more fluid, multimethodological fields of scholarly inquiry—such as the field of fashion studies.

# Fashion studies: Evolving research interests and approaches

What is today referred to as the interdisciplinary field of fashion studies is an outcome of the "blurring of genres" and disciplinary approaches that emerged with the increasing "migration" of scholars across academic fields during the 1970s and 1980s, which Norman Denzin and Yvonna Lincoln describe in their historic tracing of qualitative research practices: "Humanists migrated to the social sciences, searching for new social theory, new ways to study popular culture and its local ethnographic contexts. Social scientists turned to the humanities, hoping to learn how to do complex structural and post-structural readings of social texts" (2005, 3). With such "blurring" and "methodological diaspora" (Denzin and Lincoln 2005, 3) scholars developed new methodological practices and techniques that made them akin to a bricoleur, someone who makes do by "adapting the *bricoles* of the world" (de Certeau 1984, xv; quoted in Denzin and Lincoln 2005, 4). The development of cultural studies (see Grossberg 2010) and material culture studies (see Miller 2005) are some of the achievements of such scholarly migration and methodological "do-it-yourself" practices. The impact of these two fields—along with many others—opened up new questions and modes of inquiry for the critical study of fashion and dress in the 1990s: for example, by beginning to foreground new interests in the social, cultural, and material practices and relations that are part of the consumption and production of fashion and dress (see Breward 1998; McRobbie 1998).

## Historical roots and routes

Intellectual engagements with fashion and dress have a long history that can be traced to the contemplation on fashion in philosophy and literature (for overviews see Purdy 2004; Johnson, Torntore, and Eicher 2003; Kawamura 2005; Entwistle 2000; Wilson 1985). They can also be traced to the long existing interest in documenting people's habits and manners, including dress and appearance, in etchings and engravings that would lead to the development and publication of costume books in early modernity. For example, those that became part of European's visual mapping of "world cultures," serving as visual instruments—and methods—in the creation of social, cultural, and geographic classification and hierarchies of peoples and "races," tying together assumptions based on appearance, place, and time: such as urban versus rural or civilized/modern/Western versus primitive/traditional/other (for discussions, see Taylor 2004, 4–43; Lillethun, Welters, and Eicher 2012; Kaiser 2012, 2 and 32, Gaugele 2015). Such binary modes of thinking have been at the heart of the history of fashion in euro-modernity, where fashion came to be defined as "the prevailing style of dress or behavior at any given time, with the strong implication that fashion is characterized by change" (Steele 2005, 12), which historically has been viewed to typically occur in urban European contexts (see Steele 2005, 13). In the Romance languages as well as in many Germanic languages, though interestingly not in English, the word for fashion is *mode* or *moda* derived from the Latin word *modus* for shape or manner, which is also a root of the word "modernity," associated with the fast-paced urban life in European capitals for which fashion (or *la mode*) became a symbol or metaphor (see Baudelaire 2004).

A substantial material and institutional ground for the emergence of the academic study of fashion and dress in European and Anglo-American contexts has been formed by the history of collecting historic and "exotic" items of dress, privately, for example, in sixteenth-century cabinets of curiosities or *Wunderkammern*, and later in the nineteenth and twentieth centuries' institutionalized form of museum collections. These include ethnographic collections of "other" cultures' forms of dress ("folk," regional, rural, or non-Western dress), and later also the distinct development of collections of Western costume and dress, in particular, examples of haute couture and high fashion clothing of upper class (and mostly female) provenance (for an overview on the history of dress collections, see Taylor 2004). Academically, the study of fashion and dress is further deeply informed by theories and approaches evolving in the context of the nineteenth- and early twentieth-century formation and diversification of specialized university disciplines, such as psychology, anthropology, history, economics, and sociology, with some scholars (especially among the latter two) also paying increasing attention to understanding and explaining fashion as an overarching system and social dynamic, embedded in (or driving) the rise and conditions of capitalism and the process and discourse of "modernity" (for an overview see König, Mentges and Müller 2015).

The conceptualization of fashion as a form, or rather a "natural," inherently time-bound dynamic of social distinction through change—as theorized in various ways, for example, by the sociologist Georg Simmel (2004), economist Werner Sombart (2004), and economist Thorstein Veblen (2004)—has been perhaps the most pronounced and enduring idea in the development of fashion theory in the twentieth century. The interest in fashion as a mode of social distinction and overarching dynamic driving social life, should not only be understood to center on the class-bound vertical flow of fashion, "trickling down" from the top to the lower social strata as outlined by Simmel (2004) in the early twentieth century. But further entangled with these early theories of fashion is also the emphasis on fashion in establishing gender distinctions, including the conception and marginalizing of fashion—and its research—as an essentially "female" domain or activity (see Veblen 2004 and Flügel 2004, for further discussion, also Taylor 2004, 44–65). Moreover, the concept of fashion as a material mode of articulating distinction by spearheading or adapting to what has often been described as the "rapid" change in clothing and appearance styles was, as noted above, seen as a distinctly urban-Western phenomenon—aiding in the construction of ethnic or racial distinctions ("West vs. the rest," the lack of cultural or ethnic diversity in "Western" representations of fashion history, etc.). Other disciplines, perhaps most notably anthropology, substantially contributed to this discourse by assuming and representing "other" cultures—structured by the norms and methods of classical ethnography—as "timeless," as "an 'object' to be archived" (Denzin and Lincoln 2005, 15; for further discussion, see also Fabian 1983 and 2007).

One indicator which also points to the idea of the exclusiveness of fashion to euro-modernity was the avoidance of the use of the temporality and change implying word "fashion" or "mode" in relation to non-Western (and nonurban) contexts, and instead the use of the apparently more neutral, or universal term "dress"—to describe the human practice of adorning the body (see Entwistle 2000, 42–43; also Eicher 2001 and in this book). Furthermore, as pointed out by anthropologists in the 1970s, much early ethnographic work, while otherwise so attuned to the investigation of material culture, paid only little serious attention to dress. In part, such limited consideration of dress in early ethnographic accounts is likely due to the gendering and marginalization of clothing and dress as "unworthy" or "unserious" fields of study on the part of (historically predominantly) male anthropologists. However, it also means that such ethnographies ignored or misrepresented a part of human embodiment, which—if seriously acknowledged or considered—may likely have forced perspectives on "time" and "change" into the ethnographer's gaze. Ronald Schwarz notes in an article in 1979 "that clothing is a subject about which anthropologists should have much to say yet remain mysteriously silent. . . . Descriptions of clothing are so rare in some texts of social anthropology . . . that the casual reader might easily conclude the natives go naked" (Schwarz 1979, 23; in Taylor 2002, 195). The creation of such an image or imaginary of the "other" as naked, painted through a limited and ethnocentric view on what ethnographically depicted people wore, certainly aided in the conception or euro-modern narrative of fashion as exclusively Western-urban, which has until rather recently informed much of the writing in the field of fashion studies (for a discussion, see Niessen 2003; Hansen 2004; Lillethun, Welters, and Eicher 2012; Riello and McNeil 2010, 357 ff.).

The early theorizing of fashion or dress, both in the context of sociology and anthropology, was driven by, as Joanne Entwistle puts it, an interest in overarching "why" questions, which led to the development of meta-theories around the overarching meaning or function of fashion and dress that do not consider the time- and place-bound nuances and complexities of fashion and dress as practices (Entwistle 2000, 55–57). Such "modernist" meta-theories of fashion and dress formed a backdrop for the emergence of new feminist perspectives on fashion and dress in the latter half of the twentieth century, as demonstrated in the seminal books by Elizabeth Wilson *Adorned in Dreams* (1985) or Caroline Evans and Minna Thornton's book *Women and Fashion: A New Look* (1989); these texts critique the limitations, and inherent gender bias, of early twentieth-century theories of fashion, pointing to new directions that would broaden the study of fashion and dress in the following decades.

## Formation and expansion of fashion studies

The field of fashion studies owes its formation to a variety of approaches and perspectives that inform the study of fashion and dress, including the work of philosophers, sociologists, art and design scholars, anthropologists, economists, and historians. The term "fashion studies," however, has only been used in the more recent decades in Anglo-American contexts. Much of the scholarship that today forms the foundation of fashion studies has emerged under the umbrella terms of "costume" or "dress history," in close proximity to museum work. This is reflected also in early scholarly journals, with a predominantly historic focus (*Dress, Costume* or the former German journal *Waffen and Kostümkunde*). Another important dimension of fashion studies has developed from university programs in textile and apparel studies and also from home economics and consumer studies departments (for a discussion, see Palmer 1997; Mentges 2005; Eicher and Evinson 2014). There has been a growing academic interest in fashion and dress in the 1960s, 1970s, and 1980s (here just some selected examples: Eicher and Roach 1965 and 1973; Hollander 1978; Kaiser 1985; Steele 1985; Ribeiro 1986; Roche 1989/1994), yet a shift in the labeling of these scholarly areas of research from costume history, to dress history and dress studies (in the 1990s), to fashion studies, only occurred more recently. A shift in nomenclature, in particular from "history" to "studies" reflects the broadening of interests, most notably with increasing interests in theoretical discourse, as well as in more contemporary issues and practices.

New approaches and methods for the exploration of fashion evolved with the new art history (for a discussion, see Breward 1998; Granata 2012) and also particularly within the field of cultural studies, with a group of scholars, including Dick Hebdige, John Clark, Angela McRobbie, and Paul Willis focusing on postwar youth subcultural styles in Britain. Informed by structuralism, post-structuralism, and semiotics, and drawing on the work of Roland Barthes, Antiono Gramscy, and others, Hebdige's book *Subculture: The Meaning of Style* (1979) exemplifies the approach of reading subcultural styles as forms of resistance to the dominant order. Utilizing the idea of bricolage, as theorized by Claude Levi Strauss, he shows how hegemonic meanings of clothing (such as the suit) are not fixed but can be subverted to take on new meanings, in a symbolic fit with subcultural ideologies of resistance. This work had a substantial impact on the scholarship of fashion, by highlighting questions of identity and agency, and challenging the idea of a "trickle-down" of fashion by drawing attention to the dynamics and impact of youth cultural styles (for discussions, see Evans 1997; Hodkinson 2002). Cultural studies in particular emphasized the importance of context and constructionism, to "offer knowledge that did not claim to necessarily encompass the whole world ... to stand against scientific and epistemological universalism" (Grossberg 2010, 17). The underlying belief in the approach of cultural studies is that

> human beings live in a world that is, at least in part, of their own making, and that world is constructed through practices (of many different forms of agency, including individual, and institutional, human and non-human) that build and transform the simultaneously and intimately connected discursive and nondiscursive (both material) realities. . . . To put it simply, what culture we live

in, what cultural practices we use, what cultural forms we place and insert into reality, have consequences for the way reality is organized and lived. (Grossberg 2010, 23–24)

Building on the increased "blurring of genres" and disciplines in the 1970s and 1980s and the paradigm shift toward the emphasis on contextuality and constructionism, fashion studies started to crystallize more clearly in the context of the 1990s. These studies were deeply informed by the impact of the wider social and intellectual developments in the second half of the twentieth century, including the feminist movement, civil rights, gay and lesbian rights movements—and theoretical developments, including post-structuralism, gender, queer, and postcolonial theories, working against the "fixing" of ultimate meanings of cultures, bodies, and identities (see Kaiser 2012, 11; Breward 1998). These developments, including the critical unpacking of historical ideas such as essentialist concepts of gender, race, and ethnicity, have helped to "unframe," in Susan Kaiser's words, "some of the frameworks that had previously been taken for granted as 'natural' or 'the way it should be'" (2012, 11). One of the texts clearly signaling this turn in the scholarly inquiry of fashion in the early 1990s is Elizabeth Wilson's essay "Fashion and the Postmodern Body" in *Chic Thrills*, one of the first "reader" type publications in the field (Ash and Wilson 1992). Wilson contextualizes the rising academic interest in fashion and dress with the discourse around postmodernity and the "end of grand narratives": the breakdown of "totalizing" narratives and "overarching theories" underpinning the idea of Western modernity and "civilization" from the eighteenth century onward, in which fashion and its idea of continuous change had been conceptualized as a sign of the "progress" and "modernity" of the West and its superiority and distinctiveness from "the rest" (Wilson 1992, 6–7).

Along with a growing scholarly interest in the cultural construction of body and identity through fashion and dress, influenced, among others, by Judith Butler's theorizing of gender as a performative act, and Michel Foucault's work on self-disciplining, self-monitoring, and technologies of the self, there emerged in the 1990s an increasing acknowledgment and exploration of the relationships between fashion, body, and identity. This is evident in the title and content of Wilson's essay, in which she highlights the "postmodern fragmentation" of knowledge, histories, and identities and discusses the increasing impact of media technologies, late twentieth-century politics, and the widening scope of globalization processes following the end of the Cold War. Together, these developments culminate in what can broadly be framed as the "postmodernism debate," which in Wilson's words, "helped rescue the study of dress from its lowly status, and has created—or at least *named*—a climate in which any cultural and aesthetic object may be taken seriously" (Wilson 1992, 6). She describes dress as a constitutive component in the process of subject formation and embodiment, one that is "tactile, visual . . . colours, shapes. It embodies culture" (Wilson 1992, 14). Citing Roy Boyne, she also highlights embodiment together with the emphasis placed on practices that would inform much of the work in fashion studies in the following decades: a shift "from knowledge to experience, from theory to practice, from mind to body" (Boyne 1988, 527, cited in Wilson 1992, 14).

This emphasis on fashion in relation to the body and self became a core theme in 1990s fashion scholarship that underpins the development of this field to date. One of the publications that aided in the broadening of perspectives and approaches to fashion was Jennifer Craik's book *The Face of Fashion: Cultural Studies in Fashion* (1993), in which she argues for the need to frame fashion in broader terms, in which "designer fashion" is just one variant of multiple, coexisting, and interacting systems of fashion (1993, xi), and highlights the role of fashion in everyday life: "Styles, conventions, and dress codes can be identified in all groups, including subcultures, ethnic groups, alternative life styles, workplace and leisure cultures" (1993, xii). Her consideration of fashion, as she notes, draws parallels with ethnographic studies of non-Western dress, in order to shed light on nonelite, everyday fashion, which she finds has been only superficially researched, endeavoring in her book to methodologically "piece together fashion histories and sift available material in order to map various fields of fashion practice" (1993, xii). The perspective on fashion as practice— and as a body technique—has been further framed in her book by drawing on Pierre Bourdieu's concept of habitus and Marcel Mauss' concept of technologies of the body, which she utilizes to explore fashion and dress as techniques of femininity, and also masculinity. Erving Goffman's work on the presentation of the self in everyday life and the performance of identities was also influential in the field's increased engagement with bodily practices, opening up avenues for more experiential approaches to the study of fashion, body, and gender (see for example, Tseëlon 1995).

In the 1990s, fashion and dress were studied in a wide variety of fields and disciplines such as fashion and dress history, art history, gender and queer studies, design studies, film and media studies, literature studies, cultural geography, urban studies, postcolonial studies, history, economics, marketing, and so on. These together formed a concentrated enough area of scholarly inquiry (and an identifiable "market") that would spark the launch of the journal *Fashion Theory: The Journal of Dress, Body and Culture*, edited by Valerie Steele, and the *Dress, Body, Culture* book series edited by Joanne Eicher; both developed with Kathryn Earle at Berg Publishers (see also Eicher's chapter in this book). Published in four issues per year, and not tied to an association—such as the *Clothing and Textiles Research Journal* (1982–), *Dress: Journal of the Costume Society of America* (1975–), or *Costume: The Journal of the Costume Society* (1968–) that up to that time were leading "organs" for scholars of dress, paving the way for fashion studies— *Fashion Theory* would help to substantially expand the output and distribution of interdisciplinary research on fashion and dress (for a broader discussion and detailed numbers on the increase of publications on fashion in the last two decades, see King and Clement 2012).

The expanding academic interest in fashion during that time evolved also in response to the global expansion of the fashion industries, through the acceleration of fashion production processes, including image production, through the rise of new media and communication technologies, and the faster circulation of fashionable goods through the so-called "democratization" of fashion consumption (at the cost of cheap, outsourced production labor). While much of the work in the 1990s concentrated particularly on fashion, body, and identity often through modes of representation, for example, in film and photography, and also increasingly with a focus on consumption practices, reflecting the "acknowledging of consumption," particularly in new material culture studies at the time (see Miller 1995; Breward 1998), there also emerged the call to expand fashion studies into the exploration of production, inspiring also much of the work in this edited volume. A particularly influential work was Angela McRobbie's 1998 book *British Fashion Design: Rag Trade or Image Industry*, in which she critiqued the then predominant interest within fashion studies in meaning-making processes through fashion, in particular, on the part of middle-class consumers, while ignoring almost entirely the conditions or contexts in which fashion is produced. Through qualitative interviews with subjects working in fashion design and fashion media, McRobbie's study offered firsthand insights into the working conditions of the fashion and creative industries in England in the 1990s. The dearth of such perspectives on design and production was also noted by the fashion designer and educator Ian Griffith, who in 2000 commented on the field of fashion studies, that the "voices of practitioners, or indeed, the practice of fashion do not figure large in its academy, and consequently a whole world of information is hidden from view" (Griffith 2000, 89–90). He thus pointed to an area of fashion studies that was by the turn of the millennium still a widely underexamined one (though, for an early study, see Blumer 1969), but which has since then received increasing attention from scholars of fashion (some selected examples: Kawamura 2004; Skov 2004; Hethorn and Ulasewicz 2008; Entwistle 2009; Fletcher 2014), leading a decade later to the founding of a new platform for fashion scholarship with *Fashion Practice: The Journal of Design, Creative Process and the Fashion Industry* (2009–), coedited by Sandy Black and Marilyn de Long. This increasing interest in practice is a demonstration how the "blurring of genres" described earlier, extends beyond the humanities and social sciences, into the integration of fields of "theory" and "practice," showing the impact of design thinking and design-based research in the recent decade.

As Joanne Entwistle notes in the introduction to her book *The Fashioned Body*, understanding fashion requires understanding the relationship between "different bodies operating in fashion: fashion colleges and students, designers and design houses, tailors and seamstresses, models and photographers, as well as fashion editors, distributors, retailers fashion buyers, shops and consumers" (Entwistle 2000, 1). In addition, there are multiple systems, cultures, and markets of fashion with distinct practices, infrastructures, spatialities, and temporalities, from the fast fashion distributed by global chains (see Maynard 2013; Moon 2014) to the diversification of global secondhand markets (see Gregson and Crewe 2003; Norris 2012). Entangled with or making up this global, material scope of fashion(s) are the bodies using and making, or in the literal sense of the word "fashioning," the sites, clothes, images, imaginaries, looks—"the stuff"—to be felt, looked at, shaped, experienced and changed by. One of the most recent key publications in the field, *The Handbook of Fashion Studies* (Black et al. 2013), exemplifies the richness and breadth of the field of fashion studies today, which has evidently bridged the "divides" previously addressed by scholars in the field between the museum and the academy, theory and practice, consumption or production, etc.

*The Handbook of Fashion Studies,* along with many other recent publications including, for example, a number of special issues in *Fashion Theory* and the project of *The Encyclopedia of World Dress and Fashion,* edited by Joanne Eicher (2010, and discussed in this book), demonstrates the development of an increased international collaboration in the field, fostered in part through the initiation of more international conferences. This leads to a greater consideration and integration of broader global, or international, perspectives on fashion and dress, bringing new—or hitherto absent—insights into the Anglo-American (-centric) field of fashion studies. In the context of the ongoing multiplication of fashion studies research in this age of increased global interconnectedness, a new "organ" or publication outlet in the field—the *International Journal of Fashion Studies* launched in 2014—has made it its agenda to foster the inclusion of international scholarship and decentralize fashion studies' predominantly English-speaking point of view (see Mora, Rocamora, and Volonté 2014).

The wider academic impact of fashion studies scholarship is not only visible in the growing volume of publications dedicated to fashion or dress by, for example, publishers like I. B. Tauris, Routledge, Bloomsbury, and Intellect; the latter has also pushed the launch of further new journals that provide a forum for the diversification of and specialization within the field, including *Critical Studies in Fashion and Beauty, Clothing Cultures, Critical Studies in Men's Fashion,* or *Fashion, Style and Popular Culture.* But in addition, the academic impact of fashion studies, a field that has traditionally borrowed from many disciplines, is also demonstrated in the inclusion of special issues edited by scholars of fashion in journals of other fields, such as Eugenia Paulicelli's and Elizabeth Wissinger's special issue for *Women's Studies Quarterly* in 2013, in which they transfer the notion of "fashion's essence as constant change" to the field of fashion studies: which may "never come to rest but rather will continually evolve, reaching out and making new connections between formerly disparate ideas and considerations" (Paulicelli and Wissinger 2013, 19).

# Research as practice: Fashioning methods

Fashion and fashion studies' wide reach and also its "in-between-ness" (Granata 2012) makes for an exciting field of research, yet the "escalation of interdisciplinary research" (Taylor 2013, 23) can also feel overwhelming, not least for students and emerging scholars, who are trying to find their footing in the field. It is perhaps due to the field's dense interdisciplinary entanglements, which bring a wide range of methods to the field—and the essential need for the use, combination, and adaption of multiple methods in the exploration of fashion considering its diverse forms and practices, as will be frequently addressed in this book—that so far, only a few publications have focused in on research methods and practices in fashion studies.

Where researchers in longer established fields and disciplines are supported through an overwhelming number of research handbooks, discussions of methodology in fashion studies are still rather scattered across the literature in the field. They are usually included in the compressed form of a few paragraphs in a section of a book, in an article's introduction, or attached in an appendix, leaving students and scholars with few resources from which to learn about methodological practices in fashion studies in a more concentrated form. The two exceptional works, referenced here before, providing a foundational study of research methods in the field, are written by dress historian Lou Taylor, titled *The Study of Dress History* (2002) and *Establishing Dress History* (2004). Both books are based on a historic review of interdisciplinary methodological approaches, yet with a particular focus on dress history studies, and their adjacency to the context and history of museum collecting practices. The journal *Fashion Theory* also included a special issue on methodologies in the study of dress history one year after its launch (Jarvis 1998), as well as occasional articles dedicated to methodological discussion (Palmer 1997; Tseëlon 2001; Granata 2012), but more commonly the focus has been on historic or museum and exhibition methods (see the special issue by Steele and Palmer 2008). More recently, Joe Hancock (2015) edited an issue dedicated to methodologies in the new journal *Clothing Cultures*, with articles exemplifying a range of methodologies from historical methods to focus groups and quantitative analysis. Other than this, there are only a few publications more broadly dedicated to the discussion of methodologies in dress and fashion studies. These include publications focused on research for the fashion industry (Flynn and Foster 2009) and in fashion design (Gaimster 2011), as well as the book *Doing Research in Fashion and Dress* written by Yuniya Kawamura (2011) as an introductory guide to research methods used in fashion studies, ranging from object-based research to semiotics and mixed methods, including brief "how to" instructional guidelines.

It could be argued that because fashion studies is so interdisciplinary it is well served by drawing on the resources of the fields that inform fashion studies, including methods books in adjacent fields, of which there are many useful ones that suit research interests and sites in fashion studies (e.g., Denzin and Lincoln 2005 for qualitative methods; Rose 2012 for visual methodologies; Pickering 2008 for cultural studies methods). However, "methods books" can also have a tendency to be (like the word "method" itself) rather abstract when they isolate or decontextualize the discussion of "methods" from the broader trajectories or bodies of research. One productive way to learn about research methods in fashion studies can therefore be quite simply to carefully read the works of other scholars for their ways of doing research—by paying attention to not only what may be explicitly mapped out in an introduction or in a "methods chapter," but by looking closely into what their use of sources and methods (and theories) makes possible: What insights can an author produce through their particular modes of research and investigation, what kinds of questions and interests are formulated, and how are these methodologically approached and adjusted? What do scholars of fashion look at, how do they come to know—how do they develop insights and interpretations with and of their selected materials? Research methods are embedded in context (academically, historically, socially, culturally, personally) and the actual use of methods in the practice of research is therefore a much more dynamic or fluid undertaking than the dictionary sense of method as "rational procedure"—and its underlying temporal notion of defining and planning an activity ahead of time and following it through according to plan—implies.

For scholars of fashion "a method" emerges more likely in one's exchange with the agents (human and nonhuman) and site/s of exploration, as a tailoring and fitting of research approaches along with the shaping of research interests and contexts. According to Roy Dilley, context or rather contextualization, can be understood as a performative act, embedded in the environment, background, or disciplinary location (quoted in Coleman and Collins 2007, 8). In this conception, research is as much a situated practice as we understand fashion to be a situated practice (see Entwistle 2000). As the anthropologists Simon Coleman and Peter Collins emphasize, fields or contexts—historical or contemporary—become generated by social relationships and they can be understood as events that are in a constant process of becoming, rather than fixed in space and time. They can be created anew each time a researcher invokes a field in the process of research and writing (Coleman and Collins 2007, 12). And as such fields cannot be seen—spatially, temporarily, or ethically—disconnected from the academy (Coleman and Collins 2007, 11), the institutional or (inter-)disciplinary location in which research is embedded in turn impacts the field—they are interwoven with each other. Along with the crossover of scholars between the humanities and social sciences came the development of texts "that refused to be read in simplistic, linear, incontrovertible terms" (Denzin and Lincoln 2005, 3). This has also led to blurring the lines between text and context, or theory and practice, and the acknowledgment of the intersubjective and interpretive dynamics of research mapped out by Denzin and Lincoln in a definition of qualitative research as "a situated activity that locates the observer in the world. It consists of a set of interpretive, material practices that make the world visible. These practices transform the world. They turn the world into a series of representations, including field notes, interviews, conversations, photographs, recordings and memos to the self" (2005, 3). So researching or "locating" fashion, is also linked with locating oneself as a researcher in time and place, through the selection or shaping of specific themes and fields, the ignoring of others, the raising of certain questions, the developing or integration of particular theoretical frameworks, etc.

## The approach of this book

Equivalent to the researcher as bricoleur and "quilt maker," described by Denzin and Lincoln as someone who assembles and combines tools and techniques of research and "stitches, edits and puts slices of reality together" (2005, 3), Caroline Evans used the metaphor of ragpicking to describe her approach to the analysis of experimental fashion design in the 1990s, which she conceptualized as a "case study of what to do with a method" (Evans 2003, 11). Establishing an equivalence between the designer and the design historian, and drawing on the figure of the ragpicker who moves between the material culture of the past and present, the 1990s designers she examines, rummage "in the historical wardrobe, scavenging images for re-use just as the nineteenth century ragpicker scavenged materials for recycling"—a practice Evans utilizes to fashion her own method of "scavenging images from the past to examine and reinterpret those of the present" (Evans 2003, 13). Research in or as a practice, is a dynamic back and forth between the often distinctly conceived spheres of "theory" and "practice," and as the chapters in this book will show, it involves the interpersonal entanglements between the researching self and research subject/s. As many of the chapters and case studies in this book will also show, research is an embodied practice, located or happening in specific time/s and place/s, which also means that it can often involve a quite fluid up and down in one's own feelings and emotions (see Alford 1998, 22). Much of this fluidity of the doing of research in practice is often not conveyed in the final "products" of research. What we are presented with instead are usually the polished and orderly arrangements of words, sentences, paragraphs, and chapters that systematically present "research outcomes" in a clear narrative with a beginning and an end: a linearity that overshadows a researcher's previous (often yearlong) movements in a field of research and on the "tracks" between empirical and theoretical inquiry (Alford 1998, 23). Rarely do the research products in the form of fashion studies texts (although some examples are Entwistle and Rocamora 2006; Moon 2009) provide a reader or student with a sense of what it was like to embark on a project: how does one actually enter or begin to construct a field of research; where and how can one find, collect or produce "data," how can one for example "do fashion studies," so to speak, in the very concrete production sites of fashion—the sites that usually remain invisible behind the allure of fashion as it comes to circulate each season in new clothes, enticing images of fashionable bodies or in compelling advertising campaigns.

One of the reasons why fashion is so powerful and deeply affective is that the very practices through which the "magic of fashion" is produced are effectively hidden from view. Some of those practices that are part of the production and experience of fashion will be the focus of the chapters in this book. In particular, this book takes an interest in researching fashion as part of everyday practices— not just of the wearing of clothes—but also of the routine practices that are part of the work of and in fashion. The authors in this book will approach this by examining fashion sites and practices by foregrounding reflection on the "doing" of research. This requires, in many cases, a self-reflective mode of thinking and writing, that often does not find space in the writing of final research outcomes, that is, books or articles, often simply due to the limits of word counts, or to not distract from the narrative of presenting "outcomes" of research. Yet, the narratives of "embarking" on and "doing" research are no less valuable for scholars, especially in light of the proliferation of many diverse research practices and methods in fashion studies as they emerge through the aforementioned cross-pollination of the multiple academic fields, interests, and perspectives that make up this field.

As Lou Taylor notes in a recent introductory chapter on methods in fashion and dress history: "No one can possibly be skilled in every one of these academic fields, each of which has its own sets of specific critical approaches, interests, standpoints" (Taylor 2013, 23). Lou Taylor introduces in her overview, theoretical and methodological approaches relating to her fields of scholarship, dress history, including object-based and material culture approaches; social, economic, and business history; oral history; the use of photography and film; among others that are used in the study of dress history. To complement and further expand the perspectives on methods in existing publications on methods in fashion studies, this edited volume follows a case-study approach in which interdisciplinary scholars discuss their own research approaches and tailoring of methods with a specific focus on the use of material culture, ethnography, and mixed methods, as ways to investigate and make sense of contemporary sites and practices of fashion.

# References

Alford, Robert R. 1998. *The Craft of Inquiry*. New York: Oxford University Press.

Baudelaire, Charles. 2004. "The Painter of Modern Life." In *The Rise of Fashion*, edited by Daniel Leonhard Purdy, 213–221. Minneapolis: University of Minnesota Press.

Black, Sandy, Amy de la Haye, Agnes Rocamora, Regina Root, and Helen Thomas, eds. 2013. *The Handbook of Fashion Studies*. London: Bloomsbury.

Blumer, Herbert. 1969. "Fashion: From Class Differentiation to Collective Selection." *Sociological Quarterly* 10 (3): 275–91.

Breward, Christopher. 1998. "Cultures, Identities, Histories: Fashioning a Cultural Approach to Dress." *Fashion Theory* 2 (4): 383–90.

Coleman, Simon and Peter Collins. 2007. *Locating the Field: Space, Place and Context in Anthropology*. London: Berg.

Craik, Jennifer. 1993. *The Face of Fashion*. London: Routledge.

Denzin, Norman K., and Yvonne S. Lincoln. 2005. "Introduction: The Discipline and Practice of Qualitative Research." In *The Sage Handbook of Qualitative Research*. 3rd Edition, edited by Norman K. Denzin and Yvonne S. Lincoln, 1–32. London: Sage.

Eicher, Joanne B. 2001. "Introduction: The Fashion of Dress." In *National Geographic Fashion*, edited by Cathy Newman, 16–23. Washington, DC: National Geography Society.

Eicher, Joanne B., and Mary Ellen Roach, eds. 1965. *Dress, Adornment and the Social Order*. New York: Wiley.

Eicher, Joanne B., and Mary Ellen Roach, eds. 1973. *The Visible Self: Perspectives on Dress*. Englewood Cliffs: Prentice Hall.

Eicher, Joanne B., and Sandra Lee Evinson. 2014. *The Visible Self: Global Perspectives on Dress, Culture and Society*. New York and London: Bloomsbury.

Entwistle, Joanne. 2000. *The Fashioned Body: Fashion, Dress and Modern Social Theory*. Cambridge: Polity.

Entwistle, Joanne. 2009. *The Aesthetic Economy of Fashion: Markets and Value in Clothing and Modelling*. New York and Oxford: Berg.

Entwistle, Joanne and Agnes Rocamora. 2006. "The Field of Fashion Materialized: A Study of London Fashion Week." *Sociology* 40 (4): 735–51.

Evans, Caroline. 1997. "Dreams That Only Money Can Buy . . . or, The Shy Tribe In Flight from Discourse." *Fashion Theory* 1 (2): 196–88.

Evans, Caroline. 2003. *Fashion at the Edge: Spectacle, Modernity and Deathliness*. New Haven, CT and London: Yale University.

Evans, Caroline and Minna Thornton. 1989. *Women and Fashion: A New Look*. London: Quartet Books.

Fabian, Johannes. 1983. *Time and the Other: How Anthropology Makes Its Object*. New York: Columbia University Press.

Fabian, Johannes. 2007. *Memory Against Culture: Arguments and Reminders*. Durham and London: Duke University Press.

Fletcher, Kate. 2014. *Sustainable Fashion and Textiles: Design Journeys*. 2nd ed. London and New York: Routledge.

Flügel, John Carl. 2004. "The Great Masculine Renunciation and its Causes." In *The Rise of Fashion*, edited by Daniel Leonhard Purdy, 102–08. Minneapolis: University of Minnesota Press.

Flynn, Judith Zaccagnini and Irene M. Foster. 2009. *Research Methods for the Fashion Industry*. New York: Fairchild Books.

Gaimster, Julia. 2011. *Visual Research Methods in Fashion*. Oxford: Berg.

Gaugele, Elke. 2015. "Kostümgeschichten und frühe Modetheorien des 19. Jahrhunderts als Wissensordnungen der Moderne." In *Die Wissenschaften der Mode*, edited by Gudrun M. König, Gabriele Mentges and Michael R. Müller, 81–96. Bielefeld: Transcript.

Granata, Francesca. 2012. "Fashion Studies In-Between: A Methodological Case-Study and an Inquiry into the State of Fashion Studies." *Fashion Theory* 16 (1): 67–82.

Gregson, Nicky and Louise Crewe. 2003. *Second-Hand Cultures*. Oxford and New York: Berg.

Griffith, Ian. 2000. "The Invisible Man." In *The Fashion Business: Theory, Practice, Image*, edited by Nicola White and Ian Griffiths, 69–90. Oxford: Bloomsbury.

Grossberg, Lawrence. 2010. *Cultural Studies in the Future Tense*. Durham and London: Duke University Press.

Hancock, Joe. 2015. "Diverse Methodologies for Understanding Clothing Cultures." *Clothing Cultures* 2 (1): 3–7.

Hansen, Karen Tranberg. 2004. "The World in Dress: Anthropological Perspectives on Clothing, Fashion, and Culture." *Annual Review of Anthropology* 33: 369–92.

Hethorn, Janet and Connie Ulasewicz, eds. 2008. *Sustainable Fashion: Why Now? A Conversation about Issues, Practices, and Possibilities*. New York: Fairchild.

Hodkinson, Paul. 2002. *Goth: Identity, Style and Subculture*. Oxford and New York: Routledge.

Hollander, Anne. 1978. *Seeing Through Clothes*. New York: Viking Press.

Jarvis, Anthea, ed. 1998. Methodology Special Issue. *Fashion Theory: The Journal of Body, Dress and Culture* 2 (4).

Johnson, Kim P., Susan J. Torntore, and Joanne B. Eicher. 2003. *Fashion Foundations: Early Writings on Fashion and Dress*. Oxford and New York: Berg.

Kaiser, Susan B. 1985. *The Social Psychology of Clothing and Personal Adornment*. New York: Macmillan.

Kaiser, Susan B. 2012. *Fashion and Cultural Studies*. London and New York: Berg.

Kawamura, Yuniya. 2004. *The Japanese Revolution in Paris Fashion*. Oxford and New York: Berg.

Kawamura, Yuniya. 2005. *Fashion-ology: An Introduction to Fashion Studies*. Oxford: Bloomsbury.

Kawamura, Yuniya. 2011. *Doing Research in Fashion and Dress: An Introduction to Qualitative Methods*. London: Bloomsbury.

King, Lindsay M., and Russell T. Clement. 2012. "Style and Substance: Fashion in Twenty-First-Century Research Libraries." *Art Documentation: Journal of the Art Libraries Society of North America* 31 (1): 93–107.

König, Gudrun M., Gabriele Mentges and Michael R. Müller, eds. 2015. *Die Wissenschaften der Mode*. Bielefeld: Transcript.

Lillethun, Abby, Linda Welters, and Joanne B. Eicher. 2012. "(Re)Defining Fashion." *Dress* 38: 75–97.

Maynard, Margaret. 2013. "Fast Fashion and Sustainability." In *The Fashion Studies Handbook*, edited by Amy de la Haye, Joanne Entwistle, Regina Root, Sandy Black, Helen Thomas, and Agnès Rocamora, 542–56. London and New York: Bloomsbury.

McRobbie, Angela. 1998. *British Fashion Design: Rag Trade or Image Industry*. London: Routledge.

Mentges, Gabriele, ed. 2005. *Kulturanthropologie des Textilen*. Berlin: Edition Ebersbach.

Miller, Daniel, ed. 1995. *Acknowledging Consumption: A Review of New Studies*. London: Routledge.

Miller, Daniel. 2005. *Materiality*. Durham, NC; London: Duke University Press.

Moon, Christina H. 2009. "From Factories to Fashion: An Intern's Experience of New York as Global Fashion Capital." In *The Fabric of Cultures: Fashion, Identity and Globalization*, edited by Hazel Clark and Eugenia Paulicelli, 194–210. London and New York: Routledge.

Moon, Christina H. 2014. "The Secret World of Fast Fashion." *Pacific Standard*. March 17, accessed August 26, 2014, http://www.psmag.com/navigation/business-economics/secret-world-slow-road-korea-los-angeles-behind-fast-fashion-73956/.

Mora, Emanuela, Agnes Rocamora, and Paola Volonté. 2014. "The Internationalization of Fashion Studies: Rethinking the Peer-Reviewing Process." *International Journal of Fashion Studies* 1 (1): 3–17.

Niessen, Sandra. 2003. "Afterword: Re-Orienting Fashion Theory." In *Re-Orienting Fashion: The Globalization of Asian Dress*, edited by Sandra Niessen, Ann Marie Leshkowich, and Carla Jones, 243–66. Oxford and New York: Berg.

Norris, Lucy. 2012. "Trade and Transformations of Secondhand Clothing: Introduction." *Textile* 10 (2): 128–43.

Palmer, Alexandra. 1997. "New Directions: Fashion History Studies and Research in North America and England." *Fashion Theory* 1 (3): 297–312.

Paulicelli, Eugenia and Elizabeth Wissinger. 2013. "Introduction." *WSQ: Women's Studies Quarterly* 41 (1–2): 14–27.

Pickering, Michael. 2008. *Research Methods for Cultural Studies*. Edinburgh: Edinburgh University Press.

Purdy, Daniel Leonhard, ed. 2004. *The Rise of Fashion*. Minneapolis: University of Minnesota Press.

Ribeiro, Aileen. 1986. *Dress and Morality*. New York: Holmes and Meier.

Riello, Giorgio and Peter McNeil. 2010. *The Fashion History Reader: Global Perspectives*. London: Routledge.

Roche, Daniel. 1994 [1989]. *The Culture of Clothing: Dress and Fashion in the "Ancien regime."* Translated by Jean Birrell. Cambridge: Cambridge University Press.

Rose, Gillian. 2012. *Visual Methodologies: An Introduction to Researching with Visual Materials*. London: Sage.

Schwarz, Ronald. 1979. "Uncovering the Secret Vice: Towards an Anthropology of Clothing and Adornment." In *The Fabrics of Culture*, edited by Justine M. Cordwell and Ronald A. Schwarz, 23–45. The Hague: Mouton.

Simmel, Georg. 2004 (1901). "Fashion." In *The Rise of Fashion*, edited by Daniel Leonhard Purdy, 289–309. Minneapolis: University of Minnesota Press.

Skov, Lise. 2004. "'Seeing is Believing:' World Fashion and the Hong Kong Designer Contest." *Fashion Theory* 8 (2): 165–93.

Sombart, Werner. 2004. "Economy and Fashion: A Theoretical Contribution on the Formation of Modern Consumer Demand." In *The Rise of Fashion*, edited by Daniel Leonhard Purdy, 310–16. Minneapolis: University of Minnesota Press.

Steele, Valerie. 1985. *Fashion and Eroticism: Ideals of Feminine Beauty from the Victorian Era to the Jazz Age*. New York: Oxford University Press.

Steele, Valerie. 2005. "Fashion." In *Encyclopedia of Clothing and Fashion*, edited by Valerie Steele. Vol. 2, 12–13. New York: Scribner.

Steele, Valerie and Alexandra Palmer, eds. 2008. Exhibitionism Special Issue. *Fashion Theory: The Journal of Dress, Body and Culture* 12 (1).

Taylor, Lou. 2002. *The Study of Dress History*. Manchester and New York: Manchester University Press.

Taylor, Lou. 2004. *Establishing Dress History*. Manchester and New York: Manchester University Press.

Taylor, Lou. 2013. "Fashion and Dress History: Theoretical and Methodological Approaches." In *The Handbook of Fashion Studies*, edited by Sandy Black, Amy de la Haye, Agnes Rocamora, Regina Root and Helen Thomas, 23–42. London: Bloomsbury.

Tseëlon, Efrat. 1995. *The Masque of Femininity: The Presentation of Women in Everyday Life*. London and Thousand Oaks: Sage Publications.

Tseëlon, Efrat. 2001. "Fashion Research and its Discontents." *Fashion Theory* 5 (4): 435–452.

Veblen, Thorstein. 2004. "Dress as an Expression of a Pecuniary Culture. The Theory of the Leisure Class." In *The Rise of Fashion*, edited by Daniel Leonhard Purdy, 261–288. Minneapolis: University of Minnesota Press.

Wilson, Elisabeth. 1985. *Adorned in Dreams: Fashion and Modernity*. New Brunswick: Rutgers.

Wilson, Elisabeth. 1992. "Fashion and the Postmodern Body." In *Chic Thrills: A Fashion Reader*, edited by Juliet Ash and Elisabeth Wilson, 3–16. Berkeley, CA: University of California Press.

# SECTION ONE

# APPROACHING FASHION AND DRESS AS MATERIAL CULTURE

# INTRODUCTION

## Heike Jenss

This book is informed by the understanding that fashion forms a significant part of material culture. The English term "fashion" (or *mode* in Romance languages) refers to the dynamic of change, one that is bound up with social relationships, and also with the organization of the fashion industry, and an industrialized conception of time that drives capitalism. While fashion can be understood as a collective belief system (see Kawamura 2005) and as a value producing aesthetic economy (see Entwistle 2009), the understanding of fashion as material culture is here particularly grounded in the etymology and active meaning of fashion as a verb: "to fashion"—derived from the Latin *facere*—which means: to make, "to form, mould, shape (either a material or immaterial object)" (see *Oxford English Dictionary* 2015). In this understanding, fashion is not limited to what we may associate with "high fashion," or with an "elite," although this is a significant component of the understanding of fashion as a social dynamic; but, as the first two chapters in this book will show, fashion also encompasses everyday practices and the fashioning of body and self, using "ordinary" or "humble" clothes, as discussed in the chapter by Sophie Woodward. In people's everyday practices, fashion does not necessarily mean to be the "newest" or "latest": bought, worn, and discarded according to seasonal offerings—although these temporal rhythms affect people's relationships with fashion and clothes—but the temporalities of fashion are multiple, with some clothes in longer use, others put on hold, or returning to use etc. (see Woodward 2007; Jenss 2015).

Understanding fashion as a form of material culture has methodological implications: it involves not only the examination of fashion or dress as material objects, or through object-based research, which has a long tradition in collecting material culture and in museums (see Taylor 2002, 3–23 and 2004; Steele 1998; Kawamura 2011, 91–102; Palmer 2013), but it also involves the exploration of material practices—for example, what people do with material things, what things do with people, and how they relate to each other. And more broadly, it involves the acknowledgment of the relationship between materiality and humanity (see Mentges 2005, Küchler and Miller 2005, Miller 2005). With regard to the materiality of clothing, this has been described by anthropologist Daniel Miller, with a critique on semiotic approaches to things, or "stuff" such as clothes, that conceive these primarily as signs or symbols that "represent"—for example, the status of their wearer. As he argues in an essay titled "Why Clothing is not Superficial" (Miller 2010), such an understanding of clothing assumes a particular relationship between the interior and exterior. He shows through various ethnographic case studies that clothes affect the wearer—they "make us what we think we are" (2010, 13): clothes play a "considerable and active part in constituting the particular experience of the self, in determining what the self is"—which varies across time and place (Miller 2010, 40). Such an understanding of clothing moves beyond a (hierarchical) separation of subject and object, or human and nonhuman, and acknowledges instead the vitality, force, or agency of things—an understanding that also informs the work of scholars in the field of new materialism, developing perspectives on things as "vibrant matter" (see Bennett 2010).

The book starts out with two chapters that take an interest in the examination of the most immediate or personal relationship people have with fashion, in the material form of everyday dressing. However, the two chapters do so by focusing on different kinds and effects or implications of methods. The first chapter by Cheryl Buckley and Hazel Clark is inspired by their interest in examining the histories and roles of fashion in people's everyday lives in New York and London in the twentieth century. Provoked by the limited examples of everyday clothes in the museum collections or exhibitions of these two major fashion capitals, their chapter explores the methods of collecting and museum practice and policy to show how museums—as institutions that play a key role in the shaping of cultural memory (of a city, a nation, etc.)—privilege the "extraordinary," and impact the image or conception of fashion as well as the material memory of what people wore. Clark and Buckley's chapter highlights the need to critically reflect on the methods and sources of fashion studies, including its associated institutions or agents, such as museums, which form a substantial historical foundation of the field of fashion studies, including its methodologies (see Taylor 2004; Melchior and Svensson 2014). Buckley and Clark also point to some of the possibilities in the curation of fashion, as they emerge with new media, which—less confined by institutional policies and physical space—open up new ways "to address the nuanced realities of fashion as constituting a vital part in everyday lives." Some notable examples to mention here include Minh-Ha T. Pham's public digital archive of the fashion histories of US women of color *Of Another Fashion* on tumblr (http://ofanotherfashion.tumblr.com), the website that expanded the recent *Queer History of Fashion* exhibition at the museum at the Fashion Institute of Technology (2013), featuring a number of oral history videos, or Emily

Spivack's project *Wornstories.com*, which demonstrates the role of fash
people's everyday lives, and in people's memories (see also Spivack 2014).

The second chapter by Sophie Woodward extends this interest in everyday
fashion with a discussion of the methodologies that can be used to "grasp" and
explore the role and experience of clothes, which become at times so habitual
and ordinary that one may not have much to say about them—which presents
a methodological challenge of its own. Woodward discusses in the chapter her
use of and experiences with wardrobe studies, interviews and observations of
street fashion, as methods to explore and understand the personal relationships
people have with their clothing. But she also reflects on the use of methods and
case studies to consider the wider global dimensions of fashion exemplified by
the ubiquity of global denim, which she discusses by highlighting the advantages
of collaborative, comparative ethnographies. Informed by an anthropological
approach to material culture, Woodward offers a definition of fashion as it has
emerged from her research on what people do with their clothes, focusing in
particular on practices of consumption. Highlighting fashion as an activity—
as fashioning—she conceives of fashion "as a practice of assemblage," which
includes the assembling of clothes, as well as the development of knowledge
and competencies about how to wear, combine, and embody them. Such a
definition of fashion comes to serve here also as a methodological instrument
to help consider, and "make visible," what may—despite its everydayness—
not be easily accessible. Woodward's chapter offers insights into the use of
methods that aid in addressing the elusiveness of everyday fashion noted by
Buckley and Clark, and in its discussion of ethnographies of consumption it
builds a bridge to the second section in this book with chapters that exemplify
uses of ethnography in the exploration of diverse sites of the production of
fashion objects and images.

# References

Bennett, Jane. 2010. *Vibrant Matter: A Political Ecology of Things.* Durham and London:
    Duke University Press.
Entwistle, Joanne. 2009. *The Aesthetic Economy of Fashion: Markets and Value in Clothing
    and Modelling.* New York and Oxford: Berg.
Jenss, Heike. 2015. *Fashioning Memory: Vintage Style and Youth Culture.* London and
    New York: Bloomsbury.
Kawamura, Yuniya. 2005. *Fashion-ology: An Introduction to Fashion Studies.* Oxford:
    Bloomsbury.
Kawamura, Yuniya. 2011. *Doing Research in Fashion and Dress: An Introduction to
    Qualitative Methods.* London and New York: Bloomsbury.
Küchler, Susanne and Daniel Miller, eds. 2005. *Clothing as Material Culture.* Oxford,
    New York: Berg.

Melchior, Marie Riegels and Birgitta Svensson. 2014. *Fashion and Museums: Theory and Practice*. London and New York: Bloomsbury.

Mentges, Gabriele. 2005. "Für eine Kulturanthropologie des Textilen: Einige Überlegungen." In *Kulturanthropologie des Textilen*, edited by Gabriele Mentges, 11–54. Berlin: Edition Ebersbach.

Miller, Daniel, ed. 2005. *Materiality*. Durham, NC and London: Duke University Press.

Miller, Daniel. 2010. "Why Clothing is Not Superficial." In *Stuff*, edited by Daniel Miller, 12–41. Cambridge and Malden, MA: Polity.

Museum at FIT. 2013. *A Queer History of Fashion: From the Closet to the Catwalk*. https://www.fitnyc.edu/21048.asp.

Palmer, Alexandra. 2013. "Looking at Fashion: The Material Object as Subject." *The Handbook of Fashion Studies*, edited by Amy de la Haye, Joanne Entwistle, Regina Root, Sandy Black, Helen Thomas, Agnès Rocamora, 268–300. London: Bloomsbury.

Pham, Minh-Ha T. 2014. *Of Another Fashion: An Alternative Archive of the Not-Quite-Hidden but too Often Ignored Fashion Histories of U.S. Women of Color*. http://ofanotherfashion.tumblr.com.

Spivack, Emily. 2014. *Worn Stories*. New York: Princeton Architectural Press.

Steele, Valerie. 1998. "A Museum of Fashion is More than a Clothes-Bag." *Fashion Theory* 2 (4): 327–35.

Taylor, Lou. 2002. *The Study of Dress History*. Manchester and New York: Manchester University Press.

Taylor, Lou. 2004. *Establishing Dress History*. Manchester and New York: Manchester University Press.

Woodward, Sophie. 2007. *Why Women Wear What they Wear*. Oxford and New York: Berg.

# 1 IN SEARCH OF THE EVERYDAY: MUSEUMS, COLLECTIONS, AND REPRESENTATIONS OF FASHION IN LONDON AND NEW YORK

## Cheryl Buckley and Hazel Clark

Evolving from a collaborative research project that explores the place and significance of fashion in everyday lives in twentieth-century Britain and the United States, we consider in this chapter how fashion has been collected and represented in museums, and how these methods impact the way fashion is conceptualized. Our focus is place-bound, in that we are looking particularly at leading institutions that collect fashion in our respective research sites, New York and London: The Costume Institute at the Metropolitan Museum of Art, the Museum at the Fashion Institute of Technology (FIT), the Museum of the City of New York, the Museum of London, and the Victoria and Albert Museum (V&A). We also refer to a few smaller independent and regional museums in Britain as well as the national collection of the Smithsonian Institution in the United States, to consider varied approaches to the collection of fashionable clothes. While our shared interest lies in tracing the roles of fashion in people's everyday lives in the urban contexts of New York and London (see Buckley and Clark 2012), it is the actual paucity of ordinary, everyday fashion in these cities' major museum collections—in comparison to a privileging of fashion from named designers, couturiers, or aristocratic wearers—that has sparked our reflections on fashion collecting methods, not least because these methods form a significant historic foundation of the field of fashion studies. In tracing how everyday fashion has recently been exhibited and collected (or not), and drawing on interviews with museum curators, we want to shed light on the challenges of researching fashion in everyday lives.

## Fashion collecting policies and everyday fashion practices

A key objective of museum collecting policies is to support strategic priorities articulated in their mission statements. It is important for national museums to be at the forefront in international terms, especially if they are located in major global cities with strong fashion associations, such as New York, London, Paris, or Milan. Collections in museums beyond major urban centers, by contrast, develop agendas that must also address their local and regional constituencies, which in turn affects what they collect. At the same time, museum collecting practices are the product of specific curatorial histories and disciplinary priorities that come from academic scholarship outside the museum—such legacies are evident in fashion collecting. Museums can play significant roles in institutionalizing specific forms of knowledge; those specializing in fashion, for example, may have substantial connections with the fashion industry (Melchior and Svensson 2014). As Pamela Church-Gibson puts it, "Cheap, ubiquitous clothes, which lack artistic merit of any kind are consigned not only to landfills in the real world, but also to hinterlands beyond scholarship" (Church-Gibson 2012, 18). Today, even with the increased scholarly interest in "fast fashion" (Moon 2014), there are few examples of these ubiquitous clothes in major museum collections. This has clear implications for the representation and visibility in museum collections of fashion that has been embedded in ordinary lives. In some major national museums such as the V&A, the acquisition of fashion has had a marginal, if not precarious curatorial position, particularly when viewed alongside other aspects of design and the decorative arts such as ceramics, furniture, silver, prints, and textiles. In others such as the Costume Institute of the Metropolitan Museum of Art, acquisition originally reflected close ties to the theater and then to the fashion business. Upon scrutinizing the representations of fashion in museum collections as indicative of everyday lives, arguably both collecting practices and academic scholarship appear to have been determined in important ways by aesthetics, taste, and economics.

The central premise of this chapter is that museums have, until relatively recently, underrepresented the importance of fashion in everyday lives. Instead, their method has been to concentrate on the activities of selected designers, celebrities, and wealthy consumers, as well as extraordinary and/or avant-garde cultural practices. A related sub-point to consider is why fashion has been marginal more generally in museum collections in the twentieth century. With regard to the latter, various fashion historians, writers, and critics have pointed to the hierarchies within specific categories of design and the decorative arts to reveal the effect of these on collecting practices. They have considered questions of gender, particularly in relation to curators of fashion, but also due to fashion's assumed affinities to women. They have examined the status of the discipline of dress history within academia, including its relationship to art history, and latterly social and economic history and to fashion studies, noting the denigration of object-based analysis prior to the rise of material culture studies and ethnography. They have shown how fashion's precarious status—as low culture, entertainment, popular media, business, and commerce—has facilitated its marginalization until recent years. And they have outlined the impact of specific institutional policies, historic practices, and distinctive place identities on the lack of sustained interest in fashion.[1] Notwithstanding these points, exhibitions of fashion have proved enormously popular in major museums, and the collecting of fashion and dress in national collections has gathered pace in the last thirty years.

Writing in 1998, Lou Taylor described how the hostile attitude "to the collection of seasonally-styled European fashion for women became enshrined within the (V&A) museum's collecting policy from the very start," and how this was compounded by academic prejudice, particularly in economic and social history departments at the university, which "failed almost totally to address the significance of issues of fashion, style and seasonal change" (Taylor 1998, 340 and 346). Although one target of Taylor's criticism were those historians who failed to undertake object analysis, her observation foregrounds a common assumption made by many writers in dress and fashion history, that fashion is fundamentally about change and a specific "look." This particular thesis, dominant in academic writing on dress and fashion history, is underpinned by the notion that fashion is essentially about change, that this speeds up as the twentieth-century progresses, and that it is intrinsic to the experience of being modern and to modernization. Although there has been some rethinking of fashion's relationship to modernity by writers like David Gilbert, who calls for a more outward-looking and nuanced understanding of fashion cities that notes "the ways in which there are different modernities in different places" (Breward and Gilbert 2006, 7), the core understanding of fashion—that it is about regular cycles of change and thus intimately tied to the "project of modernity"—remains largely intact. In contrast, the central thesis of our research informing this chapter is that, in order to fully interrogate fashion in the twentieth century, investigation is necessary of the ways in which *fashion*—as opposed to *dress*—infiltrated everyday lives in an ongoing, sustained way over time and across class, gender, ethnicity, and generation.[2] In the process, this reconstitutes our understanding of fashion's relationship to time. Greater knowledge of how individuals use and wear their clothes leads to an understanding of fashion as a form of material palimpsest—created from a composite of garments and accessories that are new, with those that are reworn, altered, and generally "re-fashioned" (even if only in terms of when and where they are worn) by their users over time.

Additionally it is useful to explore how geography affected what people were wearing. As Gilbert put it, when discussing large cities in Britain such as Newcastle, Manchester, and Nottingham, although designers and companies from these cities operate globally, "the fashion cultures of these cities have often had an intensely local dimension" (Gilbert 2000, 12). A key argument underlying our research is that, while fashion in the twentieth century could be symbolic in a multitude of ways—aesthetically, culturally, socially, politically, and economically—it was (and remains) "an intimate part of embodied, everyday experience" (Breward and Gilbert 2006, 14). And, while some writers have argued that fashion does not only "come from the top," there is a new "middle ground"—neither in the salon nor the street—rather "in the wardrobe" (Woodward 2007). With the exception of a few regional museums and exhibitions, however, we found it difficult to find examples of such everyday fashion in the major and national collections. Indeed curatorial practices have reaffirmed the focus on modern, avant-garde, extraordinary, and unusual design, often for strategically important reasons. These have included a desire to reposition fashion as "art," to emphasize its aesthetic value, to stake a claim for its cultural significance, or to reiterate its economic importance. Thus it has been articulated as the output of highly creative individuals who approach fashion as an artistic practice, or that it is produced by designers who are sharply attuned to the contemporary world, or that it is the product of elusive fashion houses that are part of multinational companies locked into the global economy.

## London

The exhibition and display of fashion in London and New York from the late 1970s through to the 1990s reflected an overall climate of change in museums. In Britain, this was partly as a result of changing governmental attitudes, which stimulated anxieties about funding and declining visitor numbers (Anderson 2000, 372). Museums adopted marketing strategies to survive, such as Saatchi & Saatchi's advertising campaign for the V&A in the late 1980s, featuring the slogan "V&A: An ace caff, with quite a nice museum attached."[3] Despite such flights into populism, which did not always increase museum traffic, this was also the period when the impact of academic research methodologies and critical approaches started to become more evident generally in the museum, and in its treatment of fashion. Discussing the collecting of "contemporary design" at the V&A,[4] Christopher Wilk, chief curator of the Department of Furnishing, Textiles and Fashion, observed that its collecting of these categories of objects was "largely episodic . . . undirected by museum-wide policies until quite recently" (Wilk 1997, 345). Outlining the often controversial reasons for this that go back to one of the V&A's first donations (the Donaldson Collection in 1901) and the museum's policy to "show very little which is not at least 50 years old" and "by means of the finest examples," Wilk (1997, 345–53) observed that the interest in contemporary design was dependent upon the Circulation Department until 1977 when the director, Roy Strong (1974–87), allocated funds to departmental curators to collect excellent recent work. Although the Circulation Department had a transformative effect on curatorial practices, it collected neither large items, nor fashion, or dress as it was deemed too wide a field to collect and too difficult to display. While this chapter is not concerned with the details of the V&A's attitudes to collecting garments prior to the 1970s—this is well covered by others (Taylor 2004, 106–21)—it is worth noting how museum policy had a considerable impact not only on collecting, but also on the broader definition of fashion as part of everyday lives—particularly that which is not seen as unique, or overtly excellent, or of high artistic quality. Compounding this, curators faced a pragmatic decision: How to recognize the most "representative" fashion of a given moment? In New York, Harold Koda, the director of the Costume Institute at the Metropolitan Museum of Art, explained how one of his curator predecessors, Stella Blum, would never collect from the present moment, but preferred to wait ten or fifteen years "to see if something was really valid" (Koda and Reeder 2012). Presenting fashion as art obviated the need for this, and waiting for more than a decade before acquiring garments became one of the curatorial strategies in fashion museums in the early 1970s.

Indeed it was photographer Cecil Beaton's 1971 exhibition *Fashion, an Anthology* that has been credited as putting fashion "on the map" at the V&A (Taylor 2004, 122). The show, curated by Madeleine Ginsberg, drew together five hundred items of twentieth-century couture design and accessories. Exhibiting only high quality design and finish, this approach was reiterated in another V&A exhibition of a few years later *Fashion 1900–1939* (1975–76) when the curators aimed to show "the relationship between fashion, art and decorative arts in France."[5] While presenting fashion as part of a continuum through art and the decorative arts, the exhibition also recognized the importance of economics, and it reflected dominant academic approaches at a time, when the emphasis was on the *producers* of fashion—those who designed, illustrated, and photographed it—rather than its *wearers* and consumers. In 1983, the V&A opened its refurbished Costume Court, featuring simpler display cases focusing attention on the clothes, and providing a model for other collections internationally (Taylor 2004, 122). Yet, the approach to this display "Four Centuries of the Art of Dressing" was criticized as being "not so much cool and pure as cold, hard, snobbish and elitist" (Horwell 1983, 37). Nevertheless, the refurbishment preempted many highly popular temporary exhibitions, at a time in Britain when more media and also government attention was being paid to fashion and design. According to one reviewer, although the target audience was not evident when the space was overhauled and opened as the "Fashion Galleries" in 2012, "the grandeur and exuberance of the fashions on display will ultimately win over any critics" (Costume Society 2014). Even so, in the intervening years it was the less "grand" exhibitions that were the most innovative and that have edged the museum's collection policy away from elitist fashion. An illustration of this was the exhibition *Streetstyle: From Sidewalk to Catwalk* at the V&A (1994–95). The exhibition was accompanied by a book of the same name by Ted Polhemus (1994), informed by his anthropological approach to changes in fashion and drawing on the work of cultural studies' scholar Dick Hebdige. The V&A exhibition, based on an idea, rather than a specific historical period, or designer, focused on fashion as an intrinsically youth-oriented practice, drawn from a unique collection of subcultural clothes worn from the 1940s to the 1990s. The curators who had made the acquisition, Amy de la Haye and Cathie Dingwall, also published an object-based book to "explore the multi-faceted nature of sub-cultural identity," titled *Surfers, Soulies, Skinheads and Skaters* (1996, n.p.). Subsequently the V&A staged the exhibition *Black Style* (2004) curated by Carol Tulloch, followed by *Swinging Sixties* (2006–07) curated by Jenny Lister and sponsored by Miss Selfridge, both with their own publications. These exhibitions, revealed the shift in scholarship and curatorial practice that had taken place. While *Black Style* addressed the importance of black identities, ethnicities, and race, *Swinging Sixties* was an outcome of a UK Research Council project "Cultures of Consumption" that highlighted fashion's diffusion as well as its production. Moving closer to the realm of the everyday, the key objective remained to capture a specific historical moment when a "new look" associated with a particular group, the young, contributed to the ascendancy of London as a city that was looked to for fashion leadership. *Swinging Sixties* reasserted fashion as generational, the epitome of modernity and defined by a "look," while also presenting intellectual and curatorial challenges (Breward 2008, 88–90). *Black Style* focused more on how fashion looks and how particular garments were appropriated, redefined, and adapted to become embedded in everyday lives.

The shifting intellectual landscape has contributed to the collecting and exhibiting of fashion as dress, and to fashion history being reassessed within the context of the developing field of fashion studies. As Melchior and Svensson argue, a characteristic of this approach to fashion was, however, that it "diverted attention towards the manifestation of an underlying idea, with the clothes themselves forming no more than an illustration" (Melchior and Svensson 2014, 40)—although it is worth noting that the idea also could and did reference clothes as fashion. *Malign Muses: When Fashion Turns Back* curated by Judith Clark at the MoMU (ModeMuseum) Antwerp in 2004/05, and later at the V&A as *Spectres: When Fashion Turns Back* is indicative of this, as it drew on the ideas of fashion theorist Caroline Evans specifically as published in *Fashion at the Edge: Spectacle, Modernity and Deathliness* (2003). Evans' approach to understanding fashion was conceptually challenging as it refused a narrative history, and to articulate this

Clark deployed curatorial innovation in the staging of fashion and in its suggestion that meaning was fluid and contingent (Scaturro 2010). By this time, the Judith Clark Costume Gallery, established in Notting Hill in February 1997, had had a substantial impact in developing the conceptual parameters of the "fashion exhibition." Being independent, and run almost exclusively by Clark enabled the small gallery space to be highly innovative. Even in its rather short-lived existence from 1997 to 2003, Clark's gallery paved the way for more adventurous approaches to fashion being taken by established institutions and curators. Conceptually, innovative curation most often involved theoretically challenging ideas, rather than the presentation of a historical narrative of discrete objects. This method has attracted criticism from some dress and fashion historians, but more important for the argument here, is that it marks an intellectual shift toward theory rather than history.

# New York

The impact of individual fashion curators, some with interdisciplinary backgrounds (Judith Clark, for instance, was trained in architecture), was not insignificant on the development of fashion exhibitions. This applied equally to New York, where fashion curation added to the existing scholarship on the nature of fashion. By the end of the first decade of the twenty-first century, New York City had a small but active number of museums devoted to fashion, and others that showed fashion occasionally. An interest in everyday lives and fashion had been evident in the 1986 exhibition *The East Village* at the museum at the FIT. In a review of the show in *Time* magazine, Jay Cocks called it "an eye-scalding, rambunctious and appropriately free-spirited tour of boho fashion, Manhattan style" (see Schiro 1999). Curated by the late Richard Martin, who was subsequently appointed as chief curator at the Costume Institute, *The East Village* was unlike anything Martin and his cocurator Harold Koda would have been able to stage at the Costume Institute. Housed within an educational institution, the shows at FIT could take a broad range of approaches, which reflected the curriculum in social history, anthropology, and merchandising, as well as in art and design. Koda described how there was "the whole range" of possibilities for the FIT shows, as compared to his later work at the Costume Institute where "it really is about the mastery of the craft" and "the artistic importance of the garment" with reference to the ideas of their designers (Koda and Reeder 2012).

The FIT collection, founded in 1969 as the Design Laboratory (which originated at the Brooklyn Museum in 1915) was intended to support the educational programs of the FIT, part of the State University of New York (SUNY). The museum at FIT remains one of a small number of museums in the world devoted exclusively to fashion. In the 1970s, prior to the museum forming its own collection, FIT's exhibitions drew from a collection on long-term loan from the Brooklyn Museum of Art, comprising over 50,000 garments and accessories from the eighteenth century to the present, textiles and other fashion-related material, deaccessioned in 2009, with many pieces going to the Costume Institute. In the 1980s, FIT began to stage shows under the auspices of its Shirley Goodman Resource Center, then responsible for exhibitions and collections, under the direction, until 1993, of Richard Martin with Harold Koda. Original in content and approach, they also included the exhibitions *Fashion and Surrealism* (1987), *Undercover Story* (1982), and *Three Women: Madeleine Vionnet, Claire McCardell, Rei Kawakubo* (1987). The Design Laboratory changed to its current name The Museum at FIT in 1993, the year Martin moved to the Costume Institute. Dr. Valerie Steele was appointed to its staff in 1997, and then named its director in 2003, the year she also launched the FIT annual fashion symposium (Fashion Institute of Technology 2014). She has developed the role of The Museum at FIT as the central focus of fashion design exhibitions in New York City, as well as playing a seminal role in fashion scholarship internationally through her many publications, and as the editor of the scholarly journal *Fashion Theory*.

The Costume Institute at the Metropolitan Museum of Art has a different and longer history. Formed in 1937 as the Museum of Costume Art, it owed its origins to Irene Lewisohn, founder of the Neighborhood Playhouse, a community theater in downtown Manhattan. With financial support from the fashion industry in 1946 and under the leadership of Dorothy Shaver, the vice president of the Fifth Avenue department store Lord and Taylor, the Museum of Costume Art merged with the Metropolitan Museum of Art as The Costume Institute before becoming a museum curatorial department in 1959. This close connection between fashion as a business and as a display at the museum has been pivotal in the curatorial development of the museum. When Richard Martin was appointed curator of costume in 1993, he was following in the footsteps of Diana Vreeland, who had served as special consultant from 1972 until her death in 1989. The former editor of the American *Vogue* had been responsible for bringing more flamboyant and popular shows to the Metropolitan Museum of Art including *The World of Balenciaga* (1973), *Hollywood Design* (1974), *The Glory of Russian Costume* (1976), *Vanity Fair* (1977), and *Yves Saint Laurent* (1983). The latter exhibition proved controversial by featuring the work of a living designer who was clearly situated within the fashion system, and as such it brought accusations from some quarters that commerce was overtaking culture (Storr 1987). Yet Vreeland's approach transformed public interest in fashion exhibitions. In her wake, Richard Martin's less showy exhibitions that brought a more scholarly and critical approach added new dimensions that helped to set fashion exhibitions and scholarship on a new path. Some shows were devoted to designers—*Gianni Versace* (1997), *Christian Dior* (1996), *Madame Grès* (1994)— but others took more critical approaches, which are evident even from their titles: *Cubism and Fashion* (1998), *American -Ingenuity: Sportswear, 1930's–1970's* (1998),

*Orientalism: Visions of the East in Western Dress* (1994), *Swords into Ploughshares: Military Dress and the Civilian Wardrobe* (1995). Also, *Wordrobe* (1997) an original exhibition that took a historical look at clothing adorned with words, from poems to political slogans, which Martin described as "the reconciliation of textile and text" (Schiro 1999). Martin also added to the collection by accepting donations of clothing from designers and their clients, as well as by shopping at auctions, and flea markets. Indeed, included in what was to be his last show, *Our New Clothes: Acquisitions of the 1990's* (1999), was a John Galliano dress purchased off the rack at the discount store *Century 21* (Schiro 1999). Bringing an academic rigor from his art history background, as well as a substantial intelligence, Richard Martin treated fashion and its objects as an intriguing and valuable part of cultural study. Through their different approaches, Martin and Vreeland both contributed to increasing the visibility, interest, and profitability of fashion exhibitions at the Metropolitan Museum, though few could be deemed everyday.

Comparatively, Richard Martin had much more flexibility in the range and subjects of the exhibitions he could stage and what he could collect at FIT than when he moved to the Costume Institute. The fact that the latter was, and continues to be, underwritten by the New York fashion industry (as part of the agreement when the foundational "Museum of Costume Art" collection was acquired in 1946) has shaped its collections policy and donors. While the link was most marked under Diana Vreeland, it was always present to some extent, for example, in its "party of the year." Instituted in 1947 by Eleanor Lambert, a central figure in American fashion public relations, the annual gala was intended to contribute to the operating budget of the Costume Institute. In recent years, under the leadership of Anna Wintour, editor in chief of the American *Vogue* and artistic director of Condé Nast, it has raised so much money that it has been able to contribute to the capital funds needed for the Costume Institute's recent refurbishment, including The Anna Wintour Costume Center, as well as specific exhibitions and acquisitions (Buckley and Clark 2012).

## Fashion and city life

In marked contrast to the collections of the Costume Institute and the V&A are those of the Museum of London and the Museum of the City of New York. The Museum of London "has always seen dress as one of a variety of major cultural aspects of the life and culture of the city of London—of London's memory" (Taylor 2004, 126). Its origins lay in the Guildhall Museum founded in 1826 and the London Museum founded in 1911, and its dress collection aims to "represent London's role as a centre for the fashion and clothing industry from education through to design, production, promotion, retail and wear, [and to] reflect the diversity of life in London, recording and collecting the clothing of all London's communities"

(Museum of London, Dress and Fashion 2012). With the consolidation of the new Museum of London from the merger of the Guildhall Museum and the London Museum in 1976, it aimed to collect "only objects found in London or manufactured in London" (Museum of London, History of Collections 2012). With dress integral from the outset and a costume catalog published in 1933, the Museum of London adopted a survey approach that drew from donated collections.[6] It also houses an outstanding photographic collection depicting everyday lives in all areas of London at its disposal, which has been highly effective as contextualizing media. Typically, fashion at the museum has been shown as part of general displays and its thematic exhibitions have also included fashion. A good example of this is *Twenties London* (2003), which included numerous images, objects, and paintings that represented London as a global city—a "nerve-centre," at once modern and traditional. Integral to this exhibition, fashion was presented as embedded in Londoners' everyday lives, through displaying clothes worn by ordinary Londoners. A year later, the same museum staged *The London Look—Fashion from Street to Catwalk* (2004), an exhibition that responded to shifting scholarship within fashion history. Although some of the exhibited garments were examples of haute couture and the product of auteurs and designers, the exhibition equally included fashion that was sold by department stores and multiple stores, advertised in working women's magazines, indicative of make-do and mend during wartime, and adapted, worn, and occasionally subverted on the street. This positioning of fashion as everyday, rather than exclusive, is clearly discernible in the museum's acquisition list for 2009–10: a sweatshirt (1987), T-shirt (2004), apron (Laura Ashley, 1966–67), boots (UGG, 2009) (Museum of London, Museum of London Acquisitions 2012). Nevertheless, the exhibition of everyday fashion is more likely to be the product of a broader design, social or cultural history approach, and remains less common than the display of more showy and unusual items that are more visually appealing and instantly eye-catching to the museum visitor.

In New York City, the museum closest in mission and content to the Museum of London is the Museum of the City of New York, which was founded in 1923 to present the history of New York City and its people. Located on Fifth Avenue at the northern end of "museum mile," the institution respects its neighborhood of East Harlem and offers free admission to the local community and stages shows that capture the ethnic and racial diversity of the city. Like the Museum of London, its collection includes garments, artifacts, paintings, and an extensive collection of photographs, the latter providing a comprehensive social documentary of the city since the late nineteenth century. In the 2000s, for instance, the Museum of the City of New York presented very original fashion exhibitions staged principally by Phyllis Magidson, curator of costumes and textiles, including *Black Style Now* (2006–07), and *Stephen Burrows: When Fashion Danced* (2013). In 2008–09, it also held a "twenties" show *Paris/New York: Design/Fashion/Culture 1925–1940*, by Donald Albrecht, curator of architecture and design at the museum, featuring drawings, furnishings, decorative objects, costumes, photographs, posters, and films (Museum of the City of New York 2009). While that exhibition included what was designed, made, and consumed in the two cities, its focus was largely on the transatlantic creative "conversations" between Paris and New York, presented as centers of the artistic and cultural avant-garde. In doing so, it located fashion as part of a broader design/cultural history that touched upon everyday lives, as well as being informed by seasonal ready-to-wear and couture design in different locales. Continuing this interest in the wider cultural histories of New York, *Cecil Beaton: The New York Years* (2011–12), also curated by Albrecht, revealed the differences in curatorial approach to the V&A exhibition some 30 years earlier, as it documented—in photographs, drawings, and "costumes"—Beaton's work. It presented him not as an arbiter of taste and style as at the V&A, but as a "chronicler" of the cultural life of New York City from the 1920s through the 1960s (Museum of the City of New York 2011). Typically the Museum of the City of New York stages some exhibitions devoted specifically to fashion, and also includes garments in many of its shows. One of the most notable in recent years had a close association with the V&A. *Black Style Now* (2006–07), cocurated by Phyllis Magidson, Michael McCollum, and Michael Henry Adams, was promoted as the first American exhibition to explore black fashion, and to highlight the impact of hip-hop on style (Museum of the City of New York 2006). Featuring street style that strongly referenced New York's African American communities, in addition to high fashion represented by the work of black fashion designers, the exhibition began with Martine Barrat's impressive street photography of people in Harlem in the 1980s and 1990s. This exhibition owed its existence to the earlier show *Black British Style,* curated by Carol Tulloch at the V&A Museum (2004–05). Drawing upon written, oral, and visual biographies, this particular exhibition considered aspects of fashion in everyday lives, and it highlighted the importance of curators, and other key individuals in the formation of collections and the development of exhibitions relative to specific institutional contexts and geographies (Tulloch 2004).

# Beyond London and New York

For some curators, including those interviewed as part of this research, provenance is critical to their approach to acquisitions' policy as this allows them to show fashion as part of everyday lives. Describing her arrival at the V&A in 1957, curator of dress Madeleine Ginsburg found to her dismay that the civil service administrators of the museum had "weeded" out files that held much of the key information about the background to the acquisitions, origins and reason for their acceptance (Taylor 2004, 120). Joanna Hashagen (2012), curator of fashion and textiles at the Bowes Museum in the north of England, stressed in a recent interview the legacy of Ann

Buck, curator at Platt Hall Museum, Manchester, England (who had trained her) in capturing the who, what, when, and why of specific acquisitions and donations. Keen to capture a lifetime in a wardrobe, Hashagen (2012) insists that without provenance fashion in museums is largely meaningless, particularly in a regional museum at some distance from the metropolis. Indeed Vanda Foster, a former colleague of Hashagen's (also trained by Buck) and the successor to Madeleine Ginsburg at Gunnersbury Museum in London still retains and uses the detailed, hand and typewritten accession cards that remain her key source of information in a small local-authority funded museum on the periphery of London. Importantly regional museums in Britain such as the Bowes Museum and Beamish, the Living Museum of the North, have been assiduous in collecting fashion that is part of everyday lives, including homemade and shop-bought items, on the basis that these are indicative of individual lives in the north of England as well as of broader social and cultural change (Hashagen 2012).

Regional collections are increasingly focusing on collecting local fashion, which attempts to appeal to their local constituency of visitors; and curators such as Lou Taylor and Amy de la Haye at the Brighton Museum in Britain, as well as curators at some national museum collection departments, including Alexandra Palmer at the Royal Ontario Museum in Toronto, Canada, seek clothes worn by members in their communities. This reiterates the importance of curators and other key individuals to the formation of collections and the subject of exhibitions of fashion and dress, relative to specific institutional contexts and geographies. Curator Diana Baird N'Diaye (2012) at the Smithsonian Institution in Washington, DC, is leading a major research project, the "Will to Adorn" to document "cultural biographies of dress" among members of the African American population in a range of locations including New York City, Chicago, and the US Virgin Islands (see Smithsonian Institution 2010). Based on participant interviews and the interrogation of artifacts and photographs, N'Diaye's project is undoubtedly concerned with the everyday. What is of significance here also is N'Diaye's institutional affiliation as Folklife Curator and Cultural Heritage Specialist at the Smithsonian Center for Folklife and Cultural Heritage (CFCH), not with one of the museum's collections of dress or textiles.

# Conclusion

While definitions of the everyday have involved weighty conceptualization from a range of cultural theorists (e.g., Lefebvre 1988; de Certeau, Giard, and Mayol 1998; Benjamin 2002), the interest in fashion as part of mundane lives poses pragmatic acquisition problems and curatorial challenges as fashion is conceived as ordinary as well as extraordinary. Without examples of how ordinary people—as well as the rich, famous, and exceptional—engaged with fashion in museum collections, it remains left to photographs, film, and personal testimony to capture this. A diversity of sources exists, which can include family snapshots and albums, oral histories, items from personal wardrobes, yard sales and flea markets, editorials and advertisements from general interest magazines such as *Picture Post* in Britain and *Life* or *Ebony* in the United States, some of which are being utilized by curators of fashion exhibitions (Bivins and Adams 2013), as well as autobiographies, biographies, and fiction (for an extended discussion of historic source materials see Taylor 2002 and 2013).

Reviewing the fashion collecting practices in these selected museums, our findings have reinforced our view that it is only through the questioning, and disruption, of scholarship and curatorial practices that fashion can be rearticulated within the realm of the everyday, and as this chapter demonstrates, the collection, representation, and interpretation of fashion in museums plays a pivotal role. In this reconceptualization, fashion is defined as embedded and ongoing in people's everyday lives, rather than as an exceptional event, a one-off "look," an activity associated with a stage of one's life, or only relevant to the elite. Central to this scholarship, rather than in its hinterland, is the fashion that is not only uniquely designed, exquisitely constructed, or stylistically exceptional. To date, the realization of these ideas in museum collections and exhibitions has been uneven and limited, and when "everyday approaches" have been in evidence, they have been due to specific factors: museum policies, curatorial strategies, shifting cultural geographies, and new scholarship combined with the foresight of specific curators.

The curator remains vital, not just as institutional gatekeeper, but also as intellectual arbiter between objects, images, and ideas—one who must function within the mission and parameters of an institution. Institutional policy also remains very important; the "art" museum, for instance, will always have the visual and aesthetic dimension as a priority. Yet, in the twenty-first century, when "everyone" can "curate" fashion, especially on a personal level and in the blogosphere, it begs the question of the future role of the professional museum curator and of fashion exhibitions. If freed from the mandate of collecting and showing the most aesthetically appealing pieces and leaders of taste, exhibitions might highlight more the individual and shared stories, and the memories and evocations that lie within the folds of fashionable clothes. Museums are only starting to grapple with how to deal with "collecting" fashion in the virtual realm; this will present another valuable insight into the increasing role of fashion as representation and entertainment in everyday life. Since the end of the last century, fashion has gained much greater inroads into the lives of ordinary people, through reality television shows, internet sites such as Style.com that report on designer fashion, as well as blogs by nonprofessionals. As clothes accumulate over time—hung at the back of the wardrobe, taken back out, added to and adapted, reassembled with a new scarf or pair of shoes, as "fast fashion," or in literally fleeting images, be it a family snapshot, or in the twenty-first century a digital "selfie" in a blog—more museum collections and exhibitions must address these nuanced realities of fashion as constituting a vital part of everyday lives.

# Notes

1 There is a developing body of research on this including Melchior, Marie Riegels and Birgitta Svensson. 2014. *Fashion and Museums. Theory and Practice.* London and New York: Bloomsbury; Taylor, Lou. 2004. *Establishing Dress History.* Manchester: Manchester University Press; Styles, John. 1998. "Dress in History: Reflections on a Contested Terrain." *Fashion Theory* 2 (4): 383–90; Mendes, Valerie and Amy de la Haye. 1999. *20th Century Fashion.* London: Thames and Hudson; Palmer, Alexandra. 2008. "Untouchable: Creating Desire and Knowledge in Museum Costume and Textile Exhibitions." *Fashion Theory* 12 (1): 31–64; Breward, Christopher and David Gilbert. 2006. *Fashion's World Cities.* Oxford and New York: Berg.

2 We acknowledge that costume, dress, and fashion have different meanings: in using "costume," we refer to the way that it has historically been used for clothing and accessories of a particular country, historical period, or in the theatrical context. In using "dress," we describe the putting together and wearing of items of clothing (see also Eicher in this book). Yet, while "dress" is perhaps the most appropriate generic term to refer to clothing and to the body ("dressing" the hair for instance), this usage is nonetheless complicated by its common "female" connotation in Western societies as a specifically gendered garment. In using "fashion," we describe the making or design, and wearing and assembling of clothes that can correspond to a recognizable look that involves acts of agency either by individuals, groups, or designers. We also propose that fashion has longevity, that it exists over time, and is not just the here and now, that it can be ordinary as well as extraordinary. The terms "costume" and "fashion" tend to be those used to refer to collections of clothing items, for example, The Costume Institute at the Metropolitan Museum of Art, compared to the Department of Furniture, Textiles and Fashion at the V&A Museum, London. Terminology also changes to reflect changing attitudes in museums and scholarly discourse, which has been especially true in Britain and Europe, for example, the V&A changed the name of its display of clothing on several occasions, being instituted as the "Costume Court" in 1962, as the "Dress Court" in 1983 under the directorship of Sir Roy Strong, and the "Fashion Galleries" in 2012.

3 This poster was produced in the late 1980s as one of six in the campaign series for Saatchi & Saatchi Advertising Ltd., London.

4 By which he meant "the new or the nearly new things still available in the marketplace at the time, or manufactured objects made within the past fifteen years or so that remain in continuous production."

5 *Fashion 1900-1939,* Scottish Arts Council exhibition with the support of the Victoria and Albert Museum (London: Idea Books, 1975): 7. The exhibition was supported by Roy Strong who wrote the foreword, along with the director of the Scottish Arts Council—the exhibition opened at the Royal Scottish Museum in Edinburgh (December–January 1975–76) and then closed at the V&A (March–May 1976).

**6** Key collections included the Seymour Lucas collection acquired in 1911. Like the V&A major donated collection, the Talbot Hughes collection of 1913, Lucas was a painter of historic portraits and landscapes and amassed his costume collection to give his paintings historical authenticity.

# References

Anderson, Fiona. 2000. "Museums as Fashion Media." In *Fashion Cultures. Theories, Explorations and Analysis,* edited by Stella Bruzzi and Pamela Church-Gibson, 371–89. London and New York: Routledge.

Benjamin, Walter. 2002. *The Arcades Project.* Cambridge, MA: Harvard University Press.

Bivins, Joy L., and Rosemary K. Adams. 2013. *Inspiring Beauty: 50 Years of Ebony Fashion Fair.* Chicago: Chicago History Museum.

Breward, Christopher. 2008. "Between the Museum and the Academy: Fashion Research and its Constituencies." *Fashion Theory* 12 (1): 83–93.

Breward, Christopher and David Gilbert. 2006. *Fashion's World Cities.* Oxford and New York: Berg.

Breward, Christopher, David Gilbert, and Jenny Lister. 2006. *Swinging Sixties: Fashion in London and Beyond 1955—1970.* London: V&A Publications.

Buckley, Cheryl and Hazel Clark. 2012. "Conceptualizing Fashion and Everyday Life." *Design Issues* 18 (4): 18–28.

Church-Gibson, Pamela. 2012. *Fashion and Celebrity Culture.* Oxford and New York: Berg.

Costume Society. Accessed January 24, 2014, http://costumesociety.org.uk/journal/exhibition-review-fashion-galleries-vanda.

de Certeau, Michel, Luce Giard, and Pierre Mayol. 1998. *The Practice of Everyday Life,* vol. 2. Minneapolis, MN: University of Minnesota Press.

de la Haye, Amy and Judith Clark. 2008. "One Object: Multiple Interpretations." *Fashion Theory* 12 (2): 137–70.

Emery, Joy Spanabel. 2014. *A History of the Paper Pattern Industry: The Home Dressmaking Fashion Revolution.* London and New York: Bloomsbury.

Evans, Caroline. 2003. *Fashion at the Edge: Spectacle, Modernity and Deathliness.* New Haven, CT and London: Yale University Press.

Fashion Institute of Technology. 2014. *History of the Museum.* Accessed January 24, https://www.fitnyc.edu/3399.asp.

Gilbert, David. 2000. "Urban Outfitting. The City and the Spaces of Fashion Culture." In *Fashion Cultures: Theories, Explorations and Analysis*, edited by Stella Bruzzi and Pamela Church-Gibson, 7–24. London and New York: Routledge.

Hashagen, Joanna. 2012. "Interview" by Cheryl Buckley. January 24.

Horwell, Veronica. 1983. "A Fancy Dress Party." *The Sunday Times,* London, June 5, 1983, Look 2, 37.

Koda, Harold and Jan Reeder. 2012. "Interview" by Hazel Clark. January 26.

Lefebvre, Henri. 1988. "Toward a Leftist Cultural Politics: Remarks Occasioned by the Centenary of Marx's Death." In *Marxism and the Interpretation of Culture,* edited by Nelson, Cary and Lawrence Grossberg. London: Macmillan.

Melchior, Marie Riegels and Birgitta Svensson. 2014. *Fashion and Museums. Theory and Practice.* London and New York: Bloomsbury.

Mendes, Valerie and Amy de la Haye. 1999. *20th Century Fashion.* London: Thames and Hudson.

Metropolitan Museum of Art. *Impressionism, Fashion and Modernity*, accessed June 19, 2014, http://www.metmuseum.org/exhibitions/listings/2013/impressionism-fashion-modernity.

Moon, Christina H. 2014. "The Secret World of Fast Fashion." *Pacific Standard.* March 17, 2014, accessed August 26, 2014, http://www.psmag.com/navigation/business-economics/secret-world-slow-road-korea-los-angeles-behind-fast-fashion-73956/.

Museum of the City of New York. 2009. *Paris/New York*, accessed June 18, 2014, http://www.mcny.org/exhibition/parisnew-york.

Museum of the City of New York. *Cecil Beaton: The New York Years*, accessed February 9, 2012, http://www.mcny.org/exhibitions/current/Cecil-Beaton-The-New-York-Years.

Museum of the City of New York. *Black Style Now*, accessed February, 9 2012, http://www.mcny.org/exhibition/black-style-now.

The Museum at FIT. *History of the Museum*, accessed February 3, 2012, http://fitnyc.edu/3399.asp.

The Museum at FIT. *Mission Statement*, accessed February 3, 2012, http://fitnyc.edu/3401.asp.

The Museum at FIT. *Strategic Plan 2009–14*, accessed February 3, 2012, http://fitnyc.edu/files/pdfs/MFITStrategicPlan2009.REVISED8.10.pdf.

Museum of London. Acquisition and Disposal Policy, accessed February 3, 2012, http://www.museumoflondon.org.uk/NR/rdonlyres/F0F8E5B1-0F59-421C-AE27-2CC68A62976A/0/AcquisitionandDisposalPolicy.pdf.

Museum of London. Dress and Fashion, accessed February 3, 2012, http://www.museumoflondon.org.uk/Collections-Research/About-the-collections/History-and-archaeology-collections/Dress-fashion.htm.

Museum of London. History of Collections, accessed February 3, 2012, http://www.museumoflondon.org.uk/Collections-Research/About-the-collections/History-of-the-Collections.htm.

Museum of London. *Museum of London Acquisitions*, 2009–10, accessed February 3, 2012, http://www.museumoflondon.org.uk/NR/rdonlyres/18394EFA-74F0-4137-A009-B5BA278B9AC2/0/MuseumofLondonAcquisitions20092010.pdf.

N'Diaye, Diana. 2012. "Interview" by Hazel Clark. February 1.

Palmer, Alexandra. 2008. "Untouchable: Creating Desire and Knowledge in Museum Costume and Textile Exhibitions." *Fashion Theory* 12 (1): 31–63.

Robinson, Gillian. 2012. "Interview" by Cheryl Buckley. January 18.

Scaturro, Sarah. 2010. "Experiments in Fashion Curation: An Interview with Judith Clark." *Fashion Projects.* February 26, accessed January 24, 2014, http://www.fashionprojects.org/?p=676.

Schiro, Ann-Marie. 1999. "Richard Martin, 52, Curator of the Costume Institute." *New York Times.* November 9, accessed January 24, 2014, http://www.nytimes.com/1999/11/09/arts/richard-martin-52-curator-of-the-costume-institute.html.

Smithsonian Institution. 2010. *Smithsonian Center for Folklife and Cultural Heritage*, accessed February 10, 2012, http://www.smithsonianconference.org/expert/exhibit-hall/cfch/.

Steele, Valerie. 1998. "A Museum of Fashion is More than a Clothes-Bag." *Fashion Theory* 2 (4): 327–36.

Storr, Robert. 1987. "Unmaking History at the Costume Institute." *Art in America* 75 (2): 15–21.

Styles, John. 1998. "Dress in History: Reflections on a Contested Terrain." *Fashion Theory* 2 (4): 283-89.

Taylor, Lou. 1998. "Doing the Laundry? A Reassessment of Object-based Dress History." *Fashion Theory* 2 (4): 337–58.

Taylor, Lou. 2002. *The Study of Dress History*. Manchester and New York: Manchester University Press.

Taylor, Lou. 2004. *Establishing Dress History*. Manchester: Manchester University Press.

Taylor, Lou. 2013. "Fashion and Dress History: Theoretical and Methodological Approaches." In *The Handbook of Fashion Studies*, edited by Amy de la Haye, Joanne Entwistle, Regina Root, Sandy Black, Helen Thomas, and Agnès Rocamora, 23–43. London and New York: Bloomsbury.

Tulloch, Carol. 2004. *Black Style*. London: V&A Publications.

Victoria & Albert Museum. V&A Strategic Plan. 2011–15, accessed February 3, 2012, http://media.vam.ac.uk/media/documents/about-us/2010/v&a-strategicplan2010-15.pdf.

Victoria & Albert Museum. *V&A Mission and Objectives*, accessed February 3, 2012, http://www.vam.ac.uk/content/articles/v/v-and-a-mission-and-objectives/.

Wilk, Christopher. 1997. "Collecting the Twentieth Century." In *A Grand Design. The Art of the Victoria and Albert Museum*, edited by Malcolm Baker and Brenda Richardson, 345–53. London: V&A publications.

Woodward, Sophie. 2007. *Why Women Wear What They Wear*. Oxford and New York: Berg.

# 2 "HUMBLE" BLUE JEANS: MATERIAL CULTURE APPROACHES TO UNDERSTANDING THE ORDINARY, GLOBAL, AND THE PERSONAL

## Sophie Woodward

Among fashion's defining features are its ephemerality and its "mutability" (Wilson 1985, 58), which, as a consequence, makes it difficult to grasp. Scholars of fashion are then faced with the methodological challenge of trying to research something that is perceived to be immaterial and continually changing. One of the routes to "grasping" fashion comes from dress history approaches (Taylor 2004), which entail carrying out analyses of clothing objects to understand how fashion is materialized within particular historical and social contexts. Anthropological accounts of clothing share a focus on the materiality of clothing as a route into understanding wider social contexts (Weiner and Schneider 1989; Küchler and Miller 2005). While a focus on fashion's materiality offers a seeming concreteness, as there is "stuff" to analyze, it also poses its own methodological challenges. In this chapter, I address two particular challenges, namely, how to understand the unspoken relationship we have to clothing and also account for its simultaneously global and intimate nature, as well as the possibilities that the study of contemporary fashion and clothing as material culture opens up.

First, take the example of blue denim jeans: despite being one of the most widespread items of clothing in the world (Miller and Woodward 2007), and often the item of attire that is worn most habitually (Woodward 2007), people have very little to say about them. The garments people are able to talk about the most may instead be the ones they rarely wear—"special" clothing—or items that have been a "fashion disaster." This inability to speak about clothes that are worn almost all the time, and as a consequence are the most important to people as an embodied material practice, is encapsulated within the phrase the "humble blue jean." This is a phrase that pops up in numerous journalistic reports, such as Alexander Fury proclaiming the "return of the humble blue jean" in the *New Zealand Herald* (Fury 2014). Despite seeming like a meaningless cliché to call blue jeans "humble," when this humility is reframed through Daniel Miller's material culture perspective of the "humility of things" (Miller 1987, 85–108), it offers a route to understanding how the things we are unaware of frame our social worlds. Drawing on the work of Erving Goffman (1974) and Ernst Gombrich (1979), Miller writes that objects are important, not when we are conscious of them constraining or enabling us to act, but when we are unaware of them framing our actions. The more we are unconscious of things, the more pivotal they may be in impacting how we live our lives. Blue jeans are a perfect example of such a thing—we do not consciously reflect upon them as we wear them everyday, which is precisely why they are important. This humility of things and the way they materialize the unspoken is both a methodological challenge of looking at jeans, and also a possibility for where we can take the study of fashion.

The second challenge this chapter will address is the simultaneous global and intimate reach of fashion. Fashion is located in multiple sites and spaces, ranging from bedrooms, to streets, catwalks, magazines, design studios, and clothing factories. It is both global in structures of provision, production, and consumption, yet it is also personal and intimate as items of clothing are worn on the body as we engage with issues such as identity and sexuality. These multiple domains of fashion lend themselves to a multidisciplinary approach encompassing macro theories of fashion (Lipovetsky 2002) through to intimate ethnographies of fashion practices (Woodward 2007). As specific empirical projects may be seen as refractions of meta-theories of fashion or the global, there has been a tendency, perhaps unsurprising, for the intimate and personal to be understood through in-depth qualitative research. In an article entitled a "Manifesto for the Study of Denim" (Miller and Woodward 2007), we argued that it is possible, and important, to generate theories of fashion as global phenomenon from localized ethnographies. Practices of wearing cannot always be reduced to meta-theories of fashion, as this implies that fashion is an abstract force that people accept or reject through clothing practices (Kaiser 2003). Within this vein the Global Denim Project (Miller and Woodward 2012) took on the challenge of generating an understanding of denim through several comparative ethnographies in different global contexts. Since jeans are important to people as they are simultaneously global and personal, our approach to the topic needs to be fine-tuned to help us understand this simultaneity.

In this chapter, I will outline a series of different field sites and methods through which we can begin to understand everyday fashion as a set of material practices. I will start by outlining how fashion can be understood and defined in this context and will then explore how definitions of fashion can inform, and be developed through, different case studies: moving from the intimate space of wardrobe studies, through to observations of street fashions, to an ethnography of jeans in London, and finally to the Global Denim Project as a way to understand the globalness of fashion. By discussing the challenges and possibilities of studying fashion as material culture, I offer a way of understanding fashion with a perspective on what matters to the people wearing those clothes—which they may not always be able to verbally articulate. This approach opens up a route into the relationship between the global and intimate in fashion that is not reductive to either stance.

## Defining fashion: Everyday practices and material culture

How we define fashion is central to the approaches and methods that we adopt. My own understanding of fashion both *informs* as well as *emerges from* empirical work that I have carried out. The first empirical project I carried out on clothing practices took place in women's wardrobes (Woodward 2007) and arose from a desire to understand clothing practices, not as derived from an abstracted fashion system, but as grounded in everyday consumption, relationships, and household practices. This entailed an ethnographic approach as a means to situate the foregrounded issue of clothing practices within the wider backgrounds of people's social relationships and lives. The clothing people already owned was a resource for the construction of new looks, and even new items were bought with these already owned outfits in mind. Fashion can be defined in this context as a *practice of assemblage*—whether it is trying items on in shops or working with the things that hang in a person's wardrobe (see Hansen 2000; Tarlo 1996). Assembling includes knowledge of what is in fashion, as well as cultural competences about "how" to wear things. This is not a comprehensive definition of fashion, but it is one that fits in with an approach to fashion as a set of material practices. Fashion practices include what people do with clothing in particular contexts, including what is selected, whether from shops or markets, or from the wardrobe. Understood as a practice of assemblage, this definition of fashion includes how an outfit is chosen and worn, which is an embodied practice and thus entails bodily cultural competences (Entwistle 2000). These connected practices are intimate and material: through the feel of something we are trying on against our skin, how we look at and think about the aesthetics of different colors as they go together, or how we are able to move as we walk and lift our arms in items of clothing.

Fashion here is not understood as an abstract force, but as a series of material embodied practices. In an article engaging with the relationship between fashion, materiality, and immateriality, Tom Fisher and I explore fashion as a noun (as the system of *fashion*), as a verb (*to fashion*), and as an adjective (*fashionable*) as a means to define and understand the different facets of fashion (Woodward and Fisher 2014). In this chapter, I am predominantly concerned with the process of "fashioning"—"to fashion," which in my work mostly concerns what consumers do with clothing, but can also be applied to what designers do, among others. The process of fashioning in part produces what is fashionable, yet is also produced by the system of fashion. People are able to edit, validate, or reject what the industry produces or defines as fashionable. This is a model of fashion that is more complex than either a trickle-up (Polhemus 2010) or trickle-down (Veblen 1899) notion of fashion innovation. The complex interrelationships between different spaces for the production of fashion meanings is encapsulated in Susan Kaiser's model of the circuit of style-fashion-dress (Kaiser 2012), which highlights the multidirectional flows of innovation between consumption, production, distribution and regulation, and subject formation. This conceptualization of fashion dovetails with ideas I would like to develop here, where what is fashionable is a negotiated practice between garments that are produced and mediated by a fashion industry and consumers who wear, reject, fail to buy, or keep on wearing the same items year in and year out. This process becomes even more complicated when we factor in people's own understanding of fashion and of what is fashionable. We may come to define and understand it as academics, but consumers have their very own understanding of what fashion is (whether it is items that everyone wears, or things a few "cool" people are wearing) and, in turn what is fashionable, which may coincide or not with what is defined as fashionable in media such as cutting-edge fashion blogs.

The definition of fashion that I have outlined is concerned specifically with fashion from the perspective of what people wear and, as such, forms an orientation to fashion as a form of "ordinary consumption" (Gronow and Warde 2001) rather than as a spectacular form of differentiation. Blue denim jeans form the perfect example of this, which is one of the reasons they were chosen as a research topic, and as a redressal of an overemphasis in the literature focusing on designers or clothing that most people rarely wear. The example of denim jeans highlights a defining feature of fashion as being simultaneously global and local, generic and personal—echoing Georg Simmel's characterization of fashion as the oscillation between individuality and conformity (Simmel 1971). Jeans are "generic" as they are worn by many different sectors of the population, yet also personal as they take on the body of the wearer, becoming softer over time (a property of how they are woven and dyed). Being fashionable, or wearing clothes such as jeans that we know many other people are wearing, allows us to feel part of a wider global humanity, yet, as people talk about items of clothing being "me," fashion can be a very intimate experience. This apparently opposing tendency is a defining feature of fashion, yet also one that poses challenges to the academic researcher.

## Wardrobes and streets

Looking at fashion as a material practice is a route to seeing the intimacies of fashion as well as how and when it may be perceived as "external." In this section, I will primarily focus upon how fashion can be understood to be intimate. It is worn on our bodies, on our skin; it holds and allows bodies to move; as we are rarely unclothed, our clothes are part of who we are all of the time, and are central to how we navigate our world and social relationships. Clothes may materialize a person that we love, or memories of our cherished times, or our most humiliating failures. Clothing is also intimately linked to sexuality and the performance of gender (see Kaiser and Green in this book).

In adopting an approach to fashion that is grounded in everyday household practices and consumption, I carried out an ethnography of women's wardrobes (Woodward 2007). The first stage of this process involved the wardrobe interview, as women were asked to go through each item hanging in their wardrobe and "tell me about" it. The questions were open-ended to allow women to talk about what mattered to them. If little was forthcoming, I would prompt them to talk about how long they had had the garment, how they got it, any particular memories of wearing it, and also what they tended to wear it with. Each item was photographed so that after the interview I was able to look at the photographs when re-listening to audio-recordings. Although a photo of a garment does not capture the materiality of a garment, nor the feel, or smell of it, or how it moves, photos were useful in allowing me to spend time looking at the clothing in a way that I would not have been able to, at the risk of lingering too long in women's wardrobes.

Once I had done the initial wardrobe interview, in most cases, I asked participants to keep a clothes diary for two weeks. Participants noted what they put on in the morning, and if they changed clothes to go out, or when they came back from work. I asked women to write down things they tried on but didn't wear. I conducted a follow-up interview during which we went through the clothes diaries as they discussed what they wore and didn't wear and the reasons for this. I also carried out clothing life-history interviews in which women were asked to talk through the stages in their lives through the clothes that they wore—either as specific memories or broader styles. As I got to know these women and "hung out" in their houses, I also carried out more in-depth ethnographic observations

with many participants, watching them select outfits and how they got dr
to go out in the evening. As a consequence, the project concerned itself with
intimate experiences of choosing what to wear, seeing fashion as something that
concerns women's bodies and sense of self. Present in magazines or worn by
celebrities, fashion is both something women can feel alienated by if they cannot
"get it right," or perceive their own dressed bodies to be far removed from the
fashionable body; yet, fashion also allows them to feel good about themselves if
they have "got it right."

Someone standing in front of their wardrobe (see Figure 2.1) and usually a
mirror in their bedroom—seen by many as the most private part of the house—
is the ideal starting point for an understanding of these intimacies of fashion. A
research approach taking these intimacies into account moves away from reducing
fashion practices to just the public presentation of self, to consider the dilemmas
and anxieties, and also the hopes, behind what women end up wearing. This
includes looking at what women never wear, as well as what they try on at home

FIGURE 2.1 Clothes hanging in the wardrobe. *Photo*: Sophie Woodward.

and reject, as much as what they end up wearing in public. Clothes that are tried on and never worn are pivotal to understanding fashion aspirations—clothing that people may wish they could wear, but feel they have neither the body nor the ability to carry it off. It was only by watching what women tried on and also through their keeping of clothes diaries that this field was opened up for analysis. Wardrobe studies is an approach that has been developed by others, including Banim and Guy (2001) who looked in particular at things people keep, but no longer wore in terms of a typology of former, current, and aspirational selves. Wardrobe studies have also been used in a number of projects by Ingun Klepp who, together with Marie Bjerk (2012), has explicitly reflected on the methods and what they afford and offer to the understanding of the materiality of clothing. In addition to being a means to understand the materiality of clothing and to focus upon "inconspicuous consumption" in looking at the whole collection of clothing (van der Laan and Velthuis 2013), wardrobe studies allow an exploration of fashion as a practice of assemblage. By combining items of clothing in outfits, clothing practices are by definition practices of assemblage. When new items are combined with old ones, then the collection of clothing in the wardrobe is a possible resource through which "new" looks and fashions can be created, by reactivating old items or making new combinations.

This understanding of fashion as assemblage emerging from the wardrobe research also informed my research on street fashion. An interest in how fashion is generated lead to a project called FashionMap at Nottingham Trent University, initiated and managed by Sue Keen, which involved trained student photographers taking photos of what people were wearing in various locations in the street, in bars, and other social hubs (see Woodward 2008 for a discussion). Participants were photographed, as well as briefly interviewed, in order to access information such as where the items that people were wearing were from, or how long they had had them. The aim was to explore fashion through the lens of "street style"; alongside this aim, students developed specific projects around areas of fashion such as androgyny or masculinity and sportswear. The images and interviews were collected together and stored online as the information amassed year after year. The project had aimed to store the data in the form of a database, but due to lack of suitable funds this never fully developed. I am currently initiating a similar project at the University of Manchester, where images will be stored in a database and bear "tags," so that common themes can be accessed and will show up across the observation data.

Observations for FashionMap (see Figure 2.2) took place biannually in Nottingham and, as well as highlighting how fashions were taken up and emerged as they took place over several years, showed the multiple temporalities of fashion when seen through everyday practices. The capacities of the industry to produce clothing very rapidly, and to be responsive to what and how much is being bought, have led to a characterization of fashion as "fast." When we look at clothing through

FIGURE 2.2 Images of interviewees, "Kids in Tracksuits" from the Fashionmap Archive, Nottingham Trent University. © Nottingham Trent University.

observations of what people are wearing year after year, then while there are some rapid changes (mostly in terms of new items being matched with things that are already owned), there are also fashion "slow-burners"—items that may have been heralded as now out of fashion by magazines, but that people continue to wear (see Woodward 2009). The only way to start to access these understandings is through long-term observations as we can start to piece together a picture of what changes and what stays the same.

By carrying out observations year after year, the project strove to develop as an archive of everyday fashion, charting how it changed over time. In many ways FashionMap was an exploratory project and it raised useful issues about how we might be able to compare fashions over time. One route for comparison is through charting specific items of clothing—such as jeans—to see how they change or continue in styles over time. A second route is through comparing what people are wearing in a specific social location over different time periods. Another possible route is to compare one person over a series of observations to explore how the personal and wider fashion cycles intersect. In order to make such comparisons it is important to decide in advance what the parameters of comparison are and then ensure that information is collected from this person/location. This allows the possibility to "track" this throughout the observations.

One of the most fruitful forms of comparative data analysis in the FashionMap project was the juxtaposition of the images. After the first observations, all of the images were printed out and exhibited. This process was repeated again after three years of observations (see Woodward 2008). Seeing the images as a totality, allowed interesting connections to be made in the data, including tracing groups of similarly dressed individuals. Similarities or discrepancies could thus be seen visually through the images offering a new means of comparison. After grouping the images in this way, we then returned to the interview data to yield new insights: for example, who came to be defined as the "local celebrity" based upon how many people commented upon knowing someone who was "really cool."

Research on fashion practices that takes place in social locations such as the street or in bars remains anchored in an understanding of what people already own, and therefore can be connected to the wardrobe research. Fashion here is both intimate and also involves a negotiation of what is produced by the fashion industry and is presented to people in shops. The fashion that was documented in this project is the "everyday," and through street style documentation we are able to make visible these everyday practices. It is this interest in the everydayness of fashion and clothing that lies at the heart of the different sites and methods outlined in this chapter.

# Denim ethnography and interviews

Carrying out research into everyday clothing practices in order to *make visible* is particularly pertinent as an approach to denim jeans, the case study for the final two sections of this chapter. This section will consider an ethnography carried out in London with a focus on practices of wearing jeans, and the next section will consider the larger Global Denim Project in which it was situated. As mentioned in the introduction, denim presents us with two research challenges: how to understand the simultaneously generic and intimate nature of denim jeans and how to understand people's material relationships to jeans particularly when they may have very little to say about them. The impetus to study denim came from my initial wardrobe study and the realization that even if women only owned three or four pairs of jeans it was often the most worn item of clothing that women fell back on when they did not know what else to wear (Woodward 2007). Jeans could be both a way to blend in and a way to stand out and differentiate oneself, a way of being "individual" yet also conforming (Simmel 1971). This relationship between feeling like "me" but also fitting in was developed as the starting point for the Global Denim Project (Miller and Woodward 2007) to highlight jeans as being both personal and generic. Jeans allowed people to feel comfortable (enabled materially through how denim wears down) and were often the most personal item people owned, and fell back on when nothing else seemed right—they were there for them in times of anxiety. At the same time, jeans are also the most generic as they are such a frequently and widely worn item of clothing, worn by many different sectors of the population all over the world. As such, we set about trying to develop a more global picture of this relationship between the generic and the personal.

The ethnography of blue jeans we carried out in North London (Miller and Woodward 2012) was one of these comparative projects. The research took place on three adjacent streets over the course of two summers; we started by leafleting houses and then knocking on doors to get participants. People often responded that they had nothing to say about jeans. However, often these same people when interviewed commented in the end that they were surprised that they had so much to say about their jeans. We started interviews with a "life history" interview of their jeans: we asked them to tell us about their first pairs of jeans, and how the jeans wearing changed throughout different periods of their life, as well as about the jeans that other people wore (parents, friends). Adopting life-history interviews proved a useful strategy in getting people to talk. Everyone we interviewed was able to talk about the type of jeans they wore as, for example, a teenager, in relationship to what other teenagers were wearing. Doing life-history interviews through the clothes people wore was a useful route into exploring the links between personal biography, wider fashions, and a sense of generational identity. There is a strong tradition of doing oral-history interviews, as situated in wider social trends and notions of generation (see Allan and Jones 2003 for a discussion of this), yet it is less explored in relationship to clothing.

After life-history interviews, we focused upon the concrete practices of owning and wearing jeans, including when people tended to wear them, as well as wider attitudes over who should wear jeans. Even if participants could talk about jeans and broad styles (such as bell-bottoms and the 1970s), we noted that very few were able to talk about the details of particular jeans. In part, this is because jeans were seen as a background, everyday item of clothing, rather than as something "special." When people talked about items they wore habitually, we were able to start to understand the everyday material practices that constituted jeans wearing.

Although we were able to adopt approaches to make understanding jeans easier, they were still not something that people talked passionately about, with only a couple of exceptions of jeans aficionados. This is not just a question of adopting the right methods, but instead of appreciating that jeans matter as a form of everyday material culture that is pivotal to helping people to live their lives, which is often not verbalized. In particular, wearing plain blue jeans allowed people to "be ordinary" (see Miller and Woodward 2012). Although jeans (Figure 2.3) have the capacity to, and may be used in some contexts to differentiate people, in the main our ethnography highlighted that when people wore blue jeans, they did not want to look different or appear special. In fact they just wanted to be able to get on with their lives. This was a particularly pertinent issue for migrants in the study, as although there were occasions when they wanted to be marked as different such as on special occasions, when going to work, or to the shops they just wanted to be able to get on with things. Wearing blue jeans enabled this to happen as they were "just jeans" (a phrase used by many informants), and were not seen as being "from" anywhere in particular, as associations with the

**FIGURE 2.3** Participant's range of jeans, from special to ordinary. *Photo*: Sophie Woodward.

United States has been all but lost. People may not have eloquent speeches to give about these blue jeans, but in their humility the jeans were able to let people get on simply living their lives without marking them as different, or making them particularly visible. A core part of jeans' ability to do this is because they are so widely worn and recognizable in their appearance; I will consider this further in the final section of this chapter.

## Comparative denim ethnographies

The premise of the Global Denim Project was to develop a comparison between a range of localized ethnographies of jeans. The contexts studied ranged from China (Mcdonald 2011) to the United States (Olesen 2011), to India (Wilkinson-Weber 2011), to Germany (Ege 2011), and to Egypt (Chakravarti 2011), to name a few. Many focused upon consumption, but some also considered design (Townsend 2011) and production (Chakravarti 2011). Most studies were ethnographic in nature, yet other methods were included, such as historical approaches (Comstock 2011). To illustrate the different methods adopted and the possibilities of comparative projects, I will discuss an example from Brazil and one from Japan in relationship to the London example already discussed. Each research project within the Global Denim Project is an independent research project with its own aims and methods. However, the project aimed to be more than just a collection of related projects, and to see what a directly comparative project could allow. The challenge of comparison arises from the specificities of methods and foci within particular projects, as we are not always comparing like with like. Yet, all projects share a focus on the same topic of jeans, and a commitment to being material culture projects that place jeans at the heart of their research. We could not develop a systematic framework for comparing every project in the same way, given their differences. The process of comparison was much more organic, in the sense that thinking about similarities and differences was a way to enhance and further develop the findings of each project, and also to draw some more general conclusions (see Miller and Woodward 2011).

For us, comparison is only effective when considering the specificities of each project, its methods and its findings. The Brazilian ethnography, carried out by Mizrahi (2011), focused on the type of jeans worn by women at funk balls in the favelas of Rio de Janeiro. The ethnographic approach of participant-observation was essential to understanding how jeans enact and permit the embodied performances of gender and sexuality that take place within these specific contexts. As an ethnography of material culture, the research included an understanding of the materiality of jeans. In this example, they are not made of denim, but rather of "*moleton* stretch," which has the same constituents of denim (although much higher stretch content), cotton (around 95 percent) and elastane fibers (5 percent), and has the appearance of denim, indigo dyed, and with jean pockets. Moleton is woven differently in order to have the qualities of jersey, as it stretches both horizontally and vertically, unlike traditional denim with elastane that only stretches in one direction. This elasticity is important in allowing easy movements of the legs, knees, and hips when dancing, as well as hugging the body and revealing and holding its curves. The fabric is also thick enough to be both embellished with crystals as well as being cut into to form design features up the legs. The heart of this research was not just the materiality of jeans, as the garment cannot be analyzed separately from the wearer. Instead the methodological focus entails both observing the jeans as worn on a moving body in a specific context, and participating in the context of the events, which is a multisensory experience.

The materiality of the jeans is central to framing women's experiences as they dance, allowing them to move and to show their body. The findings of this Brazil-centered project can be developed through comparison with some of the other projects, such as the ethnography in North London. In the same way, blue jeans in north London are part of people's everyday, ordinary experiences, seeing the wearing of jeans as a set of material practices in Rio favelas highlights the ways in which these garments are part of framing the gendered, embodied experiences of dancing at these balls. The trousers are not separate from these social contexts, but they help to produce them. This inseparability of jeans, bodies, and sites can only be fully comprehended through the participant-observation that Mizrahi undertook. Had she not been present, listening to the music, feeling the heat, seeing the bodies move in the jeans, she would not have arrived at this understanding. Returning to the comparative method, when we compare the materiality of jeans in Rio and London, we can start to see some strong divergences. Unlike the example of blue jeans in London, the aesthetic at favela balls is very recognizable and distinctive. Yet at the same time, these garments have the appearance of blue jeans, generally. Thus the specificity of the jeans aesthetic and practices of wearing is both "local," and global. The resemblance of the moleton stretch jeans to denim gives them a fashionable appeal by connecting the women in this specific context to a wider global fashion sensibility. Although this is a different permutation of the personal/global discussed earlier, jeans are still valued in part here due to their capacity for creating individual comfort and the simultaneous ability to attach them to a wider global sense of fashionability.

The final project within the Global Denim Project that I will turn to is of ethnographic research into the artisan making of jeans in Kojima, Japan. One of the core features that ethnography demands, and the comparative method it enhances, is the specificity of local contexts, in this case, of jean consumption and design. In Kojima, the ethnographic study focused on observing what designers do, and to understand their practices in the local, historical context. Keet explores (2011) the cultural history of jeans to show that prior to the 1990s, if jeans were made in Japan, this was downplayed in marketing strategies because jeans were often affiliated with America. This shifts through the 1990s with an increased desire for original Levi's jeans, which are bought from the United States and dissected and analyzed in "denim laboratories" in Japan. The original looms for denim weaving are bought from the United States and used to manufacture new jeans bearing the characteristic selvedge. Further, the original techniques of stitching are adopted. Keet's focus on the designers demonstrated that in order to understand the materiality of jeans we need to see the materialities of production. An observation of these processes highlights that designers both replicate original production techniques, yet also develop innovations in distressing, dyeing, and using new washes. The localized ethnographic process that focused upon the designers working and based in Kojima (renowned for its jeans production), enabled Keet to explore a particular construction of authenticity in a Japanese context. These understandings of localized meanings are enhanced by a methodology that also incorporates the global fashion advertising of jeans brands. By studying how jeans are advertised in the United States, Keet showed that some American brands are seen to be more authentic when they use Japanese denim—such as PRPS, a denim brand based in New York, who had their jeans made in Japan (Keet 2011). An understanding of the meanings of jeans emerges in this context from a localized ethnography, from cultural histories of jeans, and the exploration of the global fashion marketing of jeans. This set of methods allows us to see an interplay between a global and a local specificity, an exchange that is further enhanced by juxtaposing and comparing other projects globally. Global comparison highlights that which is local and specific, yet also the common meanings of jeans that emerge.

# Conclusion

The global spread of jeans necessitates a project with a global scope; yet simply to have a project that covers a wide range of countries would not be enough. Jeans are not only worn throughout the world, they are also the dominant form of casual clothing in many places. Moreover, as was suggested by the initial wardrobe ethnography in London (Woodward 2007), jeans were important to women as a way of resolving anxieties over what to wear. It became clear that jeans matter to people, and so we needed to develop methods that allowed an understanding of this intimate relationship that people have with jeans, as well as the appeal of their global fashionability. We proposed that a series of local ethnographies that focused on the wearing of denim jeans throughout the world would allow an understanding of this ubiquitous garment's significance. The three examples from the Global Denim Project introduced here give a flavor of what a range of comparative ethnographies can show. Once we start to interrogate even something as seemingly "blindingly obvious" (Miller and Woodward 2007) as jeans, a complex picture emerges. "Jeans" are not always the same thing: different materialities entail different material practices. The relationship between the global and the personal and the garment's meaning is different, depending upon context. While a discipline such as anthropology is by definition a comparative discipline, often this comparison entails situating your own ethnographic research in relationship to and in comparison with preexisting ethnographic research on a related topic. Yet, what the Global Denim Project does is foment a range of ethnographic work being carried out at the same time, on the same topic. There is much to be learned from comparative ethnographic work being carried out in this manner and this method offers future possibilities for similar research in the field of fashion studies. Comparative work can focus upon different points of comparison and similarity, such as a type of clothing or a clothing practice. It could also entail a comparative method (such as carrying out wardrobe studies in several countries).

As material culture scholars, we cannot understand fashion just in terms of what people say about garments, or what we are conscious and aware of, but rather, we must think about how clothing frames and allows our social relations. The methods and approaches adopted are all involved in *making visible* these materialities, as well as what we do with them, and what they do for us. There are a range of methods that are suited to this kind of aim—such as the comparative ethnography discussed here or the interviews. While it is important that our methods and approaches "fit" the empirical topic, it is not just a question of getting the "right" method for a topic to unlock the phenomenon in question. We also need to pay heed to that which may be inaccessible and try to understand what this is telling us. In fact, often, material culture is not something that can easily be captured through particular methods, as it is not something that people themselves are aware of. It is this inaccessibility that is not simply a failure in the research process, but tells us something about the phenomenon in question—people having little to say about specific pairs of jeans is a case in point. Sometimes the methods we pick seem to be a direct match for the topic—such as a wardrobe study for looking at the intimacies of fashion and identity. In other cases, the methods are surprising—such as a wardrobe ethnography to look at the global and at fashion—yet often it is through seemingly unusual matches that new insights are permitted.

# References

Allan, Graham and Gill Jones. 2003. *Social Relations and the Life-Course*. Basingstoke: Palgrave Macmillan.

Banim, Maura and Ali Guy. 2001. "Dis/continued selves: Why do Women Keep Clothes They no Longer Wear." In *Through the Wardrobe: Women's Relationships with their Clothes*, edited by Ali Guy, Eileen Green, and Maura Banim, 203–219. Oxford: Berg.

Chakravarti, Leila. 2011. "Material Worlds: Denim on the Globalised Shop Floor". Unravelling Denim Special Issue *Textile: The Journal of Cloth and Culture*, edited by Sophie Woodward and Daniel Miller 9 (3): 62–75.

Comstock, Sandra. 2011. "The Making of an American Icon: The Transformation of Blue Jeans during the Great Depression." In *Global Denim*, edited by Daniel Miller and Sophie Woodward, 23–49. Oxford: Berg.

Ege, Mauritz. 2011. "Carrot-cut Jeans: An Ethnographic Account of Assertiveness, Embarrassment and Ambiguity in the Figuration of Working-class Male Youth Identities in Berlin." In *Global Denim*, edited by Daniel Miller and Sophie Woodward, 159–80. Oxford: Berg.

Entwistle, Joanne. 2000. *The Fashioned Body*. Oxford: Polity.

Fury, Alexander. 2014. "The Return of the Humble Blue Jean" in the *New Zealand Herald*. April 14, 2014, accessed July 9, 2014, http://www.nzherald.co.nz/viva-magazine/news/article.cfm?c_id=533&objectid=11238546.

Goffman, Erving.1974. *Frame Analysis: An Essay on the Organisation of Experience*. Harmondsworth: Penguin.

Gombrich, Ernst. 1979. *The Sense of Order: A Study in the Psychology of Decorative Art*. Oxford: Phaidon

Gronow, Jukka and Alan Warde, eds. 2001. *Ordinary Consumption*. London: Routledge.

Hansen, Karen Tranberg. 2000. *Salaula: The World of Second Hand Clothing and Zambia*. Chicago: University of Chicago Press.

Kaiser, Susan. 2003. *The Social Psychology of Clothing*. New York: Fairchild Publications.

Kaiser, Susan. 2012. *Fashion and Cultural Studies*. Oxford: Berg.

Keet, Philomeena. 2011. "Making New Vintage Jeans in Japan: Relocating Authenticity." Unravelling Denim Special Issue *Textile: The Journal of Cloth and Culture*, edited by Sophie Woodward and Daniel Miller 9 (1): 44–61.

Klepp, Ingun and Marie Bjerk. 2012. "A Methodological Approach to the Materiality of Clothing: Wardrobe Studies." *International Journal of Social Research Methodology* 17 (4): 373–86.

Küchler, Suzanne and Daniel Miller, eds. 2005. *Clothing as Material Culture*. Oxford: Berg.

Lipovetsky, Gilles. 2002. *The Empire of Fashion: Dressing Modern Democracy*. Princeton: Princeton University Press.

Mcdonald, Tom. 2011. "Cowboy Cloth and Kinship: The Closeness of Denim Consumption in a South-West Chinese City." Unravelling Denim Special Issue *Textile: The Journal of Cloth and Culture*, edited by Sophie Woodward and Daniel Miller 9 (1): 76–89.

Miller, Daniel. 1987. *Material Culture and Mass Consumption*. Oxford: Basil Blackwell.

Miller, Daniel and Sophie Woodward. 2007. "A Manifesto for a Study of Denim." *Social Anthropology* 15: 335–51.

Miller, Daniel and Sophie Woodward, eds. 2011. *Global Denim*. Oxford: Berg.

Miller, Daniel and Sophie Woodward. 2012. *Blue Jeans: The Art of the Ordinary*. Berkeley, CA: University of California Press.

Mizrahi, Milene. 2011. "Brazilian Jeans: Materiality, Body and Seduction at a Rio de Janeiro's Funk Ball." In *Global Denim*, edited by Daniel Miller and Sophie Woodward, 103–26. Oxford: Berg.

Olesen, Bodil. 2011. "How Blue Jeans Went Green: The Materiality of an American Icon." In *Global Denim*, edited by Daniel Miller and Sophie Woodward, 69–86. Oxford: Berg.

Polhemus, Ted. 2010. *Street Style*. London: PYMCA.

Simmel, Georg. 1971. *On Individuality and Social Forms*. Chicago: University of Chicago Press.

Tarlo, Emma. 1996. *Clothing Matters*. Chicago: University of Chicago Press.

Taylor, Lou. 2004. *Establishing Dress History*. Manchester: Manchester University Press.

Townsend, Katherine. 2011. "The Denim Garment as Canvas: Exploring the Notion of Wear as a Fashion and Textile Narrative." Unravelling Denim Special Issue *Textile: The Journal of Cloth and Culture*, edited by Sophie Woodward and Daniel Miller 9 (1): 90–107.

van der Laan, Elise and Olav Velthuis. 2013. "Inconspicuous Dressing: A Critique of the Construction-Through-Consumption Paradigm in the Sociology of Clothing." *Journal of Consumer Culture*, October 9, 2013, doi:10.1177/1469540513505609.

Veblen, Thorstein. 1899. *Theory of the Leisure Class: An Economic Study of Institutions*. New York: Mentor.

Weiner, Annette and Jane Schneider, eds. 1989. *Cloth and the Human Experience*. London: Smithsonian Institute Press.

Wilkinson-Weber, Clare. 2011. "Diverting Denim: Screening Jeans in Bollywood." In *Global Denim*, edited by Daniel Miller and Sophie Woodward, 51–68. Oxford: Berg.

Wilson, Elizabeth. 1985. *Adorned in Dreams: Fashion and Modernity*. London: Virago.

Woodward, Sophie. 2007. *Why Women Wear What they Wear*. Oxford: Berg.

Woodward, Sophie. 2008. "Digital Photography and Research Relationships: Capturing the Fashion Moment." *Sociology* 42 (5): 857–72.

Woodward, Sophie. 2009. "The Myth of the Street." *Fashion Theory* 13 (1): 83–102.

Woodward, Sophie and Tom Fisher. 2014. "Fashioning Through Materials: Material Culture, Materiality and Processes of Materialization." *Critical Studies in Fashion and Beauty* 5 (1): 3–22.

SECTION TWO

# EXPLORING FASHION PRACTICES THROUGH ETHNOGRAPHY

# INTRODUCTION

## Heike Jenss

Fashion studies incorporates the methods of many disciplines, including the work of cultural anthropologists who pioneered ethnographic and material culture approaches in their research on textiles and clothing in non-Western contexts (see Cordwell and Schwarz 1979; Weiner and Schneider 1989). More recently, in response to increasing global interconnectedness in the twenty-first century, a number of anthropological works on fashion and dress have further helped to broaden the understanding of fashion in cross-cultural perspectives, including the groundbreaking book edited by Sandra Niessen, Ann Marie Leshkowich, and Carla Jones, *Re-Orienting Fashion* (2003), Emma Tarlo's *Visibly Muslim* (2010), as well as many articles and special issues in the journal *Fashion Theory*: for example, on "Fashion and Orientalism," edited by Nirmal Puwar and Nandi Bhatia (2003); on "Muslim Fashion," edited by Emma Tarlo and Annelies Moors (2007), on "African Fashion/African Style" by Victoria Rovine (2009), on "Dress and African Diaspora" by Carol Tulloch (2010).

Historically the method of ethnography emerged in the context of European imperialism, colonial politics, and the project of euro-modernity, involving the development of scientific methods "to produce knowledge about strange and foreign worlds" (Denzin and Lincoln 2005, 1). In its early uses it was conceptualized, and inherently racialized, as an "objective way of representing the dark-skinned other to the white world" (2005, 1). One of the initiators of ethnography, using participant-observation as a method, was Bronislaw Malinowski (1884–1942), who conducted research by living with the Trobriand Islanders near Papua New Guinea from 1914 to 1918. Malinowski participated in and observed their everyday life, practices, routines, rituals, and forms of kinship to generate firsthand "data" that would form a basis of his ethnographic description of the Islanders' culture (see Denzin and Lincoln 2005, 15). The word "ethnography" is a combination of the terms *ethnos* (= people) and *graphere* (= writing), coming to mean "writing culture." The latter is the title of James Clifford's and George Marcus' 1983 book on the poetics and politics of ethnography, addressing the issue of representation in ethnographic accounts and the need for reflexivity to call into question issues of gender, class, and race as they are bound up with ethnography. The term "ethnography" refers to a mode of doing research, by immersing oneself in a specific cultural context, participating in and observing routine practices within the field in an attempt to understand the experiences and perspectives of those studied and collecting or writing/ producing data—and it also refers to the interpretation and representation in the final, written ethnographic account (see, for a discussion of the practices and historical moments of qualitative research, including ethnography, Denzin and Lincoln 2005). Ethnography is therefore not simply a method of data collection, but a "process of creating and representing knowledge (about society, culture, and individuals) that is based on an ethnographer's experience" (Pink 2001, 18). Today ethnography is understood—like any research—as an interpretive and intersubjective practice, acknowledging that the practice of "making sense of one's findings is both artistic and political," and that there "is no single interpretative truth" (Denzin and Lincoln 2005, 26).

As a method that allows a researcher to focus on specific sites, locations, and practices, the approach of ethnography has been instrumental to the development of more nuanced perspectives on fashion and dress in recent decades (see for earlier discussions Hansen 2004; Jenss 2005). With "globalization" as one of the central issues or concepts addressed in fashion studies, as well as in other fields of research, ethnography offers perspectives and approaches for understanding the cross-cultural dimensions and dynamics of fashion and dress—including the "encounters in the global fashion business," as, for example, mapped out in a collection of ethnographies on fashion production edited by Patrik Aspers and Lise Skov (2006) in the journal *Current Sociology*.

Ethnographies of fashion have helped to break up a totalizing, rather abstract concept of globalization—and also of fashion—by offering in-depth perspectives on how fashion is constituted in everyday practices, including how it is produced and mediated, or fashioning experiences of time and place, from a metropolitan to a small-town or rural context (see, for example, Bernstein and Kaiser 2013; Goodrum and Hunt 2013). And this does of course not imply that research must be pursued in geographically distanced locations, but rather that ethnography is also used for the exploration of fashion and dress practices "at home." In three of the following case studies the scholars embark on ethnographic research in the places where they live/d, although it needs to be acknowledged here that all of these locations are urban and American: Christina Moon and Stephanie Sadre-Orafai focus on the workings in the New York fashion industry, while Brent Luvaas explores street style photography in Philadelphia. Yet, while these studies are grounded in the research sites in proximity to the author's location, they also highlight their wider global entanglements.

This is particularly pronounced in Christina H. Moon's chapter, in which she describes her navigation through the "search for the global fashion industry." Her research on subjects working in New York fashion, and leading her to other sites, evolved in part in response to the growing scholarly interest in consumption and the "social life of things" (Appadurai 1986) during the 1990s. In her ethnography she seeks to uncover what the fashion industry would look like if described through the narratives, social relationships, and practices of fashion workers, many of whom have migrated from China or Korea to America. Her chapter offers insights into the fluid dynamics and personal entanglements between "researcher" and "research subject," where she finds herself "knee-deep, grappling with these intimate pulls and memories of fashion and garment histories," including those of her own family. The chapter provides a sense of the temporalities and affective dimensions of research, reflecting on the process from its beginnings to coming to make sense of the "findings" about the fashion industry—including its histories of migrating workers, students in fashion education, and the transitioning of local spaces of fashion along with globalization.

The experiential and affective dimensions of doing ethnography on fashion are further discussed by Brent Luvaas, who offers in his chapter insights into his own transitioning from starting to work "on" street style blogs, to becoming a street style photographer and blogger himself. He introduces the use of auto-ethnography as mode of research and describes his learning process of looking, spotting, stopping, and photographing subjects on the street, reflecting on the development of embodied knowledge that subjects the often abstracted formation of, or thinking with, social and cultural theories "to the test of practice." His chapter shows the unique insights that can be generated by "doing" fashion in the context of fashion research, including the experience of writing and curating one's own street style blog.

The focus on embodied practice and the ethnographic exploration of fashion image production is expanded in Stephanie Sadre-Orafai's chapter on model casting agencies. Her interest lies in the multisensory evaluative processes that make fashion images possible, including the manufacturing of "types" of people, including constructing ethnicity. Through field work in model casting agencies in New York, informed by the approach of ethnomethodology, she explores the discursive, visual, material, and embodied practices that go into the selection of models. In her chapter, she reflects on how she enters the field and adjusts her research questions along with her journey through different casting agencies, to not only understand the making of fashion images, but the production of mediation: that is, how to "produce a model's body as a medium."

Much of what Sadre-Orafai focuses on in her fieldwork is the interaction between casting agents and models, and how, through conversations and interactions, forms of knowledge about people are produced. This approach and interest is also part of the methodological reflection in Todd Nicewonger's chapter on fashion design education and the learning of creativity at the Antwerp Academy. His work is an example of a growing scholarly interest in the exploration of fashion design practices and pedagogy, which is timely, especially in light of the attempt to move toward more sustainable fashion practices. Creativity is perhaps one of the highest values and ideals in design practice. By reflecting on his fieldwork conducted in the studios of one of Europe's leading fashion design schools, speaking with students, observing their work, and student-teacher interactions, Nicewonger illustrates how the practices of making, the designing of fashion, and the development and learning of creativity through "communities of practice" can be ethnographically studied, opening up new insights for the field of fashion studies.

Together, the four chapters in this section exemplify the adoption, adaptation, and intersubjective nature of ethnographic methodologies, reflecting on the researchers' immersion in—and knowledge production of—some of the key sites that make up the wide material scope of fashion. They offer insights particularly into some of the less visible "backstage" practices through which fashion is produced, comes to circulate and is enacted in, or as, objects, images, and experiences. In its focus on fashion practices, including fashion design and pedagogy in Antwerp, the section also establishes points of connection to the third section in this book on mixed methods, including a chapter on the work of Belgian designer Martin Margiela, or a chapter on making and design practice as mode of research and intervention.

# References

Appadurai, Arjun, ed. 1986. *The Social Life of Things: Commodities in Cultural Perspective*. New York: Cambridge University Press.

Aspers, Patrik and Lise Skov, eds. 2006. Encounters in the Global Fashion Business Special Issue. *Current Sociology* 54 (5).

Bernstein, Sara Tatyana and Susan B. Kaiser. 2013. "Fashion out of Place: Experiencing Fashion in a Small American Town," *Critical Studies of Fashion and Beauty* 4 (1–2): 43–70.

Clifford, James and George E. Marcus, ed. 1983. *Writing Culture: The Poetics and Politics of Ethnography*. Berkeley: University of California Press.

Cordwell, Justine and Ronald Schwarz, ed. 1979. *The Fabrics of Cultures*. New York: De Gruyter Mouton.

Denzin, Norman K., and Yvonne S. Lincoln. 2005. "Introduction: The Discipline and Practice of Qualitative Research." In *The Sage Handbook of Qualitative Research 3rd Edition*, edited by Norman K. Denzin and Yvonne S. Lincoln, 1–32. London: Sage.

Goodrum, Alison and Kevin J. Hunt. 2013. "The Field as Mall: Redressing the Rural-Urban Divide in Fashion Theory through Equestrian Events." *Critical Studies in Fashion and Beauty* 4 (1–2): 17–42.

Niessen, Sandra, Ann Marie Leshkowich, and Carla Jones, eds. 2003. *Re-Orienting Fashion: The Globalization of Asian Dress*. Oxford and New York: Berg.

Pink, Sarah. 2001. *Doing Visual Ethnography*. London: Sage.

Puwar, Nirmal and Nandi Bhatia, eds. 2003. Fashion and Orientalism Special Double Issue. *Fashion Theory: The Journal of Dress, Body and Culture* 7 (3/4), September/December 2003.

Rovine, Victoria L., ed. 2009. African Fashion/ African Style Special Issue. *Fashion Theory: The Journal of Dress, Body and Culture* 13 (20), June 2009.

Tarlo, Emma. 2010. *Visibly Muslim*. Oxford and New York: Berg.

Tarlo, Emma and Annelies Moors, eds. 2007. Muslim Fashions Special Double Issue. *Fashion Theory: The Journal of Dress, Body and Culture* 11 (2/3), June/September 2007.

Tulloch, Carol, ed. 2010. Dress and the African Diaspora Special Issue. *Fashion Theory: The Journal of Dress, Body and Culture* 14 (3), September 2010.

Weiner, Anette and Jane Schneider, eds. 1989. *Cloth and the Human Experience*. Washington, DC: Smithsonian Institution Press.

# 3 ETHNOGRAPHIC ENTANGLEMENTS: MEMORY AND NARRATIVE IN THE GLOBAL FASHION INDUSTRY

## Christina H. Moon

For the past ten years, I have been studying the global fashion industry through the labor of its cultural workers, including designers, design students and interns, sample makers, factory owners, clothing wholesalers, and sewers, among many others, who play a powerful role in the making of fashion. My field sites included several different design firms in New York and Los Angeles, a multinational design corporation, a high-end fashion company, and a mass fashion wholesale company, which took me to the varied spaces of the fashion industry: design studios, factories, corporate offices, and fashion runway shows across New York, Los Angeles, Paris, Hong Kong, Guangzhou, and Seoul (see Figures 3.1–3.4). Though I arrived in New York in 2005 as a wide-eyed graduate student, lured to the city by the glamour and glossy images made by a rapidly transforming media apparatus in the global fashion industry, I left with the realization that the cultural labor of migrating subjects—immigrants and their children—had played an enormous role in transforming cities like New York, Paris, and Milan into the global fashion capitals we have come to know today. This is a thread found throughout my work; much of my research explores the working lives of these subjects, not just sewers but fashion workers, who not only perform new kinds of creative work for the industry (particularly in design), but who also form the social ties that connect design capitals and manufacturing landscapes in clothing throughout the world.

In this chapter, I explore "how it is I got there" in my initial research on the New York fashion industry of the mid 2000s: how I arrived at the research sites and subjects that make up my studies on the global fashion industry, and what implications ethnographic practice might have in drawing out new research questions and conclusions (and possibilities) for the study of fashion. It was not until the very act of writing up my research findings did I realize the importance of what my "methods" were, and how my own practice of going about and collecting information through ethnographic research—the interpretive and subjective practice of personally embedding oneself in the fashion world—would ultimately shape the kind of "global fashion industry" I would observe, interpret, and depict in written, documentary representation. In a world of fashion I had always imagined as full of glamour, luxury, and beauty, I saw an underworld of capitalist logics, abstract economics, and exploited labor. The ethnographic practice of talking to and being among communities of fashion workers enabled me to illuminate an industry run on relationships and old-world ties and connections. These were the intimate and affective sides to global connections driving the technology and innovation within the global fashion industry, often excluded in socioeconomic and political histories of fashion.

## Mapping the global commodity chain of fashion

As a student of the social sciences, I had inherited sociological maps of the industry, a global fashion industry that was imagined as a "global commodity chain" and "system of aesthetic cultural production" that produced regimes of "circulating values" and emerging "markets." The theoretical model of a global commodity chain, consisting of "nodes" and "points" in a network of labor and production processes, would have as the end result a finished commodity, and explained how a commodity was produced in a "transnational and global context" (Applebaum and Gereffi 1994; Bonacich and Applebaum 2000; Gereffi and Korzeniewicz 1994; Bair 2005). With the introduction of trade laws including the General Agreement on Trade and Tariffs (GATT), the North America Free Trade Agreement (NAFTA), and the Multifiber Trade Agreement (MTA), academics eagerly sought to apply this theoretical model of the 1990s to the fashion industry, one of the first industries to experience the increasingly *global* spatiality of its apparel firms and the development of transnational links in production processes (see Castells 2000; Bonacich 2004; Gereffi et al. 2002; Gereffi and Korzeniewicz 1994). At the same time, social and cultural theorists began to expand this literature with perspectives on the "social life of things" (Appadurai 1986)—the global commodity chain's complimentary analysis: seeking to humanize the anonymous sphere of capitalist commerce as described by economists, they increased the focus on exploring subject/object relations in the object's valorization processes, attempting to trace the whole life history of objects. Curiously, both concepts appeared at a time in the 1990s when academic scholars had begun to make claims that the primary site to study "modern capitalist economies" had shifted from sites of production to sites of consumption. Soon, studies across the social sciences would predominantly focus on the study of moving commodities, material culture, and consumption processes (Appadurai 1986; Bourdieu 1984; Carrier 1994 and 1997; Miller 1986, 1995, 1996, 1998, and 2001). It was now possible to study entire histories of objects from origins, states of becoming, circulation in trade, and meaning-making in consumption: radical approaches to the study of objects and commodities in circulation, which greatly inspired generations of ethnographers to explore the global breadth of industry through the analytical unit of the commodity (Hart 2007). In time, the burgeoning field of fashion studies would produce scholarship on the production of fashion cultures and economies (Entwistle 2009), the making of fashion cities (Breward and Gilbert 2006), emergent fashion markets, consumerism and spatiality (Aspers 2010), fashion production and business practices (Blaszczyk 2008), and the making of sustainable fashion systems in a globalizing world (Black 2012).

In 2005, I thought that I too would go out into the world and trace the "object of fashion" through its Marxist, socioeconomic categories of production as a global commodity chain. Like sugar, cars, and Coca-Cola, I too would track fashion's multiple stages of becoming, like the "T-shirt travels" in its making, through the realms of production, distribution, and consumption beyond the borders of nation (Rivoli 2009). On a more humanistic level, I would analyze the different kinds of social and cultural worlds that the object moved back and forth in, exploring how the object gained cultural value, life history, and a whole biography of its own.

**FIGURE 3.1** The author peeks into a one-room sweatshop in the Changshindong neighborhood of Seoul, South Korea to ask a garment worker for directions. *Photo:* Christina H. Moon.

From cotton to fabric, from garment to fashion, into a system of symbolic meanings, I would then explain the hierarchical structures of a global fashion world and its fashion capitals, and the accumulation of cultural value as the object "becoming" through these worlds. Yet, although this would tell me something about the object itself, its cultural value, states of becoming, and political economy—there seemed to be *no people* in these mappings, neither the room for their complicated affectations and attachments for this world, nor the very contingencies that come along with all the nuances of global encounters in the making of fashion. As the cultural historian Michael Denning notes, "Maps are ways of conceiving totalities, understanding boundaries," yet maps are also "points of view—no single map tells us all we might want to know" (Denning 2004).

## Narrative traversing

From a practical perspective, I had no clue where I would begin to go "ethnographically." Where would I go to begin to study and track such an imagined, real, and transforming thing called the global fashion industry? An industry that changes day by day, minute by minute? I would have to "embark" on a field site and physically take myself there and so, I simply chose New York because it was the closest "global fashion capital" for me, a nice antidote to the quiet graduate life I had lived while at New Haven. On my first day of "field research" I found myself in the Garment District on 39th street, the very cultural heart of fashion history in the United States, and the geographical center of its commerce.

Here I was immediately confronted with the fleeting images and the sensory rush of a bustling neighborhood, full of people going on about their ordinary workday. It felt so different to be staring at some schematic of a supply chain in fashion—claimed objective representations of a global commodity chain that I had read about and imagined from the academic literature—to an actual physical place full of sounds, colors, images, smells, experiences, and human interactions. The ephemerality of everyday life and the cultural meaning it produced came at one as a full assault on the senses that bombarded in real time and lived experience, and every passing moment seemed to be full of possibilities, of potential interactions with different people, thick and detailed descriptions, fleeting thoughts, illuminations, with communicating signs abounding. These sudden moments of thought and feeling would go against all that I thought could be described, archived, or categorized all that I had ever found to be surefooted and confident, all that I had considered as "research." Here, I would have to talk to people, have all sorts of awkward and intimidating interactions and encounters, and have to acknowledge my own subjective positioning in light of an overwhelming anthropological history of modernist critique built on ethnocentrism, relativism, and "data collection." How would any of these theoretical models and concepts I had learned about, particularly the global commodity chain, guide me through any of this: gaining "access," getting people to talk to me, making and developing relationships, and then, later on, the personal entanglements, attachments, and investments that would influence the decisions I made as I went about the research? How would "methodology" guide me through the fragmented pieces of "data" presented by people, their nonlinear stories, the scattering of their memories and various social histories, narratives that I would collect in the most haphazard ways? While theoretical models explained "how the industry worked" as an operational system, a fashion world rendered stable as sense, order, and function, what of the muddy and intimate locations that come along in global connections and field work? What of people, their relationships, the nuances and details that make up their working lives in fashion, their silences, ambivalences, and their stories? Would any of this even count as research? I had begun my own interactive process and politics of "traversing," as the anthropologist James Clifford (1997) once put it, and my field sites looked nothing like what I prepared myself to look for; there weren't any objective "nodes" of a global commodity chain, but instead just a bunch of stories.

I spent days in field research, not knowing whom I would talk to next. In an industry full of people who constantly told me that "time is money," it was impossible to expect anyone to have the time to call me, a random person, back. This went against the assumption that doing ethnography at "home" would be something of an easier task for myself as an "anthropologist." There seemed to be an underlying assumption that I would gain access to "deeper" levels of information and knowledge because I was using my own native language of English, my familiarity

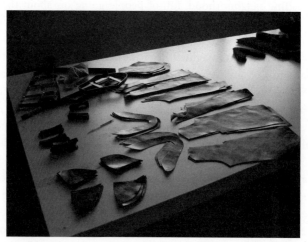

**FIGURE 3.2** Cut leather pieces sit on a table in a shoe production factory in Wuxi, China. *Photo*: Christina H. Moon.

with "American cultural practices," because I ostensibly belonged to the same "ethnic categories" as some of my potential informants ("Asian"), and because I had embarked on field research in my "own backyard" (Nader 1972). It became immediately clear, however, how difficult it would be to get anyone in fashion to talk to me at all—I was trying to get in on the "inside" of an exclusive world full of overworked people, too busy to talk. Though I made lists of potential contacts before arriving in the field, making "cold-calls" to strangers who did not know me, to trace a commodity chain was just not a practical way to maneuver within this industry, which ultimately said something larger about the way it actually works. I found early on that there needed to be a reason for somebody to call me back, beyond the fact that I was a graduate student doing research for my dissertation.

## Sticky evocations: Practices of the personal

My first route into the New York fashion industry came from my family's own personal contacts, specifically, from my parents' church in Hackensack, New Jersey, where so many of the young women from the Korean congregation were either students attending fashion design schools, or working for fashion companies in New York. While one interview came from a church friend working for Michael Kors, another came from a close friend, who works in Los Angeles's San Pedro Mart, designing and wholesaling clothes to Macy's, Urban Outfitters, and Nordstrom. Even my own parents' two closest sets of friends had something to say about fashion: one couple made their livelihood as clothing wholesalers in Korea, Argentina, and then New York, and another worked as a seamstress at a dry cleaning business for most of her working life. The global apparel trade was also tied to my father's oldest friend in the United States, a man who opened the first Korean restaurant on 32nd Street in Manhattan's Koreatown in 1983, selling classic Korean oxtail soup to the Korean laborers working and sewing in neighboring garment district factories. From my own personal networks, among those I grew up with, it seemed that everyone had something to say about fashion, clothing, and its meaning in their lives. And so, it seemed not a surprise that, while standing in the Garment District on that first day of field research, I had my own memory of "New York Fashion" from my own childhood. These memories would become embedded in the note-taking, observational, ethnographic narrative of my research:

*The smell of paint, the sight of my mother hunched over, painting jewelry with colorful enamel paint.*
*My parents ran a small workshop first in the New York Garment District painting custom jewelry. In fact, the very first job my mother ever had in the U.S.*

*after emigrating from Korea in the late 1960s, was working for a Jewish jewelry manufacturer in the district. Sponsored by her aunt, she had come to New York to study art and found a job mixing paint as a paint colorist for a factory. After working for this factory for four years, she learned all she needed to know about the business to start her own and, after meeting my father, a chemistry student sponsored by an American missionary in post-war Korea, they began their own business as a husband and wife team painting and wholesaling custom jewelry to local New York department stores. It seems to have been fate—with my father's understanding of chemical properties and my mother's sense of color, the two experimented with epoxy glue and paint and created jewel-tone colored enamels that, when applied to cheap metals, gave the illusion of expensive jewels.*

*Their small workshop was located in the Garment District and from the orders they filled, they made enough money to buy their first home in suburban New Jersey. Yet, just as soon as they began to make money, they began to look for ways out of the business. They worried that the toxic smell of paints would affect my mother's pregnancy with my brother. They could not afford the rising cost of wage labor, business was fast changing and jewelry could be made and painted for cheaper costs in other countries. Eventually, my parents closed their workshop and moved their operations into the basement of our family home, where they worked and painted along with all the other Korean friends they had in the neighborhood.*

*Heading down the basement steps I see my mother sitting alongside other Korean women, hunched over under fluorescent lights. They roll pieces of plastic cellophane into cone tubes, fill these tubes with brightly colored epoxy paint, and squeeze the paint out onto the jewelry. I help out by laying out the wooden rods, gently placing the painted earrings, belt buckles, rings out for drying. Our weekends are spent driving into the city to drop off the orders in the Garment District.*

At first I thought it was a coincidence, but now I see it is no coincidence at all, that the field sites of my research had emerged from deep pools of sentiment and attachment, recognition, and memory among the subjects I interviewed. Neither did I realize that these memories of the Garment District, the childhood church friends who were now studying or working in fashion, the friends of family working as clothing traders or sewers, and even my parents' own paths in migrating to the United States and their factory work, were part of a history of ramifications of U.S. Cold War interventions in Asia, the industrialization of Asian nations through garments, the migration of postcolonials to the metropoles, with dreams of their children becoming Americans and fashion designers. They were part of this history that saw the rise of global fashion capitals and the development of new fashion culture industries in need of designers not just in New York City, but across Asia and in global cities around the world. I had thought "ethnographic field work" would lead me to a more glamorous, fashionable, and "contemporary" research site. Yet, here I was, knee-deep in the past, grappling with these intimate pulls and memories of the fashion and garment histories of my own family. I was using "theories" and "methods" that had not equipped me to navigate any of these sticky subjective evocations—how conducting field research not only implicated my subjects' complex identities, but also spoke to my own shifting identities as a researcher.

I had come to the global fashion industry as an "outsider," as an "analyst"—*I was there to study it.* Yet, I was already unknowingly predisposed to its complicated histories and networks. The subject/object relationship of former ethnographies had not accounted for my own shifting interactions, positions, advocacies, and investments in my research, which would ultimately affect the conceptualization of my story. "The field" is not an empty site, never cleared or even a clearing, but mired in sentiment, drenched in memory, already being shaped as history, fictively produced and made. In an industry whose characterizations swing from the detached impersonal, anonymous realms of capitalist modes of production, to the unattainable objects and images of a glamorous fashion, it is ethnographic practices of the personal—relationships of familiarity and recognition, often intimate and affective ones—which would ultimately shape conceptualizations of the field sites and subjects.

Beyond family and friends, the only other way I was able to make contacts in "search of subjects" was through work and the intimate encounters of everyday labor. I offered my work for free to various companies, which gave me the opportunity to intern, be socialized into and work alongside people who I eventually interviewed and developed relationships with. Working for a minimum of a three-month period for each company, my relationships with people were forged in the daily routines and habitual repetitions of work, and those I worked closely with introduced me to other people and their already existing relationships, alliances, and networks. Although there were those who were genuinely interested in my research on the rise of New York as a global fashion capital during the 1990s and 2000s, in most cases, people called me back as an altruistic gesture toward their friend, who had introduced me in the first place, maintaining an important personal relationship (whether business or friendship) with that other person, whom they often regarded in high esteem. And strangely, by meeting people in this manner, I too would become a part of the social mesh, attachments, and networks that describe the industry.

By relying on other people's relationships, I didn't have much control over who I would be able to talk with next. I worried most days that the research had no focus around a singular "subject" that could be defined by an ethnic group or occupation. Anthropologists within the last 20 years have challenged this subject-other relationship, yet there still exists the persistent idea that subjects must be "defined," no matter how loosely by group, community, class formation, identity, social occupation, or racial and ethnic affiliation (Clifford and Marcus

1986; Clifford 1988, 1997 and 2003; Behar 1993 and 1996; Behar and Gordon 1995; Rosaldo and Appadurai 1986; Strathern 1988 and 1999; Fabian 2014). The "subjects of my study," however, were not an already given or determined group of people as outlined in an abstract of a research proposal. They were subjects who only "emerged" through other people's introductions and relationships, as I made my way through the field research. The process, in its entirety, seemed to resemble more a scattered unfolding of inarticulate intuitions and sensings, rather than a definitively outlined plan with a "control group" and "set location of fieldwork." This method of interviewing might be recognized as the "snowball" effect, but as a metaphor this term neglects the idea that the relationships formed led me to interviews with other people (Agar 1996). "Relationships" do not lead to other interviews via "momentum," but through work, labor, friendship, time, and most especially trust. Consequently, my study did not become a study of "Korean fashion designs," and the subjects of this study were not "Asian American fashion designers," using the kind of nation-bound or identity-framing that has dominated anthropological literature on fashion for the last two decades; the people I spent time with could not be reduced to such simple categories as nation, race or ethnicity, colonizer/colonized, exploiter/exploited, fashion worker/garment worker, capitalist/laborer, and so on. Furthermore, I was not sure if this band of individuals could even be considered a "community" at all—how were, for instance, fashion designers, fashion students, technical designers, curators, PR agents and marketers, sweatshop activists, rehabilitated garment workers, and migrant sewers a community of subjects? Further, could a "community" exist transnationally, globally, or even as a cultural diaspora? I spent most of my days feeling unsure, worried about how to define the subjects of my study and how to make sense of it all.

Even more confusing was my being surrounded by "informants"—fashion designers, interns, PR agents, curators at museums, fashion business owners, factory managers, sewers, etc.—who were their own ethnographers seeking maps into the industry. Just as I was trying to understand the way the industry worked, they too were in the same sort of obsessive project of trying to imagine, interpret, accumulate information, and track the fashion industry's transformations and moves. In a strange role reversal, I found myself surrounded by people who were constantly trying to mine me, "the anthropologist," "the supposed expert," for more "inside" information or connections to "get in on the inside" of a fashion world and industry that I believed they were already on the inside of. I found it surprising that even those I believed to be at the top of some perceived hierarchy of the fashion world, never came to believe themselves to be at the "center" of it all. No one I spent time with felt themselves to be completely "in it," instead they felt they were not positioned where they desired to be, and were always on the search to "penetrate" this fashion world even further. This confusion forced me to question the whole project on how to "get in on the inside of" anything at all, the project of finally knowing anything, "it," the object of study, "the way the world works" to some known degree or the end goal. Trying to depict "what this was" in texture and density, would only highlight the futile project of seeking some sort of truth value, and the "inevitable failure to represent or capture some sort of absolute real" (Stewart 1996, 22). As I moved through the field research, I had come to realize that, just as I followed and documented the complexity of their interpretations, I too was tracking and documenting my own interpretative moves in fashion.

I had become interested in the concrete or contingent relationships of people, what made up the "excesses" or "stuff" that made up their lives, the vivid stories, silences, the complicated social matrixes in which the "cultural" and "culture" emerged from—the ambivalences that had no place on a global commodity chain of fashion (Gaonkar and Povinelli 2003, 385). I was less interested in using a language of objects in circulation operating within static systems or closed totalities in distant field sites under total observation, and more interested in exploring the social practices and processes of the people participating in these

**FIGURE 3.3** Test shots taken as models wait around to walk a fashion runway show on location in New York City. *Photo*: Christina H. Moon.

global fashion worlds and industries. I wanted to begin not with how "things" were fashioning "networks" in circulation, but with how "people" formed and fashioned "relationships" in the constant making of those things, as well as the modes of attachment they affectively felt toward these complex fashion imaginaries.

## Making sense of it all: Outcomes and artifacts of discussion

And so in New York, I began work as an intern for a large multinational fashion design company located on Seventh Avenue, spending my days in and out of the Garment District running errands. In this alluring center of it all, my first interviews came not from famous fashion designers, but from a group of security guards in an old industry building, many of whom had greeted factory owners in the front lobbies of district buildings for 10, 20, or 30 years. Unlike the newspaper articles that tracked the "death of the district" through the listing of statistics, these subjects narrated instead the changes of a neighborhood as they had witnessed it—through the disappearance of the garment factory owners who once used to be their employers. My inability to gain access to the more glamorous ends of the global fashion industry, led to another research site that witnessed the effects of deindustrialization among the Garment District from the "survivors"—from factory owners to security guards. They never relayed their stories as a chronology of trade laws, but rather as palpable experiences, haunting tales, and district folklore. It was, for them, the closing down of shops, the disappearance of sewers, the nuanced changes to the daily rituals of work, the physical and geographical transformations to the street—the tangible imprints of a lived experience through a changing neighborhood and industry, of a changing people and place.

My errands in the district as a low-rung intern included dropping off and picking up samples at local factories, and I thought it curious that the majority of local factories were owned by immigrants from Korea and China, who had come to dominate district factory production throughout the 1990s. I met one such factory owner who spoke to me because I was Korean American. He told me about growing up in the countryside in Korea during the 1960s: having left school at fourteen to work in sewing factories, as an adult he sewed the clothes at American multinational companies like Nike and Reebok, and eventually made his way to New York, working as a tailor in the 1990s. After saving up money, he now runs his own sample-making factory in the Garment District, creating the runway collections for the fashion designer Marc Jacobs. While the history of the Garment District is often told as a Jewish and Italian history of America, its most recent history includes these Korean and Chinese immigrants (Waldinger

1986; Soyer 2004; Chin 2005). Their personal histories intimately tie histories and processes of other places to the New York Garment District in time and space, and their work has powerfully redefined the value of the clothing in the district today—they make *not* garments, but runway samples. Their emergence, alongside the rise of New York Fashion Week, shows that they have played, not a peripheral, but a central role in making New York into a global fashion capital. These same questions could be raised about global fashion weeks and cities around the world, looking at what the impact of these seemingly marginal/peripheral communities had on the making of these cities globally. In New York and Milan, immigrants from China are responsible for sample-making and garment work (see Ross 2004). In Paris's Le Sentier, West African immigrants dominate the garment trade (see Green 1997).

During my internships at several design firms, I worked as free labor in both the "front of the house," among design teams, public relations agents, and secretaries; and at the "back of the house" among production managers, patternmakers, sewers, and other interns. In the front of the house, I was surrounded by beautiful women who came dressed to the nines for work each day, hired to manage the appearances, impressions, and aesthetics of the company. From their styles of dress to their attitudes, to even the way they answered the phones, the labor of these fashion workers was performative in that they presented a smoothly run, "effortless," and "no sweat" operation. In their acts of self-effacement, their labor was to perform that no labor was involved—making me wonder why, when it comes to labor, it is often imagined as manual and masculine, and why the work of these fashion workers across the industry would not be considered labor at all. It was just one example of the "cultural discount" (including my own culturally discounted free labor as an intern) that pervaded the culture industries of New York. From fashion, architecture, design, media, and technology, these industries relied heavily on a free or highly casualized workforce who accepted nonmonetary rewards "as compensation for their work thereby discounting the cash price of their labor" (Ross 2009, 80).

In the back sample room, I worked among sample makers and interns who cut, sewed, and created the runway collections for New York Fashion Week and found everyday acts of communality and collective creativity in the making of runway collections. Though I originally thought that the internship would get me closer to the iconic namesake designer and the hidden, creative design practices behind her work, I watched instead an entire collective of workers design, creatively interpret, and communally produce fashions that were brandished under the designer's singular name. While I witnessed how labor is obscured with the brandishing of the label, I also found an environment that challenged the kind of "corporation" often depicted by discourse produced by the anti-sweatshop movement. Rather than a one-dimensional, anonymous, all-powerful, and unyielding entity that overshadows any possible form of political subjectivity, this multinational design corporation could be understood as the workplace setting for thousands of fashion's cultural workers.

The interns working in the back sample room were students attending either Parsons School of Design or the Fashion Institute of Technology (FIT) and surprisingly, in entirety, were students from Korea. I would learn that they were part of the post 1997 IMF crisis call for globalization, a new middle class and elite who wanted to send their students abroad for the prestige of a foreign degree, the chance to learn English language skills, get the experience of working for famous American fashion companies, with the opportunity to make powerful alumni connections upon their return to Asia. New York design schools greatly benefited from this migration of design students from industrializing manufacturing nations looking to "value up" the fashion chain and spur on fashion economies (see Tu 2011).

On their encouragement, I enrolled for a semester in the design school, which I nearly hopelessly failed, and listened to students tell me about how fashion brought them to New York, gave them the opportunity to live in this creative center of the world, where one could hone one's English, the language of globalization, graduate with an American brand-name degree, and tap into privileged alumni networks that would get them design jobs in Korea. While in New York, these design students provided substantial service to Seventh Avenue design companies: they made up a significant workforce of interns and designers—a conveniently free, casualized, temporary workforce of designers in the United States on "training" visas. Many of these designers planned to go back to Korea to develop new fashion and design culture industries the government had since poured revenue into—I learned that Korea was undergoing its own deindustrialization. This became just another example of the sticky intersections between labor, capital, and migration among globalizing institutions—schools and corporations—in the socialization, training, and recruitment of new workers into new global professional fields of fashion design.

While at design school, I met many Asian American students who had grown up in and around garment districts in New York, Los Angeles, and San Francisco, with families who had worked in some aspect of the rag trade. Not wanting to go into the corporate world of American bridge-wear, the everyday clothing sold in department stores, I met many in search of more creative outlets, wanting to start their own businesses in fashion. I followed one such Asian American designer to Los Angeles, who planned to "revamp" her parents' ailing wholesale company— she hoped to combine her design skills with their 30 years of manufacturing knowledge in South America and China, to make the kind of fast fashion clothing that would sell to powerful corporate retailers in the Americas. While those in the high-end designer fashion world in places like Paris or New York would never consider this informal market of cheaply priced clothing on the eastern edge of the LA garment district as a place that makes fashion designs, the clothing designed

**FIGURE 3.4** Model cards lay strewn on a table inside a design studio in New York City. *Photo*: Christina H. Moon.

in this part of the neighborhood made up a majority of all women's fast fashions sold in department stores, corporate retail outlets, and boutiques across the United States. The story became even more compelling when I realized that the fashions were designed and distributed by immigrant wholesalers and their children who designed, many of whom have multiple identities—ethnically Korean, born in Brazil, raised in America, and who've graduate from places like Parsons, who worked in this one area, in this one neighborhood, and for the most part down on one street (see Moon 2014).

# Conclusion: Relationships of recognition

In this thing called the global fashion industry, each field site, interview, person met, and invitation, appeared through affective and personal realms and connections. The memories, personal histories, stories, partnerships, and alliances—these relationships of recognition—shaped who I would speak to and where and what my field sites were, a "multi-sited" project which would lead to other cities and places. These relationships of affection guided me through these fashion worlds and industries, bringing me to transnational frameworks (in other times, in other spaces) of encounter and exchange, making visible the highly contingent character to fieldwork that is left unmentioned in "research" as well as the shifting dimensions of what we consider to be a "field site."

The anthropologist James Clifford, citing Michel de Certeau, writes: "An urban neighborhood may be laid out physically according to a street plan. But it is not a space until it is practiced by people's active occupation, their movements through and around it" (Clifford 1997, 54). The field too, in my research, did not become a space, place, or object until I myself had moved within it, summoned my own intimate memories and relationship to it, interacted and spoke with people working within it, and found myself intimately a part of their networks. There was nothing about my field that would be ontologically given—it was rather space that had been worked and "turned into a discrete social space, by embodied practices of interactive travel," "discursively mapped and corporeally practiced," leading me into realms of the collective and personal (Clifford 1997, 54).

The methods of my research rely a great deal on relationships—of my own and of others—which show not objective systems or totalities, but particular viewings, personal implications, and entanglements of my own and of the subjects I spent time with. These methods have created a particular, interactively and intimately made, subjective charter of how things are shaping and have shaped in the moment. The places, sites, and representations of my research have become "the contours of a specific intellectual and institutional landscape, a particular terrain" (Clifford 1997, 54), and the field sites are locations which are constantly produced, rearticulated, and in constant transformation. In this way, I tracked a moment in the fashion world, in fashion history, that cannot be recreated. My "research outcomes" became textual documents of an "irretrievable moment"—the notes, interviews, observations, my experience, and practical labor in various workplaces and institutions—created a particular mapping of experience, of "what was going on" in that moment of time. At the time of writing, I have come to feel that this was all an attempt to interpret the ephemeral and irretrievable nature of a global fashion industry shaped in the moment by ever-changing yet intimate social relationships, all through the intimacies of everyday work. What I had in front of me were the shades, shapes, tones, and stories of fashion's cultural workers, and my exploration of those intimate and affective realms of perspective that brought about social meaning, transformation, and cultural change.

If we are to understand the recent transformations in the fashion industry and therefore in global capitalism, whether it is the changes to material culture, design and aesthetic landscapes, the shifts in our nuanced sensory experiences of time, image, touch, space, the body, and materiality through fashion, perhaps "being there" would help to get us to the intimacies and contingencies of work and life among fashion's cultural workers, locations to be further explored in fashion studies. How do these subjects shape visual culture and the aesthetic material landscapes of fashion? How have their practices altered our experience of life and of fashion? How are their work relationships and imaginaries of the fashion world embodied in the everyday experience of banal materiality? Their stories, meanings, desires, relationships resonate in everyday material cultural forms, making their way into the objects, aesthetics, and practices that have cultured our world. It is this deeply complex, intimate, socializing realm that I am grasping to have an understanding for—that buried space where we might see the relationship between forms of work and forms of art, and fashion. That space from which labor transforms into the unbearable lightness of beautiful, material forms.

# References

Agar, Michael H. 1996. *The Professional Stranger: An Informal Introduction to Ethnography*. San Diego: Academic Press.

Appadurai, Arjun, ed. 1986. *The Social Life of Things: Commodities in Cultural Perspective*. New York: Cambridge University Press.

Applebaum, Richard and Gary Gereffi. 1994. "Power and Profits in the Apparel Commodity Chain." In *Global Production: The Apparel Industry in the Pacific Rim*, edited by Edna Bonacich, Lucie Cheng, Norma Chinchilla, Nora Hamilton, and Paul Ong, 42–62. Philadelphia, PA: Temple University Press.

Aspers, Patrik. 2010. *Orderly Fashion: A Sociology of Markets*. Princeton, NJ: Princeton University Press.

Bair, Jennifer. 2005. "Global Capitalism and Commodity Chains: Looking Back, Going Forward." *Competition and Change* 9 (2): 153–80.

Behar, Ruth. 1993. *Translated Woman: Crossing the Border with Esperanza's Story*. Boston: Beacon Press.

Behar, Ruth. 1996. *The Vulnerable Observer: Anthropology That Breaks Your Heart*. Boston: Beacon Press.

Behar, Ruth and Deborah Gordon, eds. 1995. *Women Writing Culture*. Berkeley, CA: University of California Press.

Benjamin, Walter. 1928. *One Way Street and Other Writings*. London: Penguin.

Black, Sandy, ed. 2012. *The Sustainable Fashion Handbook*. London: Thames and Hudson.

Blaszczyk, Regina Lee, ed. 2008. *Producing Fashion: Commerce, Culture, and Consumers*. Philadelphia: University of Pennsylvania Press.

Bonacich, Edna, ed. 2004. *Global Production: The Apparel Industry in the Pacific Rim*. Philadelphia: Temple University Press.

Bonacich, Edna and Richard P. Appelbaum. 2000. *Behind the Label: Inequality in the Los Angeles Apparel Industry*. Berkeley: University of California Press.

Bourdieu, Pierre. 1984. *Distinction: A Social Critique of the Judgment of Taste*. Cambridge, MA: Harvard University Press.

Breward, Christopher and David Gilbert, eds. 2006. *Fashion's World Cities*. Oxford: Berg.

Carrier, James, ed. 1994. *Gifts and Commodities: Exchange and Western Capitalism since 1700*. London: Routledge.

Carrier, James, ed. 1997. *Meanings of the Market: The Free Market in Western Culture*. Oxford: Berg.

Chin, Margaret M. 2005. *Sewing Women: Immigrants and the New York City Garment Industry*. New York: Columbia University Press.

Clifford, James. 1988. *The Predicament of Culture: Twentieth-Century Ethnography, Literature, and Art*. Boston, MA: Harvard University Press.

Clifford, James. 1997. *Routes: Travel and Translation in the Late Twentieth Century*. Cambridge, MA: Harvard University Press.

Clifford, James. 2003. *On the Edges of Anthropology: Interviews*. Chicago: Prickly Paradigm Press.

Clifford, James and George E. Marcus, eds. 1986. *Writing Culture: The Poetics and Politics of Ethnography*. Berkeley, CA: University of California Press.

Denning, Michael. 2004. *Globalization in the Age of Three Worlds*. New York: Verso.

Entwistle, Joanne. 2009. *The Aesthetic Economy of Fashion: Markets and Value in Clothing and Modelling*. London: Bloomsbury Academic.

Fabian, Johannes. 2014. *Time and the Other: How Anthropology Makes Its Object*. New York: Columbia University Press.

Gaonkar, Dilip Parameshwar and Elizabeth A. Povinelli. 2003. "Technologies of Public Forms: Circulation, Transfiguration, Recognition." *Public Culture* 15 (3) 3: 385.

Gereffi, Gary and Miguel Korzeniewicz, eds. 1994. *Commodity Chains and Global Capitalism*. Westport, CT: Praeger.

Gereffi, Gary, David Spener, and Jennifer Bair, eds. 2002. *Free Trade and Uneven Development: The North American Apparel Industry after NAFTA*. Philadelphia: Temple University Press.

Green, Nancy. 1997. *Ready to Work, Ready to Wear: A Century of Industry and Immigrants in Paris and New York*. Durham: Duke University Press.

Hart, Keith. 2007. "A Short History of Economic Anthropology." *The Memory Bank, A New Commonwealth* Ver 5.0., November 9, 2007, http://thememorybank. co.uk/2007/11/09/a-short-history-of-economic-anthropology/

Kaiser, Susan. 2012. *Fashion and Cultural Studies*. Oxford: Berg.

Miller, Daniel. 1986. *Material Culture and Mass Consumption*. Oxford: Basil Blackwell.

Miller, Daniel. 1995. "Consumptions and Commodities." *Annual Review of Anthropology*, 24: 141–61.

Miller, Daniel. 1996. *Capitalism: An Ethnographic Approach*. Oxford: Berg.

Miller, Daniel. 1998. *A Theory of Shopping*. Ithaca and New York: Cornell University Press.

Miller, Daniel. 2001. *Dialectics of Shopping*. Chicago: University of Chicago Press.

Moon, Christina. 2014. "Slow Road to Fast-Fashion." *Pacific Standard*. March 17, 2014, http://www.psmag.com/business-economics/secret-world-slow-road-korea-los-angeles-behind-fast-fashion-73956.

Nader, Laura. 1972. "Up the Anthropologist-Perspectives Gained from Studying Up." In *Reinventing Anthropology*, edited by Dell Hymes, 285–311. New York: Pantheon Press.

Rivoli, Pietra. 2009. *The Travels of a T-Shirt in the Global Economy: An Economist Examines the Markets, Power and Politics of the World Trade*. Hoboken, NJ: John Wiley & Sons.

Ross, Andrew. 2004. *Low Pay, High Profile: The Global Push for Fair Labor*. New York: The New Press.

Ross, Andrew. 2009. "No Collar Labor in America's 'New Economy.'" *Socialist Register*, 37: 76-87.

Soyer, Daniel. 2004. *A Coat of Many Colors: Immigration, Globalization, and Reform in New York City's Garment Industry*. New York: Fordham University Press.

Stewart, Kathleen. 1996. *Space On the Side of the Road: Cultural Poetics in an "Other" America*. Princeton, NJ: Princeton University Press.

Strathern, Marilyn. 1988. *The Gender of the Gift: Problems with Women and Problems with Society in Melanesia*. Berkeley, CA: University of California Press.

Strathern, Marilyn. 1999. *Property, Substance and Effect. Anthropological Essays on Persons and Things*. London: Athlone Press.

Tu, Thuy Linh Nguyen. 2011. *The Beautiful Generation: Asian Americans and the Cultural Economy of Fashion*. Durham, NC: Duke University Press.

Waldinger, Roger. 1986. *Through the Eye of the Needle: Immigrants and Enterprise in New York's Garment Trades*. New York: New York University Press.

# 4 URBAN FIELDNOTES: AN AUTO-ETHNOGRAPHY OF STREET STYLE BLOGGING

## Brent Luvaas

## Street style anthropology

Urban Fieldnotes is a "street style blog," a photography-based website featuring pictures of stylish "real" people shot "on the streets" of Philadelphia in their everyday clothes (see Figure 4.1). It is also a blog *about* street style blogs, an experimental, auto-ethnographic research instrument I started back in 2012 as a means of studying *other* street style bloggers. I use it to post my fieldnotes, interviews, and preliminary thoughts about the daily experience and larger social, cultural, and economic significance of street style blogging. Call it a meta-street-style blog. Call it an open-access platform for visual anthropological research. Or just call it a street style blog, because street style blogs are already sufficiently "meta" and "anthropological" to encompass these alternative classifications.

This is one of the insights I have gained through having my own street style blog for these past couple of years. Street style blogs are not just a rich subject of analysis for fashion studies; they are also a medium of it, an amateur mode of critical inquiry into the same themes, topics, and ideas that scholars of fashion hold dear. This is not, however, the only thing I have learned from having my own blog.

I have also learned how to pick a street style subject out of a crowd, to feel the subtle vibration of *style radar* signals reverberate through my body when someone "cool" walks down the street toward me. I have learned how to assess a "good" street style image, and I have learned the quick manual adjustments photographers employ to produce those images. I have learned to shoot alongside a few dozen other street style bloggers outside the runway shows of New York Fashion Week without getting in their way; how to talk like a street style blogger, how to pass in their company. I have also learned the anxieties and preoccupations of street style bloggers—concerns over lagging pageviews, or accumulating readers and followers. I have learned, in other words, to think, act, feel, and evaluate as a street style blogger does. Most of what I have learned from having a street style blog, in fact, takes the form of "practical knowledge" of this sort (Bourdieu 1977; Giddens 1979; Willis 1977), forming a pre-articulate understanding that informs my social theoretical conclusions without ever quite materializing as "data" or "fact."

This chapter explores the utility of an auto-ethnographic research practice like my own as a method of inquiry within fashion studies. Using my experiences

**FIGURE 4.1** Alexis, Chestnut Street, Philadelphia, one of the hundreds of street style subjects featured on the Urban Fieldnotes blog. *Photo*: Brent Luvaas.

as a street style blogger as a case study, I weigh the strengths and limitations of auto-ethnography for generating knowledge and developing theoretical frameworks about fashion and the fashion industry. I do not, however, pretend to do so from a position of distanced objectivity, for if there is one primary lesson of auto-ethnographic practice, it is that such a position is not possible. Indeed, it is not necessarily desirable. It presumes a disembodied, outside perspective unlike any we experience in real life, a false neutrality that threatens to bury the lived insights of fashion studies beneath the thinner top soil of factuality. Auto-ethnography strives for something "thicker" (Geertz 1977), something still humming with the breath and pulse of direct experience.

# From personal style to street style

I discovered street style blogs relatively late in the game, right as they were transitioning from online cult status to fashion world ubiquity. It was the summer of 2010, and I had just returned from Jakarta, Indonesia, where I had been working on a long-term ethnographic project on the Southeast Asian country's emerging fashion industry, and as part of that project, I had been taking all sorts of pictures of what "the kids in Indonesia" (*anak muda Indonesia*) are wearing these days. I had a hunch, as plenty of scholars of fashion have had before me, that personal style plays an important role in a nation's economic development (see Jones 2003; Gilbert 2006; Zhao 2013) and a number of shots of assorted Indonesian hipsters in tight T-shirts and skinny jeans seemed to support the case. But there I was, now back in the United States, and the research had come to a grinding halt. I needed some way to continue the work from the auspices of my office at Drexel University in Philadelphia, half a world away from my field site. So I did what any minimally technologically savvy social scientist would do in my position in this day and age: I turned to the internet. More specifically, I turned to fashion blogs, those personal style websites like Diana Rikasari's Hot Chocolate & Mint (dianarikasari.blogspot.com) and Evita Nuh's La Crème de la Crop (jellyjellybeans.blogspot.com), where the authors post images of themselves in various outfits, while posing like amateur models on bridges, in bedrooms, and on rooftops. There were hundreds of fashion blogs in Indonesia alone by 2010, peddling their cosmopolitan daydreams of a borderless fashion world. These blogs attracted tens of thousands of readers daily. I too got quickly hooked and began to follow about twelve of them regularly.

One day, I was going through my daily regimen of Indonesian fashion blogs—The Versicle, Glisters and Blisters, Afternoon Tea and Living Room—and one of the bloggers had posted a photo of themselves taken by a certain Yvan Rodic, also known as FaceHunter. "I can't believe I got to meet FaceHunter," she posted, or at least something to that effect—I have since lost sight of the original post and am paraphrasing here—"and he even took my picture." Well, I did not know who FaceHunter was back then, but I was intrigued. So I followed the link that the blogger provided and found myself on FaceHunter's website (www.facehunter. blogspot.com then, now facehunter.org). It was a stripped down, minimalist affair by website standards, composed of full-length, full-color images of "cool" people in "cool" clothes posing in "cool" places.

Rodic, it turns out, is a Swiss-born, London-based, former advertising copywriter turned photographer. He travels around the world with a point-and-shoot digital camera taking photos in up-and-coming fashion cities, including Jakarta, but also Helsinki, Dubai, Rio de Jainero, Mexico City, and numerous other places besides. He had already published one book by this time, called, appropriately, *FaceHunter*, and was now working on his second. By the time I had gotten around to shooting pictures of the sartorial idiosyncrasies of Indonesian youth, Rodic had already been through Indonesia doing the same thing twice. He has been there several more times since then.

I started to dig deeper, and through Rodic's site I became aware of dozens, and eventually, hundreds of other amateur photographers doing more or less the same thing, photographing the stylistic quirks of various cities well off the fashion map, and then posting them online for other people to observe. Some of these websites were devoted to particular cities. There was, for instance, Michelle Oberholzer's Cinder & Skylark in Cape Town, South Africa; Yael Sloma's The Streets Walker in Tel Aviv, Israel; Javi Obando and Flora Grzetic's On the Corner in Buenos Aires, Argentina; and Liisa Jokinen's Hel Looks in Helsinki, Finland. Others, like Rodic's website, were more itinerant. Their creators hopped from city to city, and often fashion week to fashion week, to report ground-level trends as they happened. Some of the best known of these websites were Tommy Ton's Jak & Jil, Adam Katz Sinding's Le 21ème, and Scott Schuman's The Sartorialist.

What interested me about these websites, which I came to know as "street style blogs," was in part the sheer phenomenon of them. They were attracting a huge amount of attention from both inside and outside of the fashion world, drawing in hundreds of thousands, and at least in The Sartorialist's case, millions of pageviews per month. Street style blogs, built largely by amateur photographers with no formal background in fashion, had become competitive with major fashion magazines over the course of a few years. Now they were attracting those magazines' advertising base. Many bloggers were getting big sponsorship deals. Many were having their content featured in print publications. Many were on the invite lists of the biggest fashion showcases. Street style blogger, it seemed, had become a potential career path in the fashion world, a back door into a notoriously closed-door industry.

I was also interested, however, in certain similarities I saw between what these bloggers did and what I do as a cultural and visual anthropologist. After a few weeks of browsing the global street style blogosphere, I became convinced that we shared a common project. These bloggers' mission in photographing South Africans, Indonesians, Fins, Jordanians, or whoever was remarkably similar to my own. We were all documenting—albeit selectively—what it looks like for a city, or a nation, to reimagine itself as a fashion capital. We were visually chronicling the formation of stylized identities, the rising of new class groups, and we were singling out those distinctive individuals in these places that we saw as capable of speaking to larger cultural processes at work, putting, that is, a local face on globalization. I was fascinated. I put my work on fashionistas in the developing world on hold, to focus instead on those bloggers photographing them. I knew there was a project to do about all of this. Now I just had to figure out how to do it.

## A method emerges

My first impulse, after years of work in Indonesia, was to study Indonesian street style blogs. But there were only a couple of those at the time, Jakarta Street Looks, which was defunct as of 2009, and Jakarta Style Journal, which was updated infrequently at best. Street style was not a significant phenomenon there yet, for reasons I have articulated elsewhere (Luvaas 2013), despite the massive popularity of fashion blogs more generally. Moreover, studying street style in Indonesia would be an arbitrary decision to make, drawing imaginary boundaries around a far more expansive network that extends across the developing and developed world alike. The very thing that makes street style interesting—at least to me—is its global ubiquity. It must, I decided, be studied globally.

The only trouble is that I am an anthropologist, and we anthropologists can be rather stubbornly place-ist in our research methodologies. We are committed, above all, to "going places" and "being there," to encountering people firsthand, rather than depending on secondary accounts and surveys. If I were going to do this project the way an anthropologist would, I would have to find some way of "being there" appropriate for street style blogs.

But how could I possibly do that? How could I possibly be surrounded by or engulfed within street style blogging? For all of the theorizing in anthropology in recent years about doing ethnography online (see Hine 2000; Boellstorff et al. 2012), I knew that online research alone would limit me in gaining that firsthand, "on-the-ground" perspective that I wanted for this project. I could only think of one possible solution. I would have to start a street style blog myself. It is the only thing that would teach me, in no uncertain terms, the lived, practical, material realities of street style blogging.

My plan was to use the blog as an open-access research platform. I would post my photographs and preliminary thoughts as they happened, invite comments and corrections from other bloggers, link to their blogs, and feature regular interviews with street style photographers. I envisioned my blog as a go-to resource for the ethnographic study of street style, an open-source model of visual fieldnotes.

I started my own street style blog, Urban Fieldnotes (www.urbanfieldnotes. com), in February of 2012, and I completed my first post as a street style blogger on March 26, 2012. I have been doing the blog as of the writing of this chapter for nearly two and a half years, and in the process, I have interviewed and posted my interviews of twenty other street style bloggers, met and interacted with many others, both online and off, and generally been enrolled in a crash course in street style blogging. I have been contacted by dozens of companies, looking to feature their products on my blog. In turn, my blog has been featured in *Nylon Magazine, Harpers Bazaar Brasil, Mojeh Magazine, Drexel Magazine, The Philadelphia Daily News, StreetStyleNews, The Guardian,* and several well-known fashion blogs. I have received gifted products, had a stint advertising for American Apparel, "partnered" with a couple of fashion brands, and watched as my blog's images circulated far and wide through Instagram, Tumblr, and other social media platforms. The blog now gets between 15,000 and 18,000 pageviews a month and has become, in essence, precisely that thing I set out to study.

Nonetheless, to clear up any potential confusion for my readers and make my intentions as clear as possible, I have posted the following statement in the upper-right-hand corner of the blog:

> Urban Fieldnotes is a street style blog, documenting fashion, style, and dress on the streets of Philadelphia and beyond. It is also a blog about street style blogging, an experiment in auto-ethnographic research and open-source fieldwork that is part of an ongoing project by Brent Luvaas entitled "Street Style 2.0: New Media and the New Politics of Fashion." This blog represents the views, perspectives, and preliminary findings of Brent Luvaas, a professional anthropologist and amateur fashion observer. This blog does not necessarily reflect the opinions and positions of Drexel University, his employer. Your comments and suggestions are welcome, but please note that any comments posted to this blog may be used in future presentations and publications, both print and digital, by Brent Luvaas.

Urban Fieldnotes, thus, is an instrument of participant-observation, a means of both interacting with and acting from the position of other street style bloggers. Starting the blog enabled me to move beyond the kinds of distanced textual analysis I see all too commonly in studies of both online phenomena and fashion and to explore street style blogging instead through the experience-near medium of auto-ethnography.

# Auto-ethnography: Using the self as the vehicle of research

Like nearly every concept in the field of anthropology, "auto-ethnography" is a contested term, with multiple, intertwined histories. When Karl Heider (1975) used it back in 1975 to describe the sixty interviews he conducted with Dani schoolchildren, he was playing with two meanings of "auto": first for "autochthonous" in that these were accounts that the Dani generated for themselves, and second for "automatic" in that the accounts they generated were straightforward and routine, lacking the discursive penetration (Willis 1977) and distanced insight of critical anthropological inquiry (cited in Reed-Danahay 1997, 4). Hayano (1979), Strathern (1987), Dorst (1989), and Pratt (1992) would later use the term to mean something more akin to "native ethnography," that is, anthropological research carried out "at home" or among "one's own people." For a decade or two, this was the primary meaning of the term. It is only in the aftermath of the postmodern critique of anthropology in the mid-1980s, articulated most famously by Clifford and Marcus in *Writing Culture* (1986), that self-reflexivity replaced earlier aims at outsider objectivity, and auto-ethnographic practice came to mean something more akin to investigating one's "self" as an embedded actor within a larger social system. Carolyn Ellis has been, perhaps, the most forceful voice for this brand of auto-ethnography. She defines the method as "systematic sociological introspection" and "emotional recall" in the service of understanding "an experience I've lived through" (Ellis 2004, xvii). Her auto-ethnographic work takes the form of self-reflexive narrative, quasi-literary accounts, and stories that connect "the autobiographical and personal to the cultural, social, and political" (Ellis 2004, xix).

In auto-ethnography, self-reflexivity is a mechanism for creating a more honest, situated, and grounded form of social scientific research. Indeed, after the postmodern critique it became a commonplace of ethnographic work in general to acknowledge how one's own background and experience have shaped the account produced. It can be argued that at least since the late 1980s, nearly all ethnography has been auto-ethnography, as it employs the "self" as the vehicle of research (Ortner 2006).

But those who have explicitly used the term "auto-ethnography" have something else in mind. Anthropologists like Ellis use it to describe an additional methodological step of focusing their project in some way on their own direct experience as lived, embodied, and interpreted through "the self," even while acknowledging that the terms and limits of what constitutes the self are by no means clear or fixed (Reed-Danahay 1997, 3). Auto-ethnography differs from ethnography, not in kind, but in the degree of self-reflexivity and focus on oneself: paying particular attention to one's thoughts, feelings, and physical sensations as a subject of inquiry. Auto-ethnography does not just use the self to do research; it is explicitly about "the self" as the medium through which research transpires.

In using the term *auto-ethnography* in this chapter, I am situating my own work within this latter meaning of the term, describing a mode of research in which, not only am I the one carrying it out, but my research takes explicit account of my thoughts, feelings, and experiences as a form of "data" in its own right. My understanding of auto-ethnography, however, also makes use of earlier understandings of the term. My work on street style bloggers is, in a sense, "native ethnography." Street style bloggers, like many scholars of fashion, are disproportionately middle or upper-middle class, highly educated, and usually urban in residence. They have a penchant for self-reflection and an interest in sartorial expression in its myriad forms, often preferring the oddball to the mainstream, the off-kilter to the on-trend. Street style bloggers tend to stand in a critical outsider position in relation to the workings of the larger fashion world, and they move through the cities they inhabit like the classic flâneurs of Baudelairean mystique, both a part of and apart from the streets they walk down. They constitute, that is, a variety of amateur anthropologist. Therefore, for me to study them is not unlike studying my own people.

Moreover, my use of auto-ethnography also relies on Heider's notion of the automatic. My process of carrying out fieldwork has gone through moments of conscious self-interrogation and other moments of unconscious acting from the position of, simply doing what a street style blogger does without thinking through what this is or means. In fact, I would argue, gaining firsthand insight into the experience of bloggers has required this sort of unconscious acting. To become a blogger is to internalize and normalize the practice of blogging to such an extent that it is no longer available to conscious thought. It must become part of one's *habitus* (Bourdieu 1977), one's automatic and embodied mode of practice. Anything short of unconscious embodiment would hardly warrant the title of "auto-ethnography" to begin with. It is unconscious, embodied acting that marks one as a blogger. I could not simply choose to be a street style blogger and then carry out my research as one. I had to engage in a slow and deliberate process of *becoming* (see Deleuze and Guattari 1987), of internalizing, embodying, and enacting, one with many starts and stops, ups and downs, all of which have ultimately contributed to my theoretical understanding of street style blogging.

## Becoming a blogger

My first day out on the streets of Philadelphia as a street style blogger drove this point home for me in as clear a way as possible. I found myself lingering on the sidewalks of Center City, camera swinging loosely around my neck, with no real conception of what I was doing or how to go about doing it. At first I couldn't bring myself to approach anyone—my teeth grinding and heart beating out of my chest—and then, when I finally worked up the courage, I couldn't decide what I was looking for in a street style subject. Was I after a street-smart cool kid in spikes and black leather of the sort who might have appeared in *i-D Magazine* circa 1981, a quirky individualist in a puffy coat and overalls a la Hel Looks, or perhaps a rakish middle-aged gentleman in a tweed jacket of the sort Scott Schuman might have stopped for The Sartorialist? Philadelphia is not exactly overflowing with any of those categories. I would have to settle for someone who was simply "cool." But how does one know that a subject is "cool" in the first place? How does one recognize "cool"? Is it an objective quality, a certain observable aestheticized indifference, itself born from the racialized streets of urban America (Leland 2004)? Or is it a measure of one's own background, one's accumulated taste as a member of a particular group (Bourdieu 1984; Thornton 1996)? And how does one settle on the brand of coolness that is right for their blog? FaceHunter's cool is not the same as The Sartorialist's cool, which has little in common with the cool of Hel Looks. Whose cool, I wondered, is closer to my own?

Bloggers tend to answer the difficult question of how they isolate appropriate models for their blogs with the conversation-stopping "I just shoot what I like." Javi Obando of On The Corner says, "We just look for someone who claims our sight, who commands our attention. If we like it, we take a picture, and that's it." Mordechai Rubinstein of Mister Mort says, "For me, it's normally that I like something. That's how it is for me, because I'm drawn to it." Adam Katz Sinding of Le 21ème told me, "I just take photos of things that I like. And things that inspire me. I don't even want to say inspire me, things that intrigue me. Things that catch my attention." But what do *I* like? I wondered, wandering the streets that day, and many days after, looking for people to photograph. What catches my attention? I thought I knew once. I thought, in fact, that I had a fairly decent sense of my own tastes and interests. But in the heat of the moment, stalking the streets of Philadelphia with a micro four-thirds camera around my neck, I couldn't seem to remember what they were. How does one know what one "likes"? The more directly you look at your likes, I discovered, the more they seem to disappear. It would take me months of shooting on the streets to develop a clear and confident sense of my own street style aesthetic, what I "like" and what represents "me." And once I had done so, my aesthetic had already evolved into something else.

Finally, walking past the Zara on Walnut Street that first day, I made a decision. *That guy,* right there, in the blue blazer, high-necked sweater, and newsboy cap. *He* is the person I want to photograph (Figure 4.2). There was no hesitation. There was no questioning of my motives. After hours of relentless thinking, second-guessing, even third-guessing, that simple knowledge was an incredible relief. The chatter in my head went mute, if only for a moment. I walked up and talked to him before I had time to change my mind.

**FIGURE 4.2** Erik Honesty, a vintage boutique owner and the very first photographic subject for the Urban Fieldnotes project. *Photo*: Brent Luvaas.

Later on I would analyze my own intentions in identifying that first photographic subject, a man I would later know by the name of Erik Honesty. He looks a little like someone who might appear on The Sartorialist. He has the dapper black gentleman vibe of an Ouigi Theodore or a Sam Lambert, a Brooklyn vintage shop owner and London tailor respectively, both commonly featured on street style blogs. My recognition of him as someone I wanted to shoot was no doubt already a preliminary embodiment of the street style aesthetic. I had seen lots of pictures of people who look like him, and I had come to "like" the look when I encountered it. But in the moment, I was not thinking of any of those things. I saw, and I reacted. And that would become my street style recipe from then on. Thinking, in these circumstances, just gets in the way.

Street style photography, at the end of that first day, seemed like an exercise in Zen big game hunting—if Zen and big game hunting were compatible things. One must be calm and collected, let go of self-doubt, and act without hesitation. One must, in other words, oneself be "cool" (see Mentges 2000), exemplifying a bodily discipline of aloof stillness. And the biggest obstacle getting in the way of that goal is mental chatter. Calming the chatter in one's mind is a difficult trick for anyone to master, but it poses a special challenge for a social scientist used to taking constant mental notes. I struggled to be quiet and receptive, open to whatever—or whoever—came my way. Form too clear an understanding of who I was looking for, I learned that first day, and I would miss out on the subjects right in front of me. Case in point: Mandi, my next photograph for Urban Fieldnotes, taken the following day (Figure 4.3). On first sight, Mandi and Erik have little in common with each other, except that I reacted to them and knew I wanted to photograph both. That is enough commonality, it turns out, for a street style blogger. After practically giving up on street style that second day, standing on Walnut Street, assessing everyone who came by, I let go of my expectations and concerns. I would either find someone or I would not. Either way I would post about it on my blog. And then along came Mandi. I saw something in her and reacted to it. I am glad

**FIGURE 4.3** Mandi, the second photographic subject for the Urban Fieldnotes project. *Photo*: Brent Luvaas.

I did. Her picture remains my most widely "pinned" image on Pinterest, a perennial virtual corkboard favorite.

Street style photography, I have had driven home for me again and again while out on the streets, is a project of honing one's intuition into a sharp visual focus. It means embodying the aesthetics of street style so deeply and so completely that they operate within you and upon you without conscious deployment. A good street style photographer knows not to overly intellectualize what she is doing or why she is doing it. She knows not to bring her embodied understanding to the surface. As Emma Arnold, blogger for the Chicago-based Trés Awesome put it, "I'll know if I want to take their picture almost immediately, but then sometimes I hesitate because I'm nervous or [because of] whatever sort of circumstances are happening inside my head."

Street style bloggers have a number of ways of talking about this delicate mental instrument I call—with some tongue in cheek—*style radar*, but their descriptions all suggest a similar underlying form: a dependency on instinct or intuition, a sense of simply "knowing" who they want to shoot, and a feeling of internal coherence between their own self-concept and the stylistic sensibility of the subject in question. *Style radar* operates outside of articulation. It is felt rather than thought, and it adheres to a variety of unmediated experience cultural theorists often describe as *affect*.

"Affect," write Seigworth and Gregg in their introduction to *The Affect Theory Reader*, consists of "those forces . . . beneath, alongside, or generally *other* than conscious knowing, vital forces insisting beyond emotion—that can serve to drive us toward movement, toward thought and extension, that can likewise suspend us (as if neutral) across a barely registering accretion of force-relations, or that can even leave us overwhelmed by the world's apparent intractability" (Seigworth and Gregg 2010, 1). Affect describes felt realities that are not translatable into any known lexicon. But their un-pin-down-able nature makes them no less keenly felt.

And here we come to the crux of the matter for auto-ethnography. It, like *style radar*, depends on attention to internal states, affective forces that are not necessarily available to social scientific analysis as we typically understand it. What kinds of generalizations are possible based on my own experiencing of the immediate sensations of street style blogging? What kinds of articulable knowledge does this practice generate?

In a sense, auto-ethnography yields none. It is experienced rather than stated, felt rather than written. Its knowledge is practical knowledge, embodied knowledge. It has few "facts" to offer. It does, however, produce a certain kind of certainty. It produces a certainty that those social scientific frames we, as scholars of fashion, use to describe everyday life start to break down in the face of direct experience. We may, as auto-ethnographers or bloggers, recognize both Erik and Mandi as "cool," but to do so tells us little about the social and economic circumstances that enable "cool"—key questions among social scientific researchers. Here we have two individuals of different genders, ethnicities, and likely socioeconomic backgrounds, and yet they both embody an affective trait generative of street style imagery that we identify as "cool." How, then, can "cool" be described as a form of socioeconomic distinction, as so many sociologists and anthropologists have argued it is (see Bourdieu 1984; Thornton 1996)? How do we classify Erik and Mandi within an existing set of sociological categories? Doing auto-ethnographic research has made me generally distrustful of such broad categorical claims. Out in the field, identifying subjects for my photos and engaging with other photographers on a peer basis, abstract sociological categories become harder and harder to assert. Everyone starts to look a little like an exception. Sure, most of the subjects of street style blogs are members of the "creative class" (Florida 2002) or "new petite bourgeoisie" (Bourdieu 1984), those cultural arbiters for whom personal style is a mode of brand distinction. But plenty of them also work in retail or management. Some of them are students. Some lawyers.

The knowledge that auto-ethnography generates might thus best be described as "anti-knowledge." It does not so much yield knowledge for social scientists to work with as it demonstrates the limits of what can be known by them in the first place. To put it differently, we can think of auto-ethnography as a sort of critical corrective to sociological abstraction. It grounds social scientific work in the lived ambiguities of everyday life, and it serves as a moral corrective to distanced academic critique. It is easy to lambast bloggers from the comfortable confines of a university office. It is easy to accuse them of selling out their passions, branding their identities, or enacting, even if only inadvertently, some "neoliberal" mode of agency (see Gershon 2011). But it is a much harder thing to do when you have felt firsthand what is at stake for bloggers. It is simply too reductive a maneuver. Auto-ethnography gives us pause, lest we judge too quickly. It immerses us in how messy real social practice is and makes any academic fantasy we may have of tidying it up into a single, universal theory seem quaint and old-fashioned.

# The more concrete kinds of knowledge auto-ethnography produces

Nonetheless, my delving into auto-ethnography has produced some more concrete forms of "data" as well, ones perhaps more subject to the critical eye of social theory as we typically understand it. I have learned, for instance, just how much time street style blogging takes. I have had to devote around six hours a week to cruising the streets, looking for people to shoot in order to generate enough images to post three times per week, another three to four hours a week to labeling and editing those photos, and an additional three to four hours a week to posting and commenting on them. And this is after two years of experience. It took considerably more time for the first six or so months. This also does not include the amount of time bloggers spend viewing other blogs, commenting on them, or engaging in a meaningful way with a larger blogging network. Nor does it include the time bloggers spend marketing their posts through social media platforms like Facebook, Twitter, Instagram, and Pinterest. These activities can easily set bloggers back an additional two to three hours a day, especially if we include in our accounting the time it takes to build a network to market the posts to. Blogging, then, is a part-time job. To do it successfully is a major commitment of time and energy. It should come as no surprise that most street style bloggers stop blogging after just a few months, some after just a few posts. Unless they build a large following, attach themselves to a network providing regular positive feedback, or find some way to monetize their efforts, most bloggers eventually decide that it is just not worth it. It should also come as no surprise that so many bloggers eventually shift their attention from the streets of their hometowns to the sidewalks of major fashion weeks. It would be easy from a distanced academic position to argue that Fashion Week's domination of street style imagery in the past few years is a case of simple cooptation. The fashion industry noticed that the street style thing was booming and pulled it into its web. Indeed, that was my explanation when I began this project. But there is an even simpler explanation, obvious to anyone who has spent time on the streets looking for people to photograph. Shooting at Fashion Weeks is *way easier* than shooting on the streets. Most people on most city streets, even in New York and London, are not that fashionable, at least according to the standards of street style blogs (see also Woodward 2009). But at Fashion Week, fashionable people stream past. You can collect months' worth of images in a single day of shooting.

I have also learned that street style blogging requires a good deal of photographic expertise and some pretty expensive equipment. The current aesthetic of street style photography involves depicting a subject in crystal clear sharpness in the foreground of an image with a heavily blurred background behind them. To do so, photographers open the aperture of their cameras to a range somewhere between f1.2 and f4. This requires using a camera with a manual or aperture-priority camera setting. It also requires a fixed focal length lens, for use only with DSLR or equivalent cameras. Neither these cameras nor their lenses come cheap. In fact, nearly all well-known street style photographers now use full-frame DSLRs with fast, fixed length 50mm or 85mm lenses with a maximum aperture of at least f1.8. I started this project with a micro four-thirds, a DSLR-like Panasonic Lumix GF-1 and a 20mm f1.7 pancake lens. In theory, I should have been able to capture the look I was seeing on blogs like The Sartorialist and Jak & Jil, but in practice, I certainly could not. It was just not camera (or lens) enough for the task. Eventually, growing frustrated with my inability to get the kind of aesthetic that other photographers were getting, I researched the cameras popular among street style bloggers and settled on a Nikon D700 with an 85mm F1.4 lens, setting me back some $4,500. Compared to what many other photographers spend on their equipment, this was a bargain. And its effects on my work were immediately apparent. The quality of my images was vastly better. My ability to emulate the styles of other photographers improved many times over. As Adam Katz Sinding of Le 21ème said to me, "It's got so much to do with the equipment. If I had a bottom of the line Nikon, we wouldn't be having this conversation right now. No one would care about my website." In street style blogging, then, equipment matters. So much for the hackneyed pro-technology sentiment that anyone can be a blogger! Most people simply cannot afford it. Not by today's standards.

I have also learned, much to my surprise, that few people object to having their picture taken and posted online by a complete stranger, regardless of whatever concerns about privacy most of us may express, and that even fewer people object to signing photo release forms handing over the rights to their image in perpetuity. Indeed, few people bother to read such forms. I get rejected by around one out of every twenty people I ask for their photo, and that number has gone down as my pitch has gained confidence. Shooting street style has driven home the utter ubiquity of digital photography to me in a way that few other experiences could.

And "experience" is the operative word here. The pieces of "hard evidence" and "fact" that I gathered through my auto-ethnographic method were gathered through—or at least supplemented by—my direct experience of street style blogging. Many are facts I could have come across by other means. I could, for instance, have asked bloggers during my interviews with them how long they spend blogging per week. In fact, I often have asked that question. But would I have thought to follow up that question with how long they spend promoting their blog through social media, if I had not known firsthand that blog posts spike in traffic primarily due to their promotion on social media? Would I have asked how their total number of pageviews had been affected by Facebook's recent change in algorithm, if I hadn't myself noticed a similar slump? And would I have thought to ask bloggers what kinds of lenses they use, if I had not run into trouble attempting for myself to capture the kinds of aesthetics they capture? Would I have even noticed the shallow depth of field preferred by bloggers, if I hadn't attempted to reproduce it for myself? Forging myself into a practitioner, has not only directly impacted my interpretation of what street style blogging is and means, but has influenced the very kinds of questions I ask about street style blogging and of street style bloggers.

It would be foolish for me to argue that auto-ethnography should replace surveys, textual analysis, semiotics, focus groups, interviews, and other methodologies for all scholars of fashion in all circumstances. These methods yield extremely valuable forms of information, many of which are only determinable from a large sample size or visible to a truly "outside" perspective. I made use of a variety of methods in my street style project, including auto-ethnography, but also photography, textual analysis of street style blogs, interviews with bloggers, and more classic ethnographic participant-observation at New York Fashion Week. When used in combination with these other methods, however, auto-ethnography is a powerful tool, grounding insights gleaned from elsewhere within the lived realities of everyday experience. It subjects theory to the test of practice.

# Conclusion: Auto-ethnography and fashion studies

This chapter has presented just a small inventory of what I have learned about street style blogging by becoming a street style blogger myself. It is no doubt specific to my subject, yet it does suggest the utility of auto-ethnography as a method in fashion studies more generally, a field in which experiential methods have so far taken a backseat. There is precedence for auto-ethnography in fashion studies. Scholars like Ashley Mears (2011) and Stefanie Sadre-Orafai (2008, and in this book) have made very effective—and very compelling—use of their own personal experiences in their studies of modeling and model-casting respectively. Neither study would have been as rich with detail or emotion if the researchers had not gone through what their research subjects go through. It is worth wondering how an expansion of the grounded, experience-near method into other domains of fashion studies would impact the kinds of insights and theoretical frameworks developed by fashion scholars.

How different would the analysis, for instance, of editorial spreads in *Vogue* be if the scholar had been an editorial photographer herself? How would this affect her insights and impact her critique of fashion representations? Are there practical reasons photographs look as they do or feature the kinds of models that they do that are not obvious through textual analysis, which might support or weaken common theoretical assumptions about the nature of the gaze or the imagined audience of *Vogue*? What are the external pressures experienced by fashion photographers to do the kind of work they do, and how keenly do these photographers feel them? What kind of equipment do they use, and how does this equipment shape, limit, and influence the images they produce? What kinds of agency do the tools of the trade exert over fashion photography?

I don't know the answers to those questions offhand, but I think it would be worth finding out. There is, after all, an important gap in fashion studies that auto-ethnography can help to fill: the first-person experience gap. It is time to see what happens when we collapse the barrier between researcher and researched and begin to do fashion studies from the perspective of those very people we study—to see what fashion looks like from the other side of the lens.

# References

Boellstorff, Tom, Bonnie Nardi, Celia Pearce, and Tracy L. Taylor. 2012. *Ethnography in Virtual Worlds: A Handbook of Method*. Princeton: Princeton University Press.

Bourdieu, Pierrre. 1977. *Outline of a Theory of Practice*. Cambridge: Cambridge University Press.

Bourdieu, Pierrre. 1984. *Distinction: A Social Critique of the Judgment of Taste*. Cambridge, MA: Harvard University Press.

Clifford, James and George E. Marcus. 1986. *Writing Culture: The Poetics and Politics of Ethnography*. Berkeley, CA: University of California Press.

Deleuze, Gilles and Félix Guattari. 1987. *A Thousand Plateaus: Capitalism and Schizophrenia*. Translated by B. Massumi. Minneapolis and London: University of Minnesota Press.

Dorst, John D. 1989. *The Written Suburb: An American Site, an Ethnographic Dilemma*. Philadelphia: University of Pennsylvania Press.

Ellis, Carolyn. 2004. *The Ethnographic I: A Methodological Novel about Autoethnography*. Walnut Creek: Alta Mira Press.

Florida, Richard. 2002. *The Rise of the Creative Class*. New York: Basic Books.

Geertz, Clifford. 1977. "Deep Play: Notes on the Balinese Cockfight." In *The Interpretation of Cultures*, 412–53. New York: Basic Books.

Gershon, Ilana. 2011. "Neoliberal Agency." *Current Anthropology* 52 (4): 537–55.

Giddens, Anthony. 1979. *Central Problems in Social Theory: Action, Structure and Contradiction in Social Analysis*. Berkeley and Los Angeles, CA: University of California Press.

Gilbert, David. 2006. "From Paris to Shanghai: The Changing Geography of Fashion's World Cities." In *Fashion's World Cities*, edited by Christopher Breward and David Gilbert, 3–32. Oxford: Berg.

Hayano, David M. 1979. "Auto-Ethnogaphy: Paradigms, Problems, and Prospects." *Human Organization* 38 (1): 99–104.

Heider, Karl. 1975. "What Do People Do? Dani Auto-Ethnography." *Journal of Anthropological Research* 31: 3–17.

Hine, Christine M. 2000. *Virtual Ethnography*. London: SAGE Publications.

Jones, Carla. 2003. "Dress for Sukses: Fashioning Femininity and Nationality in Urban Indonesia." In *The Globalization of Asian Dress: Re-Orienting Fashion or Re-Orientalizing Asia?*, edited by Carla Jones and Ann Marie Leshkowich, 185–214. Oxford: Berg.

Luvaas, Brent. 2013. "Shooting Street Style in Indonesia: A Photo Essay." *Clothing Cultures* 1 (1): 59–81.

Mears, Ashley. 2011. *Pricing Beauty: The Making of a Fashion Model*. Berkeley, CA: University of California Press.

Mentges, Gabriele. 2000. "Cold, Coldness, Coolness: Remarks on the Relationship of Dress, Body, and Technology." *Fashion Theory* 4 (1): 27–48.

Ortner, Sherry B. 2006. *Anthropology and Social Theory: Culture, Power, and the Acting Subject*. Durham and London: Duke University Press.

Pratt, Mary Louise. 1992. *Imperial Eyes: Travel Writing and Transculturation*. London and New York: Routledge.

Reed-Danahay, Deborah, ed. 1997. *Auto/Ethnography: Rewriting the Self and the Social*. Oxford: Berg.

Sadre-Orafai, Stephanie. 2008. "Developing Images: Race, Language, and Perception in Fashion-model Casting." In *Fashion as Photograph: Viewing and Reviewing Images of Fashion*, edited by E. Shinkle, 141–53. London: I. B. Tauris.

Seigworth, Gregory J., and Melissa Gregg. 2010. "An Inventory of Shivers." In *The Affect Theory Reader*, edited by M. Gregg and G. J. Seigworth, 1–27. Durham and London: Duke University Press.

Strathern, Marilyn. 1987. "The Limits of Auto-Anthropology." In *Anthropology at Home*, edited by Anthony Jackson, 16–37. London: Tavistock Publications.

Willis, Paul. 1977. *Learning to Labor: How Working Class Kids Get Working Class Jobs*. New York: Columbia University Press.

Woodward, Sophie. 2009. "The Myth of Street Style." *Fashion Theory* 13(1): 83–102.

Zhao, Jianhua. 2013. *The Chinese Fashion Industry: An Ethnographic Approach*. London: Bloomsbury.

# 5 RECASTING FASHION IMAGE PRODUCTION: AN ETHNOGRAPHIC AND PRACTICE-BASED APPROACH TO INVESTIGATING BODIES AS MEDIA

## Stephanie Sadre-Orafai

Growing up as a teenager in the mid-1990s, and living far away from any global fashion capital, images were the most accessible point of entry for me into the world of fashion. Alongside posters of my favorite musicians, I adorned the walls of my bedroom with pages I tore from fashion magazines like *Allure*, *Elle*, and *Harper's Bazaar*. While certain models appeared across several of spreads, unlike the musicians on my wall, I neither paid much attention to who they were, nor imagined what their working lives were like. I just liked the moods and feelings their images evoked—the exotic locations, the gilded makeup, the gritty styling of the shoots. It all felt very urban and glamorous, far from my daily life in Tennessee. On weekends I watched *Fashion File*, the Canadian news digest show hosted by Tim Blanks and syndicated in the United States on E! Entertainment Television. The program profiled designers and featured footage from runway presentations in New York, Paris, and Milan, including interviews with editors, stylists, and other audience members. This was before the explosion of fashion reality TV in the early to mid-2000s that aggressively packaged backstage access in a new interactive formula to teach viewers how to see and articulate their own aesthetic through modes of direct and vicarious participation (see Sadre-Orafai 2012). In the 1990s, televised fashion programs still portrayed the industry as an elite and guarded institution, amplifying the celebrity status of those who worked within it.

While I continued to be an avid reader of fashion magazines throughout college, as I pursued a degree in anthropology and studied the relationship between race and popular culture, I never thought I would work on the industry academically, let alone in it. Yet in 2002, when I moved to New York City for graduate school, I took the opportunity to write a seminar paper on the rising popularity of "ethnically ambiguous" models, visually and textually decoding coverage of the trends in women's fashion magazines. My professor liked the paper, but suggested that I "go to a photo shoot" to see how the images were "actually produced" to make my analysis more anthropological. This seemed like a daunting task. While fashion images are accessible in public spaces, the sites of their production seemed, at best, endlessly receding: the higher one ascended the fashion hierarchy, the more exclusive these spaces became. As members of an elite industry with their own means to narrate and shape the stories told about them, fashion insiders seemed to have no incentive for allowing an anthropologist to study and analyze their practices firsthand. Yet, this exhortation spurred me to start what became a four-year, multi-sited ethnographic study of fashion image production.[1]

In this chapter, I describe my entry into the field, first in 2003 at an ethnic women's lifestyle magazine, and then in 2004, 2006, and 2007 at a series of other sites, including modeling and casting agencies, and the experiences that challenged my assumptions about the fashion industry: first, about how the industry worked, and second, how best to study its dynamics. As I will describe, these encounters pushed me to find new frameworks and approaches for analyzing the various sites, practices, and individuals involved in producing fashion images, particularly casting, which, for the purposes of my research, I define broadly as the recruitment, selection, development, and marketing of models. As I followed models through the multiple circuits of discovery and development—from open calls and go-sees to the sets of photo shoots and editorial offices of magazines—I tracked both models' and casting professionals' everyday lived experiences, as well as the social lives of the images they collaboratively produced together. In this process, I discovered that more than images were being produced in these interactions.

Narrating my route through these multiple field sites, I demonstrate how a series of seeming foreclosures and false starts led to insights that helped me reframe the object of my research: from the production of fashion images to the production of what I call *bodies as media*. This reorientation allowed me to focus on not just the visual aspects of fashion image production, but also the embodied, relational, and affective dimensions, including the socialization of models and casting professionals into the industry. By focusing on how each group learned to relate to their bodies as mediums for communicating both aesthetic discernment and display, I foreground how what is typically considered preproduction can be analyzed as its own production process.

Importantly, this shift unfolded from both practical and theoretical concerns that were directly connected to my ethnographic and practice-based approach. As I moved from the photo department of an ethnic women's lifestyle magazine and a struggling boutique modeling agency to a leading casting firm and top high fashion women's modeling agency, my thinking about fashion was shaped by both my combined research and employment in the industry and unlikely comparisons outside of it. In addition to drawing on my own socialization into the industry, I looked for inspiration beyond fashion to think about how casting and modeling were part of a broader set of cultural practices of typification, classification, and performance. This helped me decenter both the fashion industry and published fashion image as the primary points of reference for understanding casting practices, enabling me to explore their broader ramifications and resonance. While the story I tell in this chapter is necessarily autobiographical, and as such, somewhat idiosyncratic, as most research processes are, it nevertheless reveals fault lines young fashion studies scholars are likely to face as they traverse fashion sites and practices, particularly those concerned with image production.

## Ethnography, ethnomethodology, and negotiating access to sites of fashion image production

While traditionally anthropologists have worked in remote areas and at the scale of an entire culture or group, contemporary researchers focus on sites both near and far and with segments more narrowly defined by shared sets of practices, including occupations. Indeed, in the past 25 years anthropologists have turned increasingly to media producers and commercial culture industries as subjects and objects of ethnographic inquiry (for overviews, see Askew and Wilk 2003; Ginsburg, Abu-Lughod, and Larkin 2002a; Mahon 2000; Spitulnik 1993). They have examined cultural producers' reworkings of social meanings and identities through the interpellation of new subjectivities and markets through various kinds of media production and circulation, including: film, music, advertising, and, more recently, fashion.

More often than not, studying a phenomenon anthropologically means analyzing it ethnographically—that is, by *being there*. Participant-observation as part of long-term ethnographic fieldwork is the hallmark of the discipline's approach. This entails embedding oneself in the everyday lives and practices of a group of people, observing what they do, talking to them about it, and doing it alongside them over an extended period of time—typically a year—with the goal of capturing the meanings and texture of their everyday experiences. This includes their unthinking routines and sentiments: the taken for granted, assumed, and deeply felt dimensions of people's lives that they either cannot or do not articulate in direct ways, or what Bronislaw Malinowski referred to as the "imponderabilia of actual life" ([1922] 2014, 18). It is the ethnographer's job to record and connect these imponderabilia to broader social, cultural, and historical contexts and patterns, to illuminate fine-grained dimensions of human experience that other methods and modes of analysis cannot grasp. Balancing insider and outsider perspectives, ethnographers use techniques of intimacy and estrangement to make the strange familiar, translating others' experiences so that they are intelligible beyond a local context, and the familiar strange, gaining enough critical distance to see underlying patterns and connections. As such, this type of research is often at least implicitly comparative in scope (for more on this tension, see Keane 2003).

As I have noted elsewhere (Sadre-Orafai 2011), while there is a relatively long tradition of deconstructing the messages, meanings, and codes of commercial and fashion images (e.g., see Barthes [1967] 1990; Goffman 1979; Jobling 1999; Williamson 1978), critical work analyzing the actual processes of its production is a more recent phenomenon (but see Kondo 1997 for an early anthropological analysis). Notably, sociologists have made strides in analyzing fashion production practices, yet they have tended to focus on more high profile producers, like models (Entwistle 2004; Mears 2011; Wissinger 2007), photographers (Aspers 2001), and designers (Skov 2002), rather than image brokers like casting and model agents (with Entwistle 2009 as an exception). This work developed largely out of cultural-economic sociology (e.g., see du Gay 1997; du Gay and Pryke 2002) and as such, its chief concerns have been questions of value, including analyses of markets, labor, and the role of creativity in a capitalist market, ultimately seeking to demystify the machinations of the fashion industry and show its "rationality" (e.g., see Crewe 2003; Entwistle and Wissinger 2006; Godart and Mears 2009).

For my part, I was less interested in how value is produced in the fashion industry—that is, how a particular look is translated into a marketable one and exchanged for monetary and other types of value—than in examining how certain forms of knowledge about people and types are produced; that a look is even recognized as an entity at all. I found that the rush to judge casting practices against their eventual outcomes (e.g., the lack of racial or body diversity in published fashion images) flattened out the multisensory evaluative processes that precede and make these images possible.

During the course of my fieldwork, I slowly began to focus on recasting these preproduction imaging practices as their own isolatable process, arguing that the work of casting professionals could not be reduced to an analysis of their published ends. My goal then became to linger during moments of recognition, typification, and classification. Ultimately this meant taking casting seriously as its own domain, one that could be separated and analyzed apart from a discussion of the final published image or outcome. As I soon found, many of these practices left less retrievable traces, thus demanding ethnographic modes of attention and analysis (cf. Gürsel 2012). They were conversations and embodied forms of knowledge, which while observable, were not always visible.

This tension between visibility and invisibility, photographic documentation and gut instinct, reverberated throughout my fieldwork. I found that despite the focus on appearances in the fashion industry, there was an intense preoccupation with where the appearances came from, how to transform them, and the limits of these changes. While there were often material solutions, such as physically transforming a model's appearance through styling or digital manipulation, there were just as often discursive and embodied solutions, changing the language one used to describe a model's appearance or encouraging a kind of inner affective shift to create differences on the surface of the body. This led me to reorient my analytic frame from wanting to understand the production of fashion images to the production of mediation itself. My guiding research question became: *How do you produce a model's body as a medium?*

This is a deeply ethnomethodological question that seeks to understand how the forms of affective and aesthetic perception, judgment, and performance that make up casting practices are interactional achievements. Ethnomethodology deflects attention away from the motivations of social actions and focuses instead on the "procedural bases through which they are produced and understood—the ways in which the actions themselves betray their own analyzability" (Heritage 1987, 235; cf. Sacks 1985). As Stephen Hester and David Francis write, "Where conventional social science takes for granted the availability of the activities it describes, ethnomethodology seeks to examine their 'possibility'" (2007, 6). Ethnomethodology attends to the knowledgeability of social actors, contextual character of ordinary understanding, integration of knowledge and action, and commonsense reasoning in mundane situations (Heritage 1987, 225–41). It analyzes everyday interaction as "a contingent accomplishment of socially organized common practices" (Garfinkel 1967, 33). Approaching casting ethnomethodologically meant underscoring the ad hoc features of practical logic and action and analyzing their recuperative, conservative, and ultimately moral dimensions; that is, how casting agents subject their aesthetic choices and modes of interaction against social expectations and norms that are not only shared across the profession but are made available and accountable to interactional participants (cf. Sacks 1984). Importantly, this is not a rule-based model of social action, but rather one that draws on "common-sense knowledge [that] is organized as a highly uneven patchwork of certainties and vague conjectures" (Heritage 1987, 230).

While ethnomethodology and other practice-based social theory informed the eventual design of my project and its focus on both the socialization of models and professional practices of casting and modeling agents, the impetus for my analysis of bodies as media came from trying to combine this literature with insights from the ethnography of media and cultural production; that is, in trying to connect situated practices to their effects. While others have tried to bridge these concerns by ethnographically attending to both producers and consumers (e.g., see Abu-Lughod 2004; Dávila 2001; Mankekar 1999), I wanted to provide a more detailed examination of exactly what casting professionals and models did. Harvey Sacks describes this as the "missing whatness" of ethnographic and sociological analyses. While studies of a particular practice may focus on its economic structure, organizational features, and social networks, few analyze exactly how the practice is accomplished (Hester and Francis 2007, 6–8).

Isolating casting as a self-contained production site made it possible to raise a number of typically unasked questions about fashion image production. For example, what can we learn about how fashion images "work" if we examine the theories of mediation that underlie their production? How do these theories reconfigure the role of both image brokers and models in this process, and what parallels and differences can we see between fashion and other domains of knowledge production? This type of practice-based approach allowed me to situate casting outside of fashion, comparing it to other forms of visual, embodied, and discursive forms of knowledge production, and connecting it to broader patterns of ways of seeing and recognizing beauty and other forms of difference.

This required not just *being there*—the guiding principle of ethnographic fieldwork—but being socialized to learn these practices in some way. Yet, to do this, I first had to gain access. The process of negotiating institutional access to workspaces of cultural producers is well-trodden territory in the ethnography of media literature. While some ethnographers have gained access by blurring the boundary between employee and researcher, as I eventually did, it is not always possible and raises its own set of constraints and negotiations; for example, questions about what can and cannot be published and to whom one then does or does not have access (e.g., see Dornfeld 1998, 19–22; Moeran 1996, 34; cf. Dávila 2001, 19). Further, "access" does not necessarily guarantee the researcher equal entry to all spaces or all situations. As anthropologist Arlene Dávila notes, despite the willingness—and indeed, enthusiasm—of her subjects in the US Hispanic advertising industry, she was still "unable to access meetings with clients, the real spaces where the commodification of Latino culture takes place" (2003, 157).

These kinds of limitations provide the impetus for creative and synthetic methodological strategies. For example, unable to penetrate the British fashion publishing industry, cultural studies scholar Anna Gough-Yates (2003) turned to analyses of trade literature; anthropologist Dorinne Kondo (1997) employed sporadic and intensive bursts of fieldwork transnationally to trace the circuits of fashion production; and sociologist Gina Neff (2005) analyzed the nightlife of digital media workers. During the course of my research, I found it necessary to supplement my own firsthand ethnographic analyses of model development and casting practices with media analyses of broader constructions of the figure of the model, particularly through reality television programs and coverage of modeling controversies (e.g., see Sadre-Orafai 2012).

Beyond issues of access, studying cultural producers raises a number of ethical, methodological, and representational dilemmas and requires negotiating a particular kind of researcher-subject relationship best summarized by anthropologists Faye Ginsburg, Lila Abu-Lughod, and Brian Larkin as "usually engaged, sometimes complicit, rarely neutral" (2002b, 21; cf. Marcus 1997). Similar to and overlapping with concerns raised by "studying up" (Nader 1972), "studying sideways" (Hannerz 2004), so-called "native" anthropology (Jacobs-Huey 2002) and ethnographic research in the United States (Moffatt 1992), some of the major issues include: negotiating access to elite and guarded institutions, representing divergent political positions, and countering re-mediations and unintended circulations of one's work. Also at stake is what anthropologists Dominic Boyer and Ulf Hannerz describe as "the challenges and opportunities at the heart of the ethnography of media, a project that is reflexive to the core in its practice of representing practices of representation" (2006, 6). Working in the New York fashion industry, I found myself dealing with several of these dimensions and more.

# From working on fashion to working in fashion

While *bodies as media* would eventually become the organizing framework for my analysis, I began with a more concrete object of study: fashion image production. As such, one of the first challenges I faced was figuring out how to access not just a one-off photo shoot, but a site (or series of sites) where I could regularly engage in observations, conversations, and practices alongside fashion image producers. While I debated how to make this happen, I took a summer internship in the editorial department of an academic press that had offices in midtown Manhattan. There I met postcollegiate editorial assistants roughly my age that had either interned at or knew someone who worked at a magazine. While none of these contacts directly led me to a field site, they introduced me to online resources, including Ed2010.com, for finding magazine internships.

That fall I applied widely, seeking positions at both men's and women's titles, niche and mainstream publications, and in a range of departments. In October 2003, I landed a photo internship at *Candy*, an ethnic women's lifestyle magazine with offices in the Flatiron district of Manhattan. Gina, the newly hired photo editor, explained that given the small size of the magazine's staff, the internship would be more like an assistant position. I would help organize contacts, proof and distribute call sheets, research stock photo requests, and assist on set.

The photo department seemed like an ideal place to explore my early research questions, which were largely practical: How are the images created? What does the editing process look like? Who makes which decisions? What kinds of considerations go into the process? Who are the most significant actors? What are their structural roles and relationships? While being on set was exciting, I found the office we shared with the two-person fashion department to be more revealing. There, I saw how ideas for fashion and beauty stories were developed, from the initial concept and collection of visual references, to finding the right creative team to execute it, to editing the resulting images for publication. While I did not have access to editorial staff meetings, I could listen to the informal conversations between Gina and other editors as they discussed plans for stories from selecting models and locations to finding the right photographer and creative team for the story concepts. I found that these exchanges often hinged on processes of mediation and translation, as well as the logistics of both.

About two months into my internship, just as I was getting down the rhythms of the photo department, the magazine folded. At a company-wide staff meeting at 4:00 p.m., the CEO made the announcement that the publisher had filed for bankruptcy protection citing the loss of its major financial backer. Earlier that day the staff had been finalizing the February 2004 issue, scheduled to be sent to the printer in less than two weeks: layouts were being edited, stock images secured, and last-minute fact-checking completed. The CEO announced that the December/January issue already on newsstands would be the last to be published.

And so I thought my time in the fashion world had ended abruptly. All of the stories I had worked on while at *Candy* were never published. At the time I felt as if this limited the potential of my analysis. I would not be able to track how the decisions and production practices I witnessed translated into a media artifact with its own social life and circulation. It felt incomplete. Originally my plan had been to factor the decisions made in the production process into my visual analysis of the final published work. It was not until later in my fieldwork that I realized this kind of comparison was not only unnecessary, but that it obscured something key about the preproduction process itself.

I spent the next few months trying, unsuccessfully, to find another magazine internship. Frustrated, I broadened my search to include other kinds of fashion production sites, looking to Craigslist for leads. I ended up at Flair, a struggling boutique modeling agency, in April 2004. The agency was a small, one-room office space with a couch and two workstations. Max, the owner and head booker, explained that Flair filled a void in the market: ethnically diverse models. While he represented a handful of white models, most were black, Asian, or of mixed race. This, he explained, was both a personal mission and shrewd business decision. These models, he said, had a difficult time finding representation because of racism in the industry. While demand for white models was greater, he felt that there was an underserved client need for nonwhite models. If he took a chance and developed them, he could exploit this gap and build a niche.

While the staff of *Candy* was small, at Flair, it was often just Max and me in the office, with models stopping by to pick up cards or have their portfolios updated.

Initially, I thought the small size and marginal status of the agency would make it an outlier, an inaccurate representation of the "real" fashion industry. Yet, it provided a unique opportunity for me to be socialized into the role of an agent with all of its attendant expectations. During the 17 months I spent there, moving from cold-calling and sending packages to clients to scouting and developing models, to actually booking them on editorial and campaign jobs (albeit small and less prestigious ones), my own socialization into the industry as a worker, not just as a researcher, became a valuable source of data. Through the trial-and-error process of learning a new skill and being fully responsible for it, I gained a better sense of the demands and pressures of working as a modeling agent.

One of my most significant lessons was learning how important it was to find the right language to describe a model and how images alone were never enough. Clients needed a narrative, either about the model's backstory or heritage, to bolster their perception about his or her suitability for a job (see Sadre-Orafai 2008). This narrative work we did with clients dovetailed with the discursive work of development, where Max and I used stories about other models and clients to teach new models how to relate to their bodies and personas as malleable and marketable resources.

Aside from working closely with Max, I also developed friendships with some of the models, getting to know what was going on in their lives and how they saw the process, what frustrated them about it, and what kind of futures they imagined for themselves in and beyond the industry. I learned about rates and the kinds of ratios of both models and clients that agencies needed to be successful, or at least profitable, which we were always struggling to achieve. More than anything, though, I saw the incredible amount of work that went into creating just the possibility for published fashion images: the invisible, uncredited labor of modeling agents, which from an analytic standpoint could only be discussed as brokering images, not producing them. Resolved, I sought a way to reframe this work as productive. Going forward, casting and model development became two parts of a single, unified process.

## Within and beyond fashion

Moving from preliminary to primary fieldwork in 2006, I faced a familiar dilemma. While I knew casting and development were the central practices I wanted to examine, I was unsure how to access the more mainstream and high-end agencies. Somewhat naively I thought that since I was now a doctoral candidate with research funding—both sources of external validation for my ability to carry out the research and the importance of the project—I could engage these sites without having to work at them. Initially, I targeted two casting directors: Phillip, a close friend of Max and former modeling agent who worked on mostly commercial projects; and Jeremy, a vocal advocate for multicultural casting with a range of high fashion and commercial clients.

Both responded warmly to my emails and agreed to meet, extending offers to let me sit in on a few castings. They were frank in their assessment of the industry: Jeremy explained that while the same creative teams often worked on commercial and editorial projects, they were less likely to use nonwhite models for editorial jobs. He dealt with this cognitive dissonance by taking a long view of his client relationships, and worked to foster mutual trust and respect, so that he could push his clients to go beyond the industry status quo.

While both Jeremy and Phillip were supportive, neither of their agencies became a tenable field site: there were scheduling conflicts with Phillip's agency, and Jeremy's business partner thought that the idea of being observed was "too weird." Both, however, gave me contacts of a few "like-minded" people who might be interested in helping. As I tried to set these new contacts and my old networks into motion, I also sent formal invitations to dozens of magazine bookings editors, casting agents, and directors of modeling agencies to participate in what I described as a research study on "multiculturalism and casting." Despite the impressive New York University letterhead, these failed to produce much interest. The exception was a tense meeting with a litigious model agency director in July. Initially sympathetic to the project, during the course of our forty-five-minute discussion she declared that it was too "dangerous" and would "get me killed," before accusing me of surreptitiously recording our conversation when I reached into my bag for a pen. While I found several individuals willing to talk about issues of race and casting "off the record," arranging for regular observations over the course of several months seemed nearly impossible.

So as summer came to an end and with it the rush of the New York Fashion Week, I returned to engaging these sites as I had before, by applying for internship positions—exchanging my free labor for access. After a handful of interviews in September, I began working at a photo agency in Soho. In addition to representing photographers and hair and makeup artists, the agency also had two producers on staff who occasionally held castings. While one producer was friendly, the other was decidedly not. I quickly realized that the castings at the agency neither occurred frequently enough, nor could I access them easily. I started looking for another internship almost immediately.

A month later, I began working at LVX, a leading fashion casting agency where I happily stayed for eleven months. LVX had a range of commercial, runway, editorial, and advertising clients and cast both models and "real people," or nonprofessional models. There were four full-time employees on staff, as well as a handful of interns and occasional freelancers and scouts. Because of the scale of the agency's business and open layout of its floor plan, I was able to see and participate in dozens of casting interactions each day, as well as editing sessions that led up to client presentations.

Before arriving at LVX I had not considered "real people" to be a meaningful category for my research. Yet, seeing the volume of nonprofessional models that came through the agency and the kinds of jobs for which they were booked, I quickly revised my perspective. I saw how the market for "real people" functioned as a disincentive for modeling agencies to represent a wider range of types. Indeed, I even found a handful of models from Flair in the agency's "real people" files. "Real people" provided a stopgap for the lack of racial, ethnic, and body diversity on high fashion agency boards. Clients' reasons for requesting "real people" were equally revealing. While some were looking for "edgier" or more authentic models, others saw it as a cost-saving strategy. This put the decline in models' rates following 9/11, which, in 2006 had not yet recovered, in sharp relief. Indeed, the more I explored this market, the more I realized how the category "real people" helped constitute the boundaries of the category "model" itself.

Viewing "real people" from the casting agents' perspectives, I also saw how the category posed different kinds of logistical issues, when compared to casting professional models. Agents needed to be able to find specific types with limited time and financial resources. To this end, they worked with scouts to collaboratively produce geographies of types in the city, which were based on their own experiences and ideas about where one might find particular types. They also devised research-based strategies for finding "real people" through associations or their own social networks. I found that these methods resonated with other kinds of embodied organizational memories based on experience, hunches, and shared wisdom, such as the low-tech profiling practices of law enforcement officers and other state agents (see Sadre-Orafai 2016).

By positioning casting practices like street scouting and booking photography beyond the frame of fashion, I was able to observe them more sharply as not just visual preproduction, but as knowledge-producing practices. This allowed me to challenge the idea that images—even casting photographs—were the primary outcome of these interactions. Instead, I found that casting agents' expertise centered more on producing knowledge about individuals, bodies, and types. And in so doing, they elaborated and refined theories of mediation—how people's appearances could be entextualized in different kinds of commercial contexts and made meaningful, as well as the limits of these translations. Just as narratives were important for securing jobs for models at Flair, casting agents drew on personal details from both "real people" and professional models to convince clients and one another about their suitability for particular jobs.

Four months into my internship at LVX, agents helped me arrange a concurrent position at DCM, a high-end women's modeling agency. DCM was a compelling site for all the reasons LVX was not. Whereas the agents at LVX emphasized the importance of "diversity," DCM had a de facto ban on nonwhite models, arguing that there was not enough of a client demand at the highest end of the market.

Echoing Jeremy and Max's critiques, when pressed about the lack of diversity on their board, agents at DCM would say, "Black girls: twice the work, half the money." This was in early 2007—the height of the "Prada exclusive," where newly discovered models were booked for the high profile show and barred from appearing on other designers' runways, and the popularity of young, Eastern European models (Luu 2013). Many of these models lasted only a few seasons, leading to more aggressive scouting and high rates of turnover on editorial boards. Development in this context was necessarily compressed.

Unlike at Flair, I was not socialized into an agent role at DCM. This allowed me to focus on the interactions between models and agents, rather than my own experiences doing this work. While there were similarities between development practices I saw at Flair and those at DCM, because of the strength of the latter's reputation, barriers to entry for its models were much lower. Instead of just seeking any booking, agents were more selective in how they managed models' careers. While other agencies took six months to a year to develop a new model—building her experience through smaller editorial jobs and less prestigious runway and advertising work—at DCM, development started at the top and unfolded in just a few months. Justin, a junior agent, explained that many of the big-name photographers wanted to shoot models first, so to have models learn by doing work at a lower level, even if it was published or paid, ultimately hampered their careers. Yet, because the stakes were higher, agents at DCM were more conservative with the kinds of models they took on, vetting them with specific high-end clients in mind.

These practices led to a reproduction of the industry status quo and helped explain the lack of diversity on their board. It also pointed to the multiple layers of mediation and refraction involved in producing models' bodies as media. More than just cultivating models' bodies as abstract, ideally mutable surfaces, development practices at DCM revealed the impact already existing infrastructure has on not just channeling but actively shaping the seemingly neutral terms by which models are developed. Looking to media studies more broadly helps sharpen this point. As Raymond Williams writes, concerning the inevitability of broadcast television: "This predestination, however, when closely examined, proves to be no more than a set of particular social decisions, in particular circumstances, which were then so widely if imperfectly ratified that it is now difficult to see them as decisions rather than as (retrospectively) inevitable results" (2005 [1975], 15). That is, while we may subscribe to ideologies concerning the neutrality of certain media forms, these ideas are outcomes of specific sociohistorical, political, cultural, and material actions. Placing models' development in this broader context allows us to deconstruct with more precision the cumulative effect of repeated selections that value some bodies as more malleable and conducive forms of media than others. It shows how abstract categories have material effects.

# Conclusion

By working at DCM and LVX at the same time, I was able to directly compare the two sides of producing models' bodies as media at the highest level of the industry. In thinking through my framework of bodies as media, I drew inspiration from anthropologist Janelle Taylor's concept "surfacing the body interior," which she uses to describe "the range of practices and processes that both materialize bodily surfaces as significant sites with broader orders, and surface that which lies hidden beneath them" (2005, 742) calling attention to the political, ethical, and social implications of the connections between mediation and appearances. Drawing on science studies and practice-based social theory, Taylor proposes that anthropologists approach "the body neither as an object nor as a text, nor only as a locus of subjectivity, but rather as a contingent configuration, a surface that is made but never in a static or permanent form" (Taylor 2005, 747). In doing so, she highlights the fluidity of both bodies and bodily surfaces amid the fixity with which we encounter them. More than just pointing to the idea that bodies are expressive mediums, Taylor highlights how, like most media forms, we ignore their mediating function in our focus on the content of their messages.

Paying attention to potential rupture, dynamism, and production of bodily surfaces—even in situations of reproduction, like at DCM—demonstrates how, despite the assumption that fashion relies on rigid categories of difference, it is a process that unfolds in looser ways that can both undo and reinscribe the explanatory power of categories of social difference. By attending to casting and model development as a single process, one can see how a practice-based, ethnographic approach can provide important insights that are not observable through a focus on publicly circulated media or on their material or economic production alone. Instead, bringing together discursive, visual, and embodied practices, it becomes possible to view the multiple ways casting professionals and models collaboratively produce models' bodies as legible types and forms that rely on existing visual referents and expectations, but are also malleable in their performance and perception. These practices, while firmly rooted within the fashion industry, have connections and analogues beyond it—from profiling practices in the context of law enforcement to the performance and management of perception in everyday interaction.

# Note

1 This research was funded in part by the Wenner-Gren Foundation for Anthropological Research (Grant #7493), the Ford Foundation, the Graduate School of Arts and Sciences at New York University, and the University Research Council and Charles Phelps Taft Research Center at the University of Cincinnati. All names of individuals and companies where I conducted fieldwork used in this chapter are pseudonyms.

# References

Abu-Lughod, Lila. 2004. *Dramas of Nationhood: The Politics of Television in Egypt.*
Chicago: University of Chicago Press.
Askew, Kelly and Richard Wilk, eds. 2003. *The Anthropology of Media Reader.* London:
Blackwell.
Aspers, Patrik. 2001. *Markets in Fashion: A Phenomenological Approach.* Stockholm: City
University.
Barthes, Roland. [1967] 1990. *The Fashion System.* Translated by M. Ward and R. Howard.
Berkeley, CA: University of California Press.
Boyer, Dominic and Ulf Hannerz. 2006. "Introduction: Worlds of Journalism." *Ethnography*
7 (1): 5–17.
Crewe, Ben. 2003. *Representing Men: Cultural Production and Producers in the Men's
Magazine Market.* Oxford: Berg.
Dávila, Arlene. 2001. *Latinos, Inc.: The Marketing and Making of a People.* Berkeley, CA:
University of California Press.
Dávila, Arlene. 2003. "Ethnicity, Fieldwork, and the Cultural Capital that Gets Us There:
Reflections from U.S. Hispanic Marketing." *Aztlan* 28 (1): 145–61.
Dornfeld, Barry. 1998. *Producing Public Television, Producing Public Culture.* Princeton:
Princeton University Press.
du Gay, Paul, ed. 1997. *Production of Culture/Cultures of Production.* London: Sage.
du Gay, Paul and Michael Pryke, eds. 2002. *Cultural Economy: Cultural Analysis and
Commercial Life.* London: Sage.
Entwistle, Joanne. 2004. "From Catwalk to Catalog: Male Fashion Models, Masculinity,
and Identity." In *Cultural Bodies: Ethnography and Theory*, edited by Helen Thomas and
Jamilah Ahmed, 55–75. Malden, MA: Blackwell.
Entwistle, Joanne. 2009. *The Aesthetic Economy of Fashion: Markets and Value in Clothing
and Modelling.* London: Berg.
Entwistle, Joanne and Elizabeth Wissinger. 2006. "Keeping up Appearances: Aesthetic
Labour and Identity in the Fashion Modeling Industries of London and New York."
*Sociological Review* 54 (4): 774–94.
Garfinkel, Harold. 1967. *Studies in Ethnomethodology.* Englewood Cliffs, NJ: Prentice Hall.
Ginsburg, Faye D., Lila Abu-Lughod, and Brian Larkin, eds. 2002a. *Media Worlds:
Anthropology on New Terrain.* Berkeley, CA: University of California Press.
Ginsburg, Faye D., Lila Abu-Lughod, and Brian Larkin, eds. 2000b. "Introduction."
In *Media Worlds: Anthropology on New Terrain*, edited by Faye D. Ginsburg, Lila Abu-
Lughod, and Brian Larkin, 1–38. Berkeley, CA: University of California Press.
Godart, Frèderic C., and Ashley Mears. 2009. "How Do Cultural Producers Make Creative
Decisions? Lessons from the Catwalk." *Social Forces* 88 (2): 671–92.
Goffman, Erving. 1979. *Gender Advertisements.* Cambridge, MA: Harvard University
Press.
Gough-Yates, Anna. 2003. *Understanding Women's Magazines: Publishing, Markets and
Readerships.* New York: Routledge.
Gürsel, Zeynep Devrim. 2012. "The Politics of Wire Service Photography: Infrastructures
of Representation in a Digital Newsroom." *American Ethnologist* 39 (1): 71–89.
Hannerz, Ulf. 2004. *Foreign News: Exploring the World of Foreign Correspondents.* Chicago:
University of Chicago Press.
Heritage, John. 1987. "Ethnomethodology." In *Social Theory Today*, edited by Anthony
Giddens and Jonathan H. Turner, 224–51. Stanford: Stanford University Press.

Hester, Stephen and David Francis. 2007. *Orders of Ordinary Action: Respecifying Sociological Knowledge.* Burlington, VT: Ashgate.

Jacobs-Huey, Lanita. 2002. "The Natives Are Gazing and Talking Back: Reviewing the Problematics of Positionality, Voice, and Accountability among 'Native' Anthropologists." *American Anthropologist* 194 (3): 791–804.

Jobling, Paul. 1999. *Fashion Spreads: Word and Image in Fashion Photography Since 1980.* Oxford: Berg.

Keane, Webb. 2003. "Self-Interpretation, Agency, and the Objects of Anthropology: Reflections on a Genealogy." *Comparative Studies in Society and History* 45: 222–48.

Kondo, Dorinne. 1997. *About Face: Performing Race in Fashion and Theater.* New York: Routledge.

Luu, Phong. 2013. "Russell Marsh: Model Maker." *Telegraph.* March 16, accessed September 1, 2014, http://fashion.telegraph.co.uk/columns/phong-luu/TMG9933193/Russell-Marsh-Model-maker.html.

Mahon, Maureen. 2000. "The Visible Evidence of Cultural Producers." *Annual Review of Anthropology* 29: 467–92.

Malinowski, Bronislaw. [1922] 2014. *Argonauts of the Western Pacific.* New York: Routledge.

Mankekar, Purnima.1999. *Screening Culture, Viewing Politics: An Ethnography of Television, Womanhood, and Nation in Postcolonial India.* Durham, NC: Duke University Press.

Marcus, George E. 1997. "The Uses of Complicity in the Changing Mise-en-Scene of Anthropological Fieldwork." *Representations* 59: 85–108.

Mears, Ashley. 2011. *Pricing Beauty: The Making of a Fashion Model.* Berkeley, CA: University of California Press.

Moeran, Brian. 1996. *A Japanese Advertising Agency: An Anthropology of Media and Markets.* Honolulu: University of Hawai'i Press.

Moffatt, Michael. 1992. "Ethnographic Writing About American Culture." *Annual Review of Anthropology* 21: 205–29.

Nader, Laura. 1972. "Up the Anthropologist—Perspectives Gained from Studying Up." In *Reinventing Anthropology*, edited by Dell Hymes, 284–311. New York: Pantheon.

Neff, Gina. 2005. "The Changing Place of Cultural Production: The Location of Social Networks in a Digital Media Industry." *The Annals of the American Academy of Political and Social Science* 597 (1): 134–52.

Sacks, Harvey. 1984. "On Doing 'Being Ordinary.'" In *Structures of Social Action: Studies in Conversation Analysis*, edited by J. Maxwell Atkinson and John Heritage, 413–29. Cambridge: Cambridge University Press.

Sacks, Harvey. 1985. "The Inference-Making Machine: Notes on Observability." In *Handbook of Discourse Analysis: Discourse Analysis in Society*, edited by Teun A. van Dijk, 13–23. Orlando: Academic Press.

Sadre-Orafai, Stephanie. 2008. "Developing Images: Race, Language, and Perception in Fashion-model Casting." In *Fashion as Photograph: Viewing and Reviewing Images of Fashion*, edited by Eugenie Shinkle, 141–53. London: I. B. Tauris.

Sadre-Orafai, Stephanie. 2011. "Fashion's Other Images: Casting Photographs and the Production of a Professional Vision." In *Images in Time: Flashing Forward, Backward, in Front and Behind Photography in Fashion, Advertising and the Press*, edited by Æsa Sigurjónsdóttir, Michael A. Langkjær, and Jo Turney, 123–30. Bath, UK: Wunderkammer.

Sadre-Orafai, Stephanie. 2012. "The Figure of the Model and Reality Television." In *Fashioning Models: Image, Text, and Industry*," edited by Joanne Entwistle and Elizabeth Wissinger, 119–33. London: Berg.

Sadre-Orafai, Stephanie. 2016. "Mug Shot/Head Shot: Danger, Beauty, and the Temporal Politics of Booking Photography." In *Fashion Crimes: Dressing for Deviance*, edited by Jo Turney. London: I. B. Tauris.

Skov, Lise. 2002. "Hong Kong Fashion Designers as Cultural Intermediaries: Out of Global Garment Production." *Cultural Studies* 16 (4): 553–69.

Spitulnik, Debra. 1993. "Anthropology and Mass Media." *Annual Review of Anthropology* 22: 293–315.

Taylor, Janelle S. 2005. "Surfacing the Body Interior." *Annual Review of Anthropology* 34: 741–56.

Williams, Raymond. 2005 [1975]. *Television: Technology and Cultural Form*. Edited by Ederyn Williams. London: Routledge.

Williamson, Judith. 1978. *Decoding Advertisements: Ideology and Meaning in Advertising*. London: Boyars.

Wissinger, Elizabeth. 2007. "Always on Display: Affective Production in the Modeling Industry." In *The Affective Turn: Theorizing the Social*, edited by Patricia Ticentio Clough, 231–60. Durham, NC: Duke University Press.

# 6 EXPLORING CREATIVITY: AN ETHNOGRAPHIC APPROACH TO STUDYING FASHION DESIGN PEDAGOGY

## Todd E. Nicewonger

Early in my fieldwork at the Antwerp Academy, a curious student approached me.[1] Having heard her teacher introduce me earlier that morning as an "anthropologist" interested in writing about the school, she asked me rather bluntly: "What exactly are you going to write about?" In my eagerness to reply, I tried to escape all the jargon I had accumulated through my graduate studies, explaining simply that I was interested in how students learn to design, which I hoped would help me better understand what people mean when they talk about creativity in design. A little surprised and slightly taken aback she responded: "But that's impossible! How can you study creativity? It's in people's heads!"

As would become common, this line of questioning, and the reaction that often followed my explanation, turned on the highly pervasive belief that creativity is an inherent cognitive ability. As this student seemed to express, creativity—at least in the West—is understood to be some*thing* with which some*one* is born (cf. Lavie, Narayan, and Rosaldo 1993). And because it is seen as an inherent and internal quality, the line of thinking goes, it is impossible, or at least foolish, to study creativity by observations alone. The only way to study these processes then is by taking a highly cognitive approach. Studying creativity by observing designers doing mundane things, like sketching a design, is absurd. Or is it?

In this chapter, I directly challenge the idea that it is impossible to study creativity in fashion design through firsthand observation and participation—the primary methodological tools used by cultural anthropologists to conduct ethnographic fieldwork. I argue that in an educational setting the social aspects of design creativity can be examined by observing interactions between novice designers (students) and advanced practitioners (design teachers) (cf. Chaiklin 2003; Chaiklin and Lave 1993). When carried out over an extended period of time, these observations, along with related qualitative methods, provide a unique view into the processes and practices of makers. This approach, then, is not rooted in questions about what designers are thinking about as they design their collections. Rather, the focus of this chapter is on what is observable: the social interactions between actors, as well as the use of tools and artifacts of their profession (cf. Goodwin and Harness 1996).

In taking up these concerns this chapter seeks to highlight how ethnographic analyses of design learning in fashion can reveal important insights about the socialization of expertise (cf. Carr 2010). As Heike Jenss argues in her introduction to this book, one of the "reasons why fashion is so powerful and deeply affective is that the very practices through which the 'magic of fashion' is produced are effectively hidden from view" (see Jenss in this book). But as Jenss goes on to argue, when the creative practices, forms of sociality, and institutional forces of fashion are examined in detail, rich and critical insights into the complex interrelationship of fashion and the wider social world emerge. This includes assumptions about creativity, material culture, and the interrelationship between embodied practices and material creations in fashion. In this way, analyses of the educative work of fashion producers, like those studying and teaching in design schools, cannot only shed critical light onto the sociocultural history of fashion pedagogies, but also raise important questions about knowledge production, more generally. For instance, as cultural anthropologists Tim Ingold and Elizabeth Hallam write, creativity is often associated with innovation and not improvisation (2007, 2). As a result, creativity receives a great deal of attention from the public sector because it is seen as a means to an end, a way to innovate new products and services that will strengthen the economy, advance technology, improve life, and so forth (Ingold and Hallam 2007, 1–2). But in lumping creativity and innovation together, Ingold and Hallam argue, the creative process is dimmed so that the end "product" becomes the focal point (ibid.). This, they write, is "read[ing] it backwards, in terms of its results, instead of forwards, in terms of the movements that gave rise to them" (2007, 3). The effect of this is that the improvisational aspects of making and the knowledge practices that animate this work are downplayed or less attended to (ibid. cf. Bruner 1993; Keller and Keller 1993; Wilf 2011).

Before I could even begin to propose questions and identify methods for studying the improvisational practices of fashion designers I had to recognize that fashion pedagogy was something I wanted to, and could, study. In retrospect, I now grasp the significance of this initial stage in my development as a critical first step in what would become my long-held interest in the ethnographic investigation of making (cf. Ingold 2013; Murphy 2013). For this reason, in the following section I will first sketch out a description of the pre-fieldwork research I carried out, prior to conducting ethnographic fieldwork at the Antwerp Academy—a perspective that often goes unwritten. Nevertheless, as I will show in this chapter, it is during this period that many of the conceptual ideas that guided my study were first identified.

Next, I want to reflect on the following ideas: communities of practice and discourses of expertise. These concepts, while often theoretically informed, did not determine what I studied, but acted as organizing principles that helped me to understand how to approach and observe the pedagogical experiences of aspiring fashion designers. Thus, in keeping with the theme of this edited volume, I tack back and forth between my pre-fieldwork and fieldwork experiences in order to illustrate how the two perspectives are intertwined from both a conceptual and methodological standpoint.

## Serendipitous encounters: The pre-fieldwork/fieldwork nexus

Like many graduate students in anthropology, my research interests developed over time, drawing influences from both what I was studying and my observations and experiences in the real world. I can trace my journey to Antwerp to the latter (at least partially) as I was inspired by growing public discourses about the social impact of designed goods and services. From exhibitions in London and New York City on the interrelationship between design and culture, and museum talks I attended, my interest in the social aspects of design grew in tandem with my studies in cultural anthropology. At this time, however, I had not decided to focus on studying fashion design yet. My interests instead emerged through a series of serendipitous encounters, which in retrospect, I realize I likely would have ignored if not for the guidance of my doctoral advisor.

My advisor, himself a well-traveled ethnographer, counseled that being amenable to the unexpected was what being an ethnographer was all about. By this he was referring to the open-ended nature of ethnographic research and its focus on generating both emic and etic (or insider and outsider) points of views through cultural immersion and descriptive analysis (cf. Harris 1976; Malinowski 1922). As he explained, ethnographic investigations often take many twists and turns because social life is never static but always in a state of change. For this reason, happenstance is likely to color almost any field experience.

Consequently, ethnographers need to be open to exploring opportunities as they arise, because it is within such experiences that important insights may be hidden. As Isabelle Rivoal and Noel B. Salazar write, serendipity in ethnographic fieldwork refers to "the very experience of suddenly coming to 'see' something that had previously been out of sight: the striking realization that 'this is what it is about'" (2013, 179).

My first lesson in serendipity occurred when I stumbled upon a museum exhibition celebrating the milliner Philip Treacy and his muse Isabella Blow in 2002. The exhibit, "When Philip Met Isabella: Philip Treacy's Hats for Isabella Blow," was held at the Design Museum in London. What grabbed my attention about this show was the way Treacy's designs pushed the boundaries of conventional thinking. The material and visual affordances of his work produced more than material forms; they also generated affective experiences that challenged my thinking about what a hat could be. Knowing very little about design or fashion, this exhibition stirred my imagination and I began to think more deeply about fashion design as not just a site for turning culture into things, but as a staging ground for generating new social imaginaries, new ways of experiencing social life. Treacy himself makes a similar point when he talks about "rule breaking":

> You know that scenario where roses are red, leaves are green, I love arguing that. "Why should they be?" I hate rules and formulas. That's boring. It's the opposite of creativity. Rules are ridiculous things that are meant to be broken. (Design Museum 2002)

In a very real sense then, this experience marked a critical moment when I began to "see" the creative practices of fashion designers in a completely new way. As a result, my growing fascination with fashion design began to meld with my studies in anthropology. I started to weave the varying perspectives I was learning into what has become my enduring interest in fashion design education as a site of cultural production—a concern with the "practices and productions of cultural producers in their social context" (Mahon 2000, 468). Of course at this point in my studies, my ability to articulate these ideas in detail had yet to fully develop. Nevertheless, my interest in fashion design had begun to take root, and in turn, raised further questions about where and how I could actually go about carrying out such a study.

Not surprisingly, the answers to many of these questions would again come out of another serendipitous encounter: this time a friend, having heard about my newly discovered interest in fashion design, suggested I check out "what the Belgian designers in Antwerp were doing." By this he was referring to fashion designers who had studied at the Antwerp Academy. At the time I knew absolutely nothing about the Belgian fashion scene. Yet, I immediately followed up on his advice, never suspecting that I would eventually move to Antwerp and spend 15 months there conducting ethnographic fieldwork.

This was in the early 2000s, when I was still taking graduate courses. I knew then that before I could even begin to conceive of pursuing my study, I needed to identify a research question or concern that would allow me to articulate why this site would be a particularly good place to ethnographically examine the creative practices of fashion designers.

So, I voraciously studied everything that I could find, which at that time was largely written by fashion journalists (e.g., Givhan 2001; Spindler 1993). I also began talking to people I met in the fashion industry about both the Antwerp fashion scene and fashion education more generally. In the process, I identified through these interactions a pattern in how the work of Antwerp-trained fashion designers was being described. There was a tension between what distinguished the designs being produced in this region from other sites. On one hand, many of the narratives I encountered evoked descriptions focused on the influence of certain aesthetic aspects associated with the region's culture and landscape. While on the other hand, sociological explanations were used to show how these same ideas were a by-product of Antwerp's local infrastructure—a tension that to this day continues to color accounts about Belgian fashion.

For instance, in "A Sense of Place" the fashion journalist Suzy Menkes (2013a) offers an array of descriptive examples, that wind, almost dizzyingly, through the varying sources of inspiration that are often attributed to Belgian fashion. These examples extend from the region's red-bricked architecture, to Antwerp's village-like atmosphere. While each of these references offers an alluring, if somewhat enigmatic, vantage point into the contemporary character of Belgian fashion, it is what she writes at the end of her story that I want to highlight here:

> Belgian style has a certain puritan modesty that must come from upbringing or teaching. Van Noten has indelible memories of the rules laid down by Mary Prijot, the "severe" head of fashion during his days at the Academy. He believes that these rules formed his own style and that the restrictions even pushed him ahead. "We could not show the female body and we couldn't show the knee—she didn't like it," Van Noten says. "She hated long hair—for her it was untidy—she had a chignon. Then jeans—she said they were for poor people." (Menkes 2013a, 46)

In this brief yet nonetheless revealing quote, Menkes moves away from making use of impressionistic forces of landscape or ubiquitous notions of cultural identity that she so vividly draws out in the other parts of her essay. Instead, in just a few deftly worded sentences, she depicts a potent scene of a young fashion designer, who revolts against the aesthetic sensibilities of his teacher and in the process, develops his own, unique approach to designing fashion. In doing so

Menkes ties this particular aesthetic characteristic of Belgian fashion to lived experience—specifically that of Dries Van Noten—and to the impact of fashion pedagogy.

When I first read Menkes' article, it reminded me of the varied accounts I had encountered prior to and while carrying out my fieldwork in Antwerp. In the process, I became intrigued with the story of the "Antwerp Six," which describes how, in the early 1980s, six young designers who had studied in the fashion department at the Antwerp Academy would go on to gain international acclaim for their inventive design styles (Van Godtsenhoven 2013; cf. Furnis 2002). This group of designers included Ann Demeulemeester, Walter Van Beirendonck, Dirk Van Saene, Marina Yees, Dirk Bikkembers, and Dries Van Noten (Martin Margiela is also associated with this group; cf. Debo and Berloot 2007; Granata 2012 and in this book). To this day this story operates as a kind of origin myth, historicizing, but also valorizing the aesthetic sensibilities perpetuated by these designers and the preceding generations that have followed them (Van Godtsenhoven 2013; Menkes 2013b).

As I have written elsewhere, this story can also be interpreted as a theory of practice that emerged out of the efforts of a small, but influential cadre of design educators (Nicewonger 2013 and 2014; cf. Heynssens 2013). This group, many of whom concurrently taught at the Antwerp Academy while working in the fashion industry, has actively promoted Belgian fashion, while also reforming the local educational system so that it reflected certain philosophical ideas that both the Antwerp Six and other avant-garde fashion designers in Europe and Asia at that time had helped to popularize (cf. Vinken 1997; Evans 2003). In doing so, they sought to extend the international notoriety of the Antwerp Six to future generations of Antwerp/Belgian trained fashion designers and in the process to galvanize Antwerp's reputation as a capital of high fashion (Heynssens 2013; for more information about the history of contemporary Belgian fashion see Martinez 2007; Teunissen 2011).

Read this way, while the contributions of the Antwerp Six are undeniably valid and historically important in their own right, the fact that a wider set of actors have actively worked across varying institutional domains to generate a localized infrastructure for reproducing Belgian fashion intrigued me. What insights, I wondered, might be gained by ethnographically approaching fashion education as a site of cultural production? It was in this light that I realized that I wanted to carry out my research at the Antwerp Academy, as it is an integral site for both the reproduction and transformation of knowledge both within the Belgian fashion community and beyond. But to do so I would need to identify methodological frameworks for studying the practices of fashion designers.[2]

To this end, in the following section I reflect on two important ideas that informed my research and allowed me to examine student-teacher interactions, which in turn enabled me to gain a better grasp on how creativity was being operationalized through curricular activities and exchanges: communities of practice and discourses of expertise. I was first introduced to the ideas behind both of these concepts prior to entering the field in a graduate course I took, exploring the acquisition of cultural practices. The shift, however, from learning about a concept to actually applying that idea in one's own work can be challenging. This was certainly true for me in part because the case studies included in the articles and monographs I was reading were based on largely nonfashion oriented contexts. This was in itself not a major problem, but it definitely left much to the imagination—particularly for someone who had never carried out long-term ethnographic research.

Nevertheless, once I arrived at the academy and began my study I found the work I had read on the socialization of knowledge and the role that communicative practices played in these processes extremely productive. Not only did this work help me recognize—as I stated in the introduction of this chapter—that creativity was observable, but it also helped me organize how I positioned myself as an ethnographer.

While I would carry out archival research, interviews, and socialize with students outside of the classroom, when I was at the academy during the school year the majority of my time was focused on observing student-teacher interactions and individualized student work. These observations were carried out across all four years of instruction. In this way I was able to move from one grade level to another and identify how techniques taught, for example, in the first year were related to activities being pursued in the other years.[3] Subsequently, it was in making these observations that I drew on the conceptual frameworks I now turn to.

## Communities of practice and discourses of expertise

On any given day while I was conducting fieldwork, I could enter the academy and observe students and teachers talking to one another about the "volume" of their designs.[4] Having no background in fashion design, the term at first perplexed me. To further complicate matters, when I asked students to explain what the concept meant, I received a series of overlapping, yet somewhat varied and slightly vague answers. Adding to my confusion was the fact that there were no formal lectures I could attend, nor texts I could consult to learn more about this concept; the academy largely relied on one-on-one instruction. But what I could do was observe how these terms were being applied in daily interactions.

My own interest in the relationship between design expertise and language emerged prior to my fieldwork while I was reading the literature on ethnomethodology and ethnographic studies on expertise (cf. Francis and Hester 2004). What drew me to this work was its focus on how shared sets of practices could be used to define specific communities. Consequently, I began to develop a methodological framework for studying the socialization of design expertise, in a way that would also allow me to relate my observations of pedagogical practices to wider sociocultural concerns. In doing so, I have drawn heavily on the concept *communities of practice*, developed by cultural anthropologist Jeanne Lave and educational theorist Etienne Wenger. As Wenger explains:

> Communities of practice are an integral part of our daily lives. They are so informal and so pervasive that they rarely come into explicit focus, but for the same reasons they are also quite familiar. Although the term may be new, the experience is not. Most communities of practice do not have a name and do not issue membership cards. (Wenger 1998, 7)

Lave and Wenger have argued that the pervasiveness of these communities does not mean that they are not exclusionary. Rather, belonging to a community of practice means being able to actively and competently participate in that community (Wenger 1998, 136). For instance, becoming a designer in many educational contexts requires learning to express/communicate one's design ideas in a way that other design professionals will be able to interpret. In this way, membership requires actors to obtain a degree of expertise, and one of the ways that new members gain this knowledge is by apprenticing with advanced practitioners (e.g., design teachers). Lave and Wenger refer to this process as *legitimate peripheral participation*:

> Mastery of knowledge and skill requires newcomers to move toward full participation in the socio-cultural practices of a community. "Legitimate peripheral participation" provides a way to speak about the relations between newcomers and old-timers, and about activities, identities, artifacts, and communities of knowledge and practice. A person's intentions to learn are engaged and the meaning of learning is configured through the process of becoming a full participant in a socio-cultural practice. This social process includes, indeed it subsumes, the learning of knowledgeable skills. (Lave and Wenger 1991, 29)

For an ethnographer with a particular interest in design education, this model of socialization interests me because design schools, like apprenticeships, are purposely structured to do just that: to bring members with extensive experience in a particular design community together with those who desire to become active members of that community. From an ethnographic standpoint this also means that I could shift my attention away from individualistic descriptions of design creativity, and instead, focus on the interactional dynamics of students and teachers to ask: *How is creativity, including notions of individuality in design, theorized through institutional frameworks for practicing design?* Such a focus centers on the transmission and reproduction of design expertise, but does so by using this position as a way to understand how creativity in fashion design is socially defined and produced within that community.

Take for instance the following interaction between a first-year student and her design teacher that I observed during my research. The design work being evaluated here is part of a series of exercises used to teach students how to conduct research and then draw on that research to develop a design concept, which the student must express/communicate through a design sketch. Prior to the evaluation of the design sketch the instructor also reviewed the research that the student had collected and presented in the preceding pages of her sketchbook.

| | |
|---|---|
| Instructor: | It's rather quiet; it's not a strong statement, not a point of view. |
| Student: | *[The student stands silently staring down at the illustrations.]* |
| Instructor: | Armor is really good research. |
| | *[The instructor begins flipping the pages of the sketchbook and silently examines the different sketches.]* |
| | It's about the waist, okay but then you have to show something. |
| | *[The instructor then looks up at the student and then returns to looking at the sketches in the student's design book before continuing.]* |
| | I think now you have to push harder. I really want to push you to do something strong, because this is strong and impressive. |
| | *[The instructor points to an image of armor that the student had photocopied as inspiration for her design and then continues with her critique.]* |
| | But that doesn't mean it has to be tough [looking, it] can be feminine. |
| Student: | *[The student nods her head and stares at the instructor's hands tracing the picture of armor.]* |
| Instructor: | You can interpret it in the cut. |
| | *[She starts to mark the strongest parts of different designs in the student's sketchbook.]* |
| | Use belts to bring the fabrics together; that would be beautiful. |
| Student: | *[The student stands tensely, her eyes focused on the area of her sketch that the instructor is discussing, and then she slightly nods her head.]* |

| Instructor: | [Instructor continues looking at the sketches, sorting through the different designs, and then she says:] |
| | Try to feel what you are going to express. Try and feel for yourself if it's fragile. Do one fragile and one strong [design] then ask what your [style/inclination] is? |
| Student: | Okay. |

As this interaction illustrates, knowledge about the design process and more specifically, how it is practiced within this particular setting is made observable through the teacher's instruction, where she conveys her analysis of this student's work. This student-teacher interaction allows a view into certain aspects of the curricular process that enabled me to gain a deeper understanding of how students learn to approach the design process along certain conceptual and improvisational lines.

In a sense, both "communities of practice" and "legitimate peripheral participation," do relational work similar to what Menkes evoked through her description of how Dries Van Noten's earlier social experiences as a student shaped his later work as a designer (2013a). This is not to suggest that Van Noten's creativity has been determined by his schooling, but instead, that through this experience he acquired a particular kind of aesthetic outlook that he would go on to build and refine in his later life as a professional designer.

With that said, not all educational experiences share the same forms of continuity. As Menkes' story further attests, students can rebel against their teachers and in the process inspire new modes of practice. In either case, whether one is focusing on tensions over what qualifies as expertise in a particular community of practice or how new members come to be advanced practitioners in these communities, there has to be some form of social exchange. And one of the main places where this happens is in apprenticing or educational contexts, where novices attempt to complete design exercises, and in the process, receive feedback on what they did correctly and what they failed to comprehend.

What also distinguishes these processes is the fact that they are highly marked by specialized language that allows designers to convey both social and technical knowledge (cf. Duranti and Black 2011; Keane 2003; Murphy 2012). These markers allowed me to realize early on in my research at the academy that I could ethnographically track how students and teachers were employing terms, like "volume." In turn, this perspective allowed me to generate important insights, including how by learning to communicate design ideas in certain ways, student designers came to embody certain dispositions and outlooks about design that reflected their involvement as members of a particular kind of community of practice. In this way such exchanges can be understood to index both institutional ideals and context-specific meanings (cf. Garrett and Baquedano-López 2002).

I first grasped the significance of these ideas one afternoon while observing a class of upper level students working on muslin mock-ups of their silhouettes, also referred to as *toiles*, which function like rough, three-dimensional drafts or early iterations of their final projects. Like on any other day, the design teacher and one of the pattern instructors, along with the student whose design was being evaluated, gathered together and began visually measuring, questioning, and experimenting with the proportions and material properties of the student's toile. In these interactions the designs were evaluated by comparing different sections of the illustration with the corresponding parts of the design, while using talk and gesture to mark the discrepancies between the design sketch and the toile. It was in such an interaction that I heard the design teacher critiquing the "volume" of the student's skirt: "Your *volume* is not right, see here." Pointing to a section of the illustrated design and then to the corresponding section of the toile, the teacher explained: "The waist is too low, raise that to here." The instructor then gestured toward a section of the skirt and stated "and you'll get the right volume."

This exchange raised a number of questions that I had been mulling over while witnessing the use of terms like "volume." Was this discourse unique to the academy? Where did this concept come from and what exactly did it refer to? Moreover, how did students learn to use this term and what insights might an analysis of such socializing processes offer?

Curious to gain a deeper understanding of the meaning of such exchanges and how they relate to the wider goals of the pedagogy, a couple of days later I asked the design teacher: What were some of the academy's underlining aims for teaching fashion design? To which the instructor replied: "We try to start from their idea and then figure [out] how to use it." In emphasizing the importance of working with "their ideas," the instructor affirmed my suspicions that one of the ways in which the academy theorized creativity was by embedding the materialization of design ideas in discursive and socially interactive contexts. From my study of social interactions between students and teachers I could see that this was in part facilitated through discursive concepts like volume.

For instance, in the beginning of the design process students are pushed to let their imaginations run free and not worry about the technical aspects of their designs. "Don't worry about how you'll make it," the teachers would tell students, "That comes later, just try to get your ideas out for now." But when the design is being translated into a material form the creative focus is placed on the design's technical realization. This point is evidenced in the previous example, when the teacher judged the toile's merits by comparing it to the student's illustrated design. It is through such interactions that the subjective perceptions of both instructor and student are aligned and the aesthetic intentions of the design form become socially recognizable.

In this light, attempts to describe volume as purely an aesthetic or design principle miss the point. Instead we can look to how volume is being positioned within these pedagogical exercises as a generative framework for aligning varying aesthetic opinions, desires, and beliefs into a common viewpoint. Through this premise the logic of volume reveals itself in ways that are seemingly unpredictable, yet structured and organized. Through the discursive practice of volume, students are able to produce patterns of practice that give meaning to form.

In analyzing these exchanges, I have attempted to illustrate how language events shape the improvisational processes of design. By learning how to interpret and apply the discursive practices of expert discourses, like volume, students come to embody certain institutional ideologies about the meaning and value of avant-garde fashion. Such thinking draws together the ideological, pragmatic, and semiotic functions of language used to consider not only the material qualities of social forms, but also how materializing practices reflect the history and politics of a particular community of artisans and subjects (cf. Barber 2007; Shankar and Cavanaugh 2012).

# Conclusion

In this chapter, I have reflected on my use of ethnographic research methodologies to examine pedagogical interactions in fashion. At the time when I entered the field, there were only a handful of anthropological examples examining the cultural production of fashion (e.g., Kondo 1997; cf. McRobbie 1998; Hansen 2004). But since the early 2000s, ethnographic work on fashion design has greatly expanded. From the behind-the-scenes look at the creative work of US-based Islamic fashion designers in the 2009 ethnographic film, *Fashioning Faith*, to the sociohistorical terrain of the Los Angeles-based fast fashion industry explored by Christina Moon (2014), these ethnographic studies, while topically diverse, challenge popular beliefs about fashion by bringing the experiences of the fashion producers they studied into conversation with wider social issues (e.g., identity politics, stereotypes, globalization, cf. Jones 2010; Luvaas 2012; Tu 2011; Tarlo 2010; Thomas 2013).

In a similar way, in my research practice and ongoing projects I attempt to link the social aspects of fashion pedagogy to larger debates on how making shapes and is shaped by the aesthetic and material aspects of social life (Nicewonger 2011). But identifying connections between creative practices in fashion design and ideological concerns can take many forms. In the case of Antwerp fashion, one could ask how social policymaking, nationalism, or market forces—for example—figure into the academy's pedagogy (cf. Julier 2009; Makovicky 2010; Martinez 2011; Skov 2011; Reinach 2011). But since no singular investigation can attend to all of these issues, or the myriad of others that could be raised, and because research sites are composites of social, political, and economic processes, I had to mark out the parameters of my study. This meant that I needed to identify both methodological and conceptual frameworks that would guide my ethnographic observations and allow me to study the creative practices of student designers. In this way, I see the ideas discussed here as complementary to those being explored by fashion scholars working at the intersection of education and design.

There is now a growing body of research exploring the sociocultural processes of curricular activities, like the creation of mood boards or life drawings, that has raised a number of important questions about how the training of young designers is organized across varying institutional sites, including how the production of knowledge in these sites both differs from and reflects sociopolitical concerns as well as makes critical contributions to the work on design expertise (Cassidy 2011; Dirix 2013; cf. Bill 2012; Dieffenbacher 2013). It has also led fashion scholars, like Clemens Thornquist, to caution against over relying on theories and methodologies imported from other disciplines (2014). In doing so, Thornquist calls for the development of conceptual frameworks that are based on endogenous practices in fashion. Others, like the scholar/practitioner Alexandra Verschueren have employed auto-ethnographic research techniques to reflect on her own creative processes as a designer and relate these reflections back to more generalizable questions about creativity in fashion design (2013).

My research, of course, takes an outsider's perspective, one that ethnographically examines the role of educational institutions in organizing the production of creative pursuits and expert knowledge in fashion. Such a perspective, I maintain, can provide critical understanding into how institutional sites for training fashion designers become assemblages of competing interests, forms of knowledge, and subjective aspirations. In such a light, it is possible to begin to see how particular forms of social relations are constituted at these intersections. For these reasons ethnographic studies of curricular practices, like my work at the Antwerp Academy, can generate further insights into the ways pedagogical institutions both produce knowledge and are connected to wider flows of politics, economics, and social imaginaries (e.g., globalization, sustainable design movements, nationalism, etc.)[5]

It is my hope that in the future more long-term, ethnographic studies of fashion design pedagogy will be conducted and that these studies will beget a rich comparative vantage for debating and exploring the creative work of fashion producers. To this end the concepts *community of practice* and *discourses of expertise* can be of critical assistance for those studying the creative practices of fashion designers.

# Notes

1   My fieldwork was generously supported by research grants from the Fulbright Program and Wenner-Gren Foundation for Anthropological Research (Grant # 7638). All the names of the actors I mention from my classroom observations have been described using pseudonyms/generic descriptors.

2 Belgium has multiple fashion design programs. The focus of this chapter, however, is on Antwerp-trained designers.

3 See: Wood, Bruner, and Ross (1976) about how learning is distributed across time and spaces (i.e., scaffolding).

4 While definitions on what counts or does not count as volume may overlap or differ from one design context to another, the emphasis here is on studying how volume is created/produced through improvisational practices.

5 While this chapter is expressively focused on fashion pedagogy the theories and concepts discussed here could also be applied to other institutional sites. See: Lave and Wenger (1991).

# References

Barber, Karin. 2007. "Improvisation and the Art of Making Things Stick." In *Creativity and Cultural Improvisation*, edited by Elizabeth Hallam and Tim Ingold, 25–41. Oxford: Berg.

Bill, Amanda. 2012. "'Blood, Sweat and Shears:' Happiness, Creativity, and Fashion Education." *Fashion Theory* 16 (1): 49–66.

Bruner, Edward M. 1993. "Epilogue: Creative Persona and the Problem of Authenticity." In *Creativity/Anthropology*, edited by Smadar Lavie, Kirin Narayan, and Renato Rosaldo, 321–34. Ithaca: Cornell University Press.

Carr, E. Summerson. 2010. "Enactments of Expertise." *Annual Review of Anthropology* 39: 17–32.

Cassidy, Tracy. 2011. "The Mood Board Processes Modeled and Understood as a Qualitative Design Research Tool." *Fashion Practice* 3 (2): 225–52.

Chaiklin, Seth. 2003. "The Zone of Proximal Development in Vygotsky's Analysis of Learning and Instruction." In *Vygotsky's Educational Theory in Cultural Context*, edited by Alex Kozulin, Boris Gindis, Vladmir S. Ageyev, and Suzanne M. Miller, 39–64. Cambridge: Cambridge University Press.

Chaiklin, Seth and Jean Lave, eds. 1993. *Understanding Practice*. Cambridge: Cambridge University Press.

Debo, Kaat and Geert Bruloot, eds. 2007. *6+ Antwerp Fashion*. Belgium: Ludion.

Design Museum. 2002. "When Philip Met Isabella Design Museum Touring Exhibition," accessed October 7, 2015. http://design.designmuseum.org/design/philip-treacy.

Dieffenbacher, Fiona. 2013. *Fashion Thinking: Creative Approaches to the Design Process*. London: AVA Publishing.

Dirix, Emmanuelle. 2013. "The Role of Drawing in Fashion." In *Fashion Antwerp Academy 50*, edited by Bracha De Man, Anne Haegeman, and Judith Van Doorselaer, 125–34. Belgium: Lannoo.

Duranti, Alessandro and Steven Black. 2011. "Socialization and Verbal Improvisation." In *Handbook of Language Socialization*, edited by Alessandro Duranti, Elinor Ochs, and Bambi Schieffelin, 443–63. Cambridge: Cambridge University Press.

Evans, Caroline. 2003. *Fashion at the Edge: Spectacle, Modernity and Deathliness*. New Haven, CT: Yale University Press.

*Fashioning Faith*. 2009. DVD. Directed by Yasmin Moll. Watertown, MA: DER Documentary.

Francis, David and Stephen Hester. 2004. *An Invitation to Ethnomethodology: Language, Society, and Interaction*. London: Sage.

Furniss, Jo-Ann. 2002. "Fashion: Paris. Milan. Antwerp . . ." *The Independent*, September 14, 6.

Garrett, Paul B., and Patricia Baquedano-López. 2002. "Language Socialization: Reproduction and Continuity, Transformation and Change." *Annual Review of Anthropology* 31: 339–61.

Givhan, Robin. 2001. "The Antwerp Aesthetic; Out of Belgium Have Come a Flock of Fashion Designers Who Go Their Own Ways. Together." *The Washington Post*, August 12, F. 1.

Goodwin, Charles and Marjorie Harness. 1996. "Formulating Planes: Seeing as a Situated Activity." In *Cognition and Communication at Work*, edited by David Middleton and Yrjö Engestrom, 61–95. Cambridge: Cambridge University Press.

Granata, Francesca. 2012. "Deconstruction Fashion: Carnival and the Grotesque." *Journal of Design History* 26 (2): 182–98.

Hansen, Karen Tranberg. 2004. "The World in Dress: Anthropological Perspectives on Clothing, Fashion, and Culture." *Annual Review of Anthropology* 33: 369–92.

Harris, Marvin. 1976. "History and Significance of the Emic/Etic Distinction." *Annual Review of Anthropology* 5: 329–50.

Heynssens, Sarah. 2013. "Between Avant-Garde & Tradition." In *Fashion Antwerp Academy 50*, edited by Bracha De Man, Anne Haegeman, and Judith Van Doorselaer, 13–28. Belgium: Lannoo.

Ingold, Tim. 2013. *Making: Anthropology, Archaeology, Art and Architecture*. London and New York: Routledge.

Ingold, Tim and Elizabeth Hallam. 2007. "Creativity and Cultural Improvisation: An Introduction." In *Creativity and Cultural Improvisation*, edited by Elizabeth Hallam and Tim Ingold, 1–24. Oxford: Berg.

Keane, Webb. 2003. "Semiotics and the Social Analysis of Material Things." *Language and Communication* 23 (2–3): 409–25.

Keller, Charles and Janet Dixon Keller. 1993. "Thinking and Acting with Iron." In *Understanding Practice*, edited by Seth Chaiklin and Jean Lave, 125–43. Cambridge: Cambridge University Press.

Kondo, Dorinne. 1997. *About Face: Performing Race in Fashion and Theater*. New York: Routledge.

Jones, Carla. 2010. "Images of Desire: Creating Virtue and Value in an Indonesian Islamic Lifestyle Magazine." *Journal of Middle East Women's Studies* 6 (3): 191–201.

Julier, Guy. 2009. "Responses to Globalization: The Rebranding of City-Regions and Nations." In *Design Studies: A Reader*, edited by Hazel Clark and David Brody, 433–37. Oxford: Berg Publishers.

Lave, Jean and Etinne Wenger. 1991. *Situated Learning: Legitimate Peripheral Participation*. Cambridge: Cambridge University Press.

Lavie, Smadar, Kirin Narayan, and Renato Rosaldo. 1993. "Introduction: Creativity in Anthropology." In *Creativity/Anthropology*, edited by Smadar Lavie, Kirin Narayan, and Renato Rosaldo, 1–10. Ithaca: Cornell University Press.

Luvaas, Brent. 2012. *DIY Style: Fashion, Music, and Global Digital Cultures*. Oxford: Berg.

Mahon, Maureen. 2000. "The Visible Evidence of Cultural Producers." *Annual Review of Anthropology* 29: 467–92.

Makovicky, Nicolette. 2010. "'Erotic Needlework': Vernacular Designs on the 21st Century Market." In *Design Anthropology: Object Culture in the 21st Century*, edited Allison J. Clarke, 155–68. New York, NY: Springer.

Malinowski, Bronislaw. [1922] 1914. *Argonauts of the Western Pacific: An Account of Native Enterprise and Adventure in the Archipelagoes of Melanesian New Guinea*. London: Routledge.

Martinez, Javier Gimeno. 2007. "Selling Avant-garde: How Antwerp Became a Fashion Capital (1990–2002)." *Urban Studies* 44 (12): 2449–62.

Martinez, Javier Gimeno. 2011. "Restructuring Plans for the Textile and Clothing Sector in Post-industrial Belgium and Spain." *Fashion Practice* 3 (2): 197–224.

McRobbie, Angela. 1998. *British Fashion Design: Rag Trade or Image Industry?* London: Routledge.

Menkes, Suzy. 2013a. "A Sense of Place." In *Fashion Antwerp Academy 50*, edited by Bracha De Man, Anne Haegeman, and Judith Van Doorselaer, 41–46. Belgium: Lannoo.

Menkes, Suzy. 2013b. "A Rare Reunion for the 'Antwerp Six.'" *The New York Times*, June 17, accessed September 4, 2014, http://www.nytimes.com/2013/06/18/fashion/a-rare-reunion-for-the-antwerp-six.html?_r=0.

Moon, Christina H. 2014. "The Secret World of Fast Fashion." *Pacific Standard*. Accessed September 4, 2014, http://www.psmag.com/navigation/business-economics/secret-world-slow-road-korea-los-angeles-behind-fast-fashion-73956/.

Murphy, Keith M. 2012. "Transmodality and Temporality in Design Interactions." *Journal of Pragmatics* 44: 1966–81.

Murphy, Keith M. 2013. "A Cultural Geometry: Designing Political Things in Sweden." *American Ethnologist* 40 (1): 118–31.

Nicewonger, Todd. E. 2011. "Fashioning a Moral Aesthetic: An Ethnographic Study of the Socialization of Antwerp Trained Fashion Designers." PhD diss., Columbia University.

Nicewonger, Todd. E. 2013. "The Fashion Designer as Artist: Reflections on 50 Years of Pedagogy." In *Fashion Antwerp Academy 50*, edited by Bracha De Man, Anne Haegeman, and Judith Van Doorselaer, 171–95. Belgium: Lannoo.

Nicewonger, Todd. E. 2014. "Belgian Designers and the Antwerp Academy." In the *Berg Encyclopedia of World Dress and Fashion*, Volume 8, West Europe. Berg Fashion Library. http://www.bergfashionlibrary.com/.

Reinach, Simona Segre. 2011. "National Identities and International Recognition." *Fashion Theory* 15 (2): 267–72.

Rivoal, Isabelle and Noel B. Salazar. 2013. "Contemporary Ethnographic Practice and the Value of Serendipity." *Social Anthropology/Anthropologie Sociale* 21 (2): 178–85.

Shankar, Shalini and Jillian R. Cavanaugh. 2012. "Language and Materiality in Global Capitalism." *Annual Review of Anthropology* 41: 355–69.

Skov, Lise. 2011. "Dreams of Small Nations in a Polycentric Fashion World." *Fashion Theory* 15 (2): 137–56.

Spindler, Amy M. 1993. "Coming Apart." *The New York Times*, July 25, accessed February 11, 2014, http://www.nytimes.com/1993/07/25/style/coming-apart.html.

Tarlo, Emma. 2010. *Visibly Muslim: Fashion, Politics, and Faith*. Oxford: Berg Publishers.

Teunissen, José. 2011. "Deconstructing Belgian and Dutch Fashion Dreams: From Global Trends to Local Crafts." *Fashion Theory* 15 (29): 157–76.

Thomas, Kedron. 2013. "Brand 'Piracy' and Postwar Statecraft in Guatemala." *Cultural Anthropology* 28 (1): 144–60.

Thornquist, Clemens. 2014. "Basic Research in Art: Foundational Problems in Fashion Design Explored through the Art Itself." *Fashion Practice* 6 (1): 37–58.

Tu, Thuy Linh Nguyen. 2011. *The Beautiful Generation*. Durham: Duke University Press.

Van Godtsenhoven, Karen. 2013. "The Wonder Years of the Antwerp 6 + 1." In *Fashion Antwerp Academy 50*, edited by Bracha De Man, Anne Haegeman, and Judith Van Doorselaer, 65–105. Belgium: Lannoo.

Verschueren, Alexandra. 2013. "The Autoethnography of Creative Design: From Medium to Shift." *SemioticX Design, Style and Fashion*, accessed September 7, 2014, http://fashion.semiotix.org/2013/02/the-autoethnography-of-creative-design-from-medium-to-shift/.

Vinken, Barbara. 1997. "Eternity—A Frill on the Dress." *Fashion Theory* 1 (1): 59–68.

Wenger, Etienne. 1998. *Communities of Practice: Learning, Meaning, and Identity*. Cambridge: Cambridge University Press.

Wilf, Eitan. 2011. "Sincerity Versus Self-Expression: Modern Creative Agency and the Materiality of Semiotic Forms." *Cultural Anthropology* 26 (3): 462–84.

Wood, David, Jerome S. Bruner, and Gail Ross. 1976. "The Role of Tutoring in Problem Solving." *Journal of Child Psychology and Psychiatry* 17: 89–100.

SECTION THREE

# MIXED METHODS

# INTRODUCTION

## Heike Jenss

For the exploration of fashion in its multifaceted dimensions, research methods are most productive when used in combination. This need for a multimethodological approach has been a theme throughout this book, with previous chapters discussing the use of various methods and sources. Cheryl Buckley and Hazel Clark include in their chapter, for example, ideas on where to look and search out source materials that may help to counter the paucity of everyday fashion they encountered in major museum collections. Their list includes sources such as family snapshots and albums, oral histories, items from personal wardrobes or yard sales, or editorials from general interest magazines. All the sources they name already imply the use of diverse methods that usually come together in the exploration of fashion—as object, image, practice, or discourse. Sophie Woodward has also discussed the necessity for combining various approaches to understanding the way people relate to fashion; her examples include wardrobe studies, interviews, and participant-observation. In the section on ethnographic explorations of fashion, each project relies on different sources and methods, as they emerge from the scholars's engagement with their research sites, including the historical study of the site itself, for example, the New York fashion industry, or the Antwerp Academy, in order to understand its current practices. Or, as Brent Luvaas pointed out, in his exploration of street style blogging, auto-ethnography is one mode of research he combines with other methods, including photography, as visual research, or textual analysis of street style blogs and interviews with bloggers.

Research is usually inspired by a lack of existing documentation, or the "gap" in research, which one seeks to help fill. An example that relates to the paucity of everyday dress in museum collections is the case of the history of men's fashion, which has been even more rarely collected (in comparison to women's clothes). In his research culminating in the book *The Hidden Consumer: Masculinities, Fashion and City Life 1860–1914* Christopher Breward (1999) therefore turned to a breadth of alternative sources to tackle the long held assumption that nineteenth-century men were only minimally interested in clothing (Breward 2010, 301–03). His research led him to, as he describes it, a "rich seam of visual and textual representation . . . to be found in novels, autobiographies, *cartes des visite* and street photographs, retail catalogues and advertisements, popular songs and theatre programs" (Breward 2010, 303). These sources offer glimpses into the way men "looked" in the nineteenth century, and a sense of the way "representations act to give meaning to consumer's relationship with commodities and other consumers" (Breward 2010, 303). Moreover, these visual and textual traces offer insights into an "imagined identity . . . something that has been made-up . . . but has real effects in the world of everyday relationships" (Dawson 1991, 181–82; cited in Breward 2010, 303). Methodologically Breward utilized these diverse sources to examine the relationship between fashion, mediation, subjectivity, and practices of the self—including constructions of masculinity.

The chapters in this third section focus specifically on the integration of varied source materials and multimethodological approaches to fashion research, including the need for a dynamic exchange between "theory" and "practice." The section begins with Francesca Granata's study of experimental fashion design of the Belgian designer Martin Margiela in the 1990s. Granata's chapter relates to the first section in this book, in particular to the issues addressed by Buckley and Clark with regard to fashion archiving and questions of temporality. In Granata's study, one of the issues in analyzing near contemporary fashion design was that due to—or despite—its timeliness, actual visual or material evidence of such recent experimental design works was not easy to locate. This required using a wide range of sources: from online image databases to fashion periodicals, press releases, exhibition catalogs, and actual garments. Bringing in her study the materialities (and temporalities) of Margiela's designs together with theoretical ideas, including Bakhtin's notion of the grotesque and carnivalesque concepts of time and nostalgia, the chapter exemplifies the fluidity across empirical research and theory building—or the use of theory as method. Granata frames theory dynamically as "applied," or in practice, manifesting itself not only in texts, or serving as a tool for deduction, but also seen as inherent in the materiality of garments and in the practice of design—establishing a bridge to Nicewonger's preceding discussion of the working of "ideas" as material and discursive forms of knowledge.

The importance of mixing sources, methods, and theories is further elaborated in Susan Kaiser's and Denise Green's chapter based on a collaborative, multiyear research project on the fashioning of masculinities in the United States. Their discussion demonstrates the complexities involved in interdisciplinary research, and in the mixing or synthesizing of methodological approaches grounded in different research philosophies. The field of fashion studies in the United States (and beyond) encompasses a substantial number of scholars who are located in academic programs that bring together social science approaches, economics, and the physical or natural sciences. These include, for example, textile and apparel programs, which are located in university departments for human development, family and nutrition sciences, or in the departments for design, technology and management, marketing and merchandizing, or consumer studies—fields in which quantitative studies are used frequently. Sparked in particular by a rise of "big data" studies and a "positivist turn," Kaiser and Green observed in fashion scholarship in recent years in the United States and at transnational conferences, their chapter outlines the different philosophies that underpin positivist, interpretative, and critical approaches to research—and focuses in on the integration of qualitative and quantitative methods.

Despite the growth of the men's fashion and beauty market, the rise of men's magazines, and of academic studies on men's fashion (selected examples include Breward 1999; Reilly and Cosbey 2008; McNeil and Karaminas 2009; or the journal *Critical Studies in Men's Fashion*), Kaiser and Green's discussion reveals that in everyday life, "fashion" is still a term steeped in binary thinking, suggesting that "there is gender trouble." Furthermore, their project sought to move methodologically beyond hegemonic conceptions of identity or masculinity, to shed light on the experience of plural masculinities—highlighting the intersectionalities among gender, sexuality, age, race, place, etc. It was only through the combination of diverse methods, ranging from a large-scale national survey, qualitative interviews, ethnographies, visual analysis as well as historical and contemporary discourse analysis, that their project was able to facilitate "opportunities for many voices," which are so crucial to illuminate the role of fashion in people's everyday lives.

The interest in creating methods and opportunities to bring in many voices, to engage with conflicting issues in fashion, is also demonstrated in Otto von Busch's chapter on practice-based modes of research as forms of intervention. His chapter addresses the contradictions and complexities that are part of fashion in everyday lives: that is, fashion as an activity, as practice, as making—which alludes to a sense of agency—and fashion as a social and political dynamic, as a hierarchical system, as a mode of exclusion and inclusion, or as he puts it, "as a violent playground," a site of conflict. Such a political dimension is already inherent in the etymology of the English term "fashion" as a noun: which is derived from the old French term *façon* for shape, pattern, or design, but which has also roots in the Latin word *factio* (= "a group of people acting together"): the basis of the political term "faction," which can also refer to a state of conflict within an organization (see *Oxford English Dictionary* 2015).

Framed by a critical discussion of the realpolitik of fashion, bridging political theories and design agency, von Busch introduces in his chapter Donna Haraway's method of diffraction and Preben Mogensen's concept of the provotype. He utilizes these conceptual tools in the creation of two projects to "manifest," or to make apparent, fashion's contradictions, and to provoke and make a difference through experience. The first is the creation of a fashion safehouse, based on Thoreau's

*Walden*, to create a space for making fashion and sharing skills and experiences. The second project takes the form of a quasi-embassy or border control, situated at The New School's Parsons School of Design during New York Fashion Week, manifesting the "exclusivity" of fashion. Both methodological concepts and projects facilitate new experiential modes of research, learning, and thinking that help to expand not only the understanding of the intersections between fashion and politics, but also to highlight further the political dimensions or implications of methods and research practices.

Rounding off the discussion on mixed methods the final chapter in this section, and in this book, returns to a reflection on the development and interdisciplinary scope of the field of fashion studies. It does this specifically with the focus on the development and editing of one of the milestone publications in this field: *The Encyclopedia of World Dress and Fashion*, published in 2010. Just within the last ten years, the field of fashion studies has seen the publication of several new academic journals, handbooks, second editions of key readers and comprehensive reference works that together demonstrate the growth and "academic dignity" the scholarship of fashion and dress has reached (a few selected examples: Steele 2005; McNeil 2009; Lillethun and Welters 2011; Black et al. 2013, Bruzzi and Church-Gibson 2013; Barnard 2014; Fletcher and Tham 2015; Hethorn and Ulasewicz 2015).

One of the scholars rigorously committed to the academic growth of the field is Joanne Eicher, who published in 1965 together with Mary Ellen Roach the book *Dress, Adornment and the Social Order*, described as "the first attempt to systematically study the social significance of clothing"—followed by many more. Her work began in a time context when scholars of dress and fashion fought many battles for the academic recognition of their field of scholarship and began to build the research concentrations in universities, professional associations, and museums—which form today the ground for scholars who confidently call themselves "fashion" scholars.

As editor of the *Dress, Body, Culture* series (initiated by Berg Publishers and now at Bloomsbury), Joanne Eicher has created a platform for hundreds of scholars to have their work on fashion and dress published in monographs and edited collections. She fostered the formation of an international and interdisciplinary network of scholars, who contributed to the major achievement of the ten-volume encyclopedia that spans diverse histories of fashion and dress items across time and place. This encyclopedia has received a comprehensive review in a special supplement in *Fashion Theory*, edited by Peter McNeil (2012). In the same spirit as the other chapters in this book, Joanne Eicher offers insights into her own practice and the "backstage" work involved in "doing fashion studies," through editorial work and academic publishing. Her chapter tells the story behind *The Encyclopedia of World Dress and Fashion*, outlining its methods for the formation and organization of knowledge, and the methods that are needed in the interdisciplinary and cross-cultural study of fashion and dress. In doing so, Eicher's chapter rounds off this book, pointing toward recent and future developments in the field of fashion studies—as well as to the impact of shifting terminologies, with "fashion" being no doubt an aid that has increased the relevance and value (in the widest sense) of the critical study of fashion.

# References

Barnard, Malcolm. 2014. *Fashion Theory*. London and New York: Routledge.

Black, Sandy, Amy de la Haye, Agnes Rocamora, Regina Root, and Helen Thomas, eds. 2013. *The Handbook of Fashion Studies*. London and New York: Bloomsbury.

Breward, Christopher. 1999. *The Hidden Consumer: Masculinities, Fashion and City Life 1860-1914*. Manchester: Manchester University Press.

Breward, Christopher. 2010. "Modes of Manliness: Reflections on Recent Histories of Masculinities and Fashion." In *The Fashion History Reader: Global Perspectives*, edited by Giorgio Riello and Peter McNeil, 301–07. London and New York: Routledge.

Bruzzi, Stella and Pamela Church-Gibson, eds. 2013. *Fashion Cultures Revisited: Theories, Exploration and Analysis*. London and New York: Routledge.

Eicher, Joanne and Mary Ellen Roach. 1965. *Dress, Adornment and the Social Order*. New York: Wiley.

Fletcher, Kate and Mathilda Tham, eds. 2015. *The Routledge Handbook of Sustainable Fashion*. London and New York: Routledge.

Hethorn, Janet and Connie Ulasewicz, eds. 2015. *Sustainable Fashion: What's Next? A Conversation of Issues, Practices and Possibilities*. Second Edition. London and New York: Bloomsbury.

Lillethun, Abby and Linda Welters, eds. 2011. *The Fashion Reader: Second Edition*. London and New York: Bloomsbury.

McNeil, Peter, ed. 2009. *Fashion: Critical and Primary Sources*. Oxford and New York: Berg.

McNeil, Peter, ed. 2012. "Special Supplement Berg Encyclopedia of World Dress and Fashion." *Fashion Theory: The Journal of Dress, Body and Culture* 16.

McNeil, Peter and Vicki Karaminas, eds. 2009. *The Men's Fashion Reader*. Oxford and New York: Berg.

Reilly, Andrew and Sarah Cosbey, eds. 2008. *The Men's Fashion Reader*. New York: Fairchild.

Steele, Valerie, ed. 2005. *Encyclopedia of Clothing and Fashion*. New York: Scribner.

# 7 FITTING SOURCES— TAILORING METHODS: A CASE STUDY OF MARTIN MARGIELA AND THE TEMPORALITIES OF FASHION

## Francesca Granata

In this chapter, I retrace the methodological and theoretical strands that underpin my research on the grotesque and carnivalesque in experimental fashion at the turn of the millennium. I then move the focus to my exploration of selected 1990s collections and presentations by Belgian designer Martin Margiela, investigating the relation between fashion and time, followed by a discussion of my research process and the way I teased out meanings from Margiela's designs via a method I refer to as "applied theory." This approach places the objects and images in dialogue with a theoretical framework derived primarily from fashion studies, critical theory, cultural history, feminist theory, as well as film studies and material culture. It is also based on the belief that fashion is itself theoretical and not an inert matter to which theories are merely applied. As Alison Gill warned, fashion should not be thought of "as a passive reflection and measure of agencies found elsewhere in (deeper) social concerns" (Gill 1998, 35), but rather as having a theoretical dimension that intervenes with and influences the theoretical discourse.

I started my research project by observing a proliferation of grotesque bodies within "experimental fashion" at the turn of the millennium. I use this term to describe the kind of fashion that, as the word suggests, experiments with established forms, patterns, textiles, and modes of presentation. Drawing on the work of Russian cultural historian and literary theorist Mikhail Bakhtin (1895–1975), I set out to investigate the reasons behind this proliferation. In *Rabelais and His World,* a study from the 1930s and 1940s of the sixteenth-century French author François Rabelais, Bakhtin describes the open-ended, collective body of carnival as the grotesque body par excellence, in contrast to the classical body of official culture: "an entirely finished, completed, strictly limited body, which is shown from the outside as something individual" (Bakhtin 1984 [1965], 320). He theorizes the grotesque as chiefly a phenomenon of reversal and of unsettling ruptures of borders, particularly bodily borders. A constant transgression, merging, and exceeding of borders constitutes the central attribute of the Bakhtinian grotesque. In an endnote, he writes that it would be "interesting to trace the struggle of the grotesque and classical concept in the history of dress and fashion" (Bakhtin 1984 [1965], 322–23). My research took on this task within the limited framework of experimental fashion that had been established by the turn of the millennium within European fashion capitals, specifically Paris and London, though produced and circulated globally.[1]

## Finding sources and tailoring methods

When setting out to study experimental fashion at the turn of the millennium, I thought that it would be quite simple to reconstruct and access such a recent past. However, I found the opposite to be the case. In fact, it was specifically because it belonged to a relatively recent past that it was, at times, difficult to find actual visual and material evidence of the garments, as well as of fashion show recordings and lookbooks produced within those years as they had not yet been fully collected and archived. Materials produced in the 1980s and early to mid-1990s, prior to the widespread usage of the internet, were particularly difficult to find, thus making photos, let alone videos, hard to locate in the image databases dedicated to designer fashion, such as style.com, or more specialized ones, such as firstVIEW.com and Catwalking.com—two image databases specifically created for the industry. The only database that had some (albeit incomplete) information on 1980s and 1990s experimental fashion was the Contemporary Fashion Archive (contemporaryfashion.net): an information network created by five European fashion institutions to document contemporary fashion design. (The archive was a shared initiative of the Austrian-based organization UNIT F, Central Saint Martins College of Art and Design in London, the Dutch Fashion Foundation in Amsterdam, the Flanders Fashion Institute in Antwerp, and the University of Applied Sciences in Pforzheim.) The project, which is still accessible online, was started in response to the multimedia nature of contemporary fashion and as a testament to its increasing centrality as a cultural force. The Contemporary Fashion

Archive ran from 2002 to 2007 and received funding from the Culture 2000 program of the European Union. Unlike industry databases, the archive served an educational purpose and thus, it contextualized the images of the presentations through designers' descriptions of their work and other relevant materials. It is also free to access, which makes this archive an important and practical tool for teaching such material.

Exhibition catalogs provided an important corrective to such gaps in the documentation of experimental fashion of the 1980s and 1990s, though for the most part they did not provide an exhaustive account of designers' work, and especially in the case of less known designers, they simply did not exist. Additionally, some very important documents of fashion of this period were style magazines published in the 1980s and 1990s. Particularly relevant to a study of experimental fashion were British independent magazines such as *i-D* and, later *The Face*—which, unlike the various editions of *Vogue*, covered independent designers from the very beginning of their careers. These were joined in the 1990s by avant-garde publications, such as *Purple* and *Visionaire*, which gave ample coverage to more experimental designs, as well as the magazines produced by designers themselves as with *Six,* published by Rei Kawakubo and her Japanese fashion design company, *Comme des Garçons.* The press record of the period not only serves as documentation of the collections, but also traces their early reception. Margiela's work, for instance, was discussed in a number of newspaper articles. Particularly influential was an article titled "Coming Apart" by the *New York Times* fashion critic, the late Amy Spindler, which discussed the deconstructive aspects of his work (Spindler 1993, A1). Literary theorist Barbara Vinken was also an early commentator on Margiela. Published in German in 1993, and later translated into English, her book *Fashion Zeitgeist* includes one of the first academic accounts of the Belgian designer's work (Vinken 2005, 142).

The New York-based, independent magazine *Details* also featured extensive coverage of Margiela's first few collections, which were otherwise not as thoroughly commented upon and photographed as the Belgian designer's later work. (During the 1980s and early 1990s, *Details* was strikingly different from its current Condé Nast incarnation as a men's style magazine. It was a fashion magazine featuring extensive editorial and photographic coverage of the Paris shows—often exceeding thirty pages—all written and photographed by Bill Cunningham.) Besides newspapers, gaining access to style magazines of the period was rather unstraightforward as they had not, for the most part, been digitized and had been scantily collected. As a result, in order to find documentation of fashion from this period, further review of individual titles in specialized universities or museum libraries was still needed.

However, since 2012, the European Union also sponsored the Europeana Fashion project. Part of this initiative is to generate "an online collection of millions of digitized items from European museums, libraries, archives and audiovisual collections," which makes Europeana Fashion the widest repository of private and public dress and costume collections and archives across Europe (see http://www.europeanafashion.eu). Among its content providers, too numerous to mention here, is the ModeMuseum in Antwerp, which holds a very important collection of experimental fashion of the 1980s and 1990s (including garments from Martin Margiela), as well as the Victoria and Albert Museum in London, whose contemporary fashion holdings are also substantial. Europeana Fashion was started precisely as an acknowledgment of fashion's "research value." It allows access, free of charge, to over 700,000 digital fashion objects ranging from historical and contemporary dress to accessories, photographs, sketches, and lookbooks, providing an invaluable research and teaching tool. A similar trend toward digitization has also opened up some museum collections to the general public in the Unites States, chiefly that of the Costume Institute at the Metropolitan Museum of Art, which holds important examples of experimental fashion from the 1980s and 1990s. Also, underway is the digitalization of British photographer Niall McInerney's archives to be available through Bloomsbury's Fashion Central (www.bloomsburyfashioncentral.com) starting in 2016. His photographic archive of runway shows from the 1980s and 1990s, including independent and experimental ones, is substantial and during my research I contacted him to find documentations of some of the least accessible of Margiela's collections.

Although I began my research by looking at images in the form of photographs and fashion show recordings, as well as videos and films produced by designers in lieu of or in addition to fashion shows, I soon integrated it with a close study of objects understood both as garments and as accessories. Object-based research was central to my project and was employed as a way to build and test theories against examples of actual garments and accessories. I closely examined, photographed, measured, and whenever possible, handled, surviving dress in museums and private collections. To augment my study of Martin Margiela, I repeatedly visited the collection of the ModeMuseum in Antwerp, the Metropolitan Museum of Art's Costume Institute in New York, and the Victoria and Albert Museum in London, as well as the home of a private Margiela collector. Access to museums and private collections was certainly time consuming and required much advance planning, and it was in some cases, as with the New York-based collections such as the Costume Institute, restricted to doctoral students and scholars. I had access to the Costume Institute through a one-year fellowship at the Metropolitan Museum of Art, which was crucial for my project. In the case of my work, a close examination of the garments and accessories I discussed was, in fact, necessary to "unveil" their construction techniques, which were often impossible to ascertain from photographs. It was also indispensable to establish, with a level of certainty, the textiles and alternative materials used in a number of experimental garments produced within the period, and the effects that these materials might have ultimately produced. For instance, with Margiela's enlarged collections 2000 and 2001, it was only through a close examination that I was able to observe the lack of respect for grading techniques. Unlike graded clothes, the garments were enlarged equally in width and length when adapted from a size 42 to a 72, resulting in gargantuan dimensions and a general lack of proportionality (Figures 7.1 and 7.2). Only after a close and detailed analysis, which involved

**FIGURE 7.1** Examining Margiela's garments at the MoMu Archives, Antwerp. *Photo*: Francesca Granata, with permission of the Mode Museum, Antwerp.

**FIGURE 7.2** Oversized wool sweater and label detail indicating a nonexistent garment size. Maison Margiela, Autumn/Winter 2001. *Photo*: Francesca Granata, with permission of the Mode Museum, Antwerp.

measuring and handling the garments, was I able to deduct how some of the knits and coats were in fact molded and rendered stiff thus retaining their shape when worn, and further ensuring their gigantic size. Following this material discovery as well as contextualization of the garments through runway photography, I was able to see and speculate the ways in which such garments were read at times as "fat suits," thus allowing a theorization of the collections' relation to normative sizes and body types.

The methodology just briefly described was developed from Valerie Steele's article in the methodology issue of *Fashion Theory* (1998) entitled "A Museum of Fashion is More Than a Clothes-Bag," which is based on research methods developed by the art historian Jules Prown, and is thus deeply indebted to a material culture approach. Material culture is a "mode of investigation" common to the field of cultural history and cultural anthropology, which uses objects as its primary data, seen as the articulation of culture through material productions (Prown 1974, 1980, and 2000). Steele, following Prown, breaks down the process of garment analysis into three main stages: "Description, Deduction and Speculation," and suggests that these stages should be kept relatively discrete (Steele 1998). Lou Taylor has also discussed the importance of museum collections and object-based research to the study of fashion in her books *Establishing Dress History* and *The Study of Dress History* (Taylor 2002 and 2004). A more recent and very thorough example of object-based analysis in action is given by Alexandra Palmer's article "Looking at Fashion: The Material Object as Subject" (Palmer 2013). Although object-based research played a significant role in my methodology, I did not privilege this approach over others. Nor did I establish a hierarchy in favor of object over theory—one which, as Prown's methods prove, is unnecessary—rather, I attempted to place this empirical study within a theoretical framework.[2]

My methodology also involves, albeit to a lesser extent, oral history. Whenever possible, I conducted interviews with practitioners and their surviving collaborators that proved helpful, and often necessary, in providing additional information about the production of the work, which was often insufficiently cataloged and documented. Moreover, this method allowed for a "dialogical encounter" between practitioner and interviewer, in which new meanings and interpretations developed. However, as discussed by a number of oral historians, there are obvious limitations and common pitfalls to this approach (Sandino 2006; Thompson 1988; Taylor 2002). Of particular relevance to my research was the "intentional fallacy": the misreading of the practitioners' intentions as the work's primary meaning. Instead, it has been suggested that interviews with practitioners provide not a direct or more authentic reading of the work, but rather an instance of "the author's" self-reception (Proctor 2006). In the case of Margiela, due to the reclusiveness of both him and his team, it was not possible to conduct an in-person interview, however, I was able to use the Maison's detailed press releases, lookbooks, and the exhibition catalog that the Maison produced on the occasion of its 1997 retrospective to take into account the designer's perspective.

## Applied theory: Margiela's work and alternative temporalities

In addition to formal analysis of images/videos and object analysis of garments and accessories, my approach combines fashion and design history and theory, along with critical theory, cultural history, feminist theory, as well as film studies. I position my project as a work of "applied theory" (Evans 2003, 3): the theories enable a greater understanding of the garments and performances discussed, while in turn the work discussed opens up new possibilities for theories of fashion. This becomes evident in the analysis of a number of Margiela's collections from the 1990s and his exhibition from 1997, which suggests new ways of theorizing time in relation to fashion and its histories.

Bakhtin argued that cyclical time played an extremely important role within the carnival and the culture of folk humor, and was opposed to official time, which was characterized by an apparent stability and pretensions to eternity:

> [c]arnival celebrated temporary liberation from the prevailing truth and from the established order: it marked the suspension of all hierarchical rank, privileges, norms, and prohibitions. Carnival was the true feast of time, the feast of becoming, change, and renewal. It was hostile to all that was immortalized and completed (Bakhtin 1984, 10). The culture of folk humour conceives all these false pretences of immovable stability and eternity in the perspective of ever-changing and renewed time. (Bakhtin 1984, 213)

Bakhtin's conception of time, expounded in relation to the carnival and the ever-becoming nature of the grotesque, brings to mind the constantly changing nature of "fashion time," characterized by ephemerality as opposed to the stability and immortality traditionally claimed by other cultural forms. Thus, one could argue that, to some extent, all fashion partakes of the carnival and the grotesque in its relation to time, yet Margiela's work makes this argument most convincingly: by recycling his own collections, as well as old clothes from various past decades, he highlights the cyclical nature of fashion, which is sometimes denied by the linear and progressive teleological narrative of Western history, and fashion history in particular. The latter often follows traditional art history and art historical survey texts in their dependence on strict chronology and suggestions of progress.[3] Margiela's interest in transience and in the recycling of old garments, however, is shared by a great number of artists and designers of this period, and can be partially read as a response to anxieties surrounding ever-accelerating times of production and consumption, as well as a rejection of the aesthetic of excess characterizing the preceding decade. These anxieties over progressively faster temporalities occurred concomitantly across design and art disciplines—including fashion—and Margiela's work can be seen as part of this larger debate occurring simultaneously across theory and practice (Sandino 2004, 283–93; Evans 2003, 36–39 and 249–60).

As the literary and psychoanalytical theorist Julia Kristeva points out, cyclical time stands in opposition to "time as project, teleology, linear and prospective unfolding time; time as departure, progression and arrival—in other words the time of history" (Kristeva 2001, 30). Kristeva adds that cyclical time is "traditionally linked to female subjectivity," a point which reveals a continuum between fashion, the feminine, and the grotesque. The concept of cyclical time, in fact, dovetails with Kristeva's discussions of the subject-in-process, which presupposes constant and endless change. This temporal modality is also central to the "ever-becoming" grotesque body of carnival. The cyclical nature of fashion history, which contradicts popular understandings of fashion as a chronological progression in search of the *new*, can be observed in Barbara Burman Baines's account of fashion's endless revivals, which she explored within the context of the English dress in her book *Fashion Revivals from the Elizabethan Age to the Present Day* (Burman Baines 1981). This concept has also been theorized in three-dimensional form by Judith Clark's exhibition "Malign Muses: When Fashion Turns Back," which was dialogically developed with theorist Caroline Evans. The exhibition employed a system of interlocking cogs on which garments from different periods were placed to explore the cyclicality and nonlinearity of fashion time (Clark 2004).

Margiela, however, takes this process a step further and produces what could be described as a carnivalized time. I use the expression "carnivalized time" as a further elaboration of Bakhtin's theories of the carnival to mean not only the cyclical time of carnival festivities but, more specifically, an inverted and topsy-turvy time when temporalities of past, present, and future are reversed and/or thoroughly confused.[4] Through a close material and visual analysis of his work and, in particular, his Theatre Costumes and Trompe l'oeil collections, I observed how Margiela's work denies the ineluctable linearity of Western industrial time, and literally inverts past and future, thus carnivalizing time. Margiela's garments and performances invert and accelerate time, as well as confound both the aging process of the garments and the historical time of fashion history. He inverts and refutes teleological and progressive notions of time and history, by making the old anew and rendering the new as old. These tendencies, however present in the majority of his work, can be best observed in his Spring/Summer 1993 and Spring/Summer 1996 collections—two collections that have been largely ignored within the literature on the designer—captured in the designer's ten-year retrospective at the Museum Boijmans Van Beuningen in Rotterdam in 1997.

# Theater costumes collection: Spring/Summer 1993

The designer's Spring/Summer 1993 collection presented "historically inspired underwear and skirts" alongside "reworked and over-dyed jackets of Renaissance and eighteenth century style theater costumes in velvet and brocade worn on bare torsos, closed with safety pins or belted with scotch tape" (La Maison Martin Margiela 1997). Besides the obvious irony of using Scotch tape and safety pins to "style" historical theater costumes, their inclusion adds another layer to Margiela's play with temporalities. These costumes, which were transformed and further aged through an over-dying process, in fact, already carry a reference to historical time. Not unlike historical film costumes, they approximate a historical past by often resorting to established conventions of how the past has come to be represented (i.e., puffed sleeves and velvets become a shorthand for the Renaissance, neck ruffs for the Elizabethan era). In the case of this collection, very scant examples of clothing were available and, with the exception of two pieces from the aforementioned private collection, I had to base my analysis on photographic documentations of the clothes comprising the collection. These were examined alongside the Costume Institute's curatorial notes for the deconstruction section of the exhibition "Infra-Apparel" from 1993, which included material analysis of some of Margiela's Theatre Collection pieces. The analysis was also further informed by the Maison's own detailed press release, which I was able to access in the museum collections.

Theater costumes present a simplified and emphasized version of "history," even more so than cinematic ones, distilled in a few immediately readable signs, which need to be recognizable by an audience at a distance. As a result, they often shed more light on contemporary rather than past fashions, and on the way the conventions, according to which we represent and imagine various historical periods, are, in fact, rooted in the present. This is particularly evident in the theater costumes that Margiela included in his 1993 collection, whose historical approximation and vagueness are furthered by the reworking of the garments, which ultimately look rather contemporary and vaguely pan-historical. The reworked theater costumes, having been taken out of the context of an entire ensemble and undergoing photographic close-up, give away their lack of historical accuracy: snap buttons, which are often used in theater costume to allow for quick changes, are visible on "Renaissance" jackets worn open and on a vaguely military eighteenth-century jacket. A waistcoat, once taken out of context, conveys a nineteenth-century riding habit, such as a Redingote à la Hussarde. Stomachers and corsets paired with exposed belly buttons underscore contemporary mores rather than whatever period they were originally meant to represent.

Margiela's Spring/Summer 1993 collection brings to mind the complex filmic time of historical movies, where the past is imagined via the present. Historical films, such as the 1967 gangster/romance film *Bonnie and Clyde*'s portrayal of 1930s America, merge fashion from different decades and convey how a decade, be it our own or, in the case of *Bonnie and Clyde*, the 1960s, represented a particular past. This process is in great part achieved via costumes and mise-en-scène. Similarly, Margiela's reconstructed theater costumes highlight the ways in which history is constructed and makes visible how the past is mediated and available only through the present. His designs reinforce an understanding of history—or better, histories—as reflexive, interpretative, and thus necessarily mediated and culturally constructed, rather than a stable and unmediated reconstruction of the past, which could be fully disinterested or objective.

It is through my material and visual analysis of the collection that I build my argument that the Belgian designer's garments constitute visual and material theorizations of "new history," and its attendant historiographical methods, which developed with particular force from the 1970s onward to debunk the so-called "Master Narratives" and the traditional paradigm of history.[5] Written from a Western vantage point, this paradigm was highly dependent on official documents in its quest for causality and objectivity, and was characterized by an interest in the chronological unfolding of national and international political events (needless to say, this mode of history had very little space for fashion). Margiela's reconstructed theater pieces instead forcefully point to the ways in which reality is socially and culturally constructed, and expose how one "cannot avoid looking at the past from a particular point of view" (Burke 2001, 6). Such a reading of Margiela's work opens up the field of inquiry and suggests new theoretical models for the study of fashion histories, which, as with Kristeva's conceptualization of temporalities, understand histories as nonlinear, as well as inevitably mediated. Thus, ultimately, Margiela's reworking of theater costumes provides further evidence that fashion has a theoretical dimension.

Under closer scrutiny, and as the suspension of disbelief afforded by the stage is removed, Margiela's garments reveal themselves for what they are: obviously "fake" replicas and approximations of a historical past often achieved by quoting more recent pasts; such is the case with his eighteenth-century-like, small fur jacket, which seems to be adapted from a 1940s garment, and a Renaissance-like blouse whose laced sleeves seem to be quoting the nineteenth century, and were possibly made of textiles of that period.

Frequently, due to budgetary restrictions and the unavailability of materials such as old laces, theater costumes adapt old clothes and materials from a more recent past to make reference to an older past. For instance, nineteenth-century lace is often used for Renaissance costumes, which might have been the case with the Renaissance jacket from the 1993 collection. These layering of pasts in Margiela's garments is confirmed by Richard Martin and Harold Koda's research for the exhibition "Infra-Apparel," in which they date one of Margiela's reconstructed eighteenth-century theater costumes to the 1940s (Martin and Koda 1993, 28). And, as fashion historian Alexandra Palmer has shown by studying eighteenth-century garments in the collection of the Royal Ontario Museum, clothes often retain layers of histories (Palmer 2010).

Rendering the conflation of various historical periods explicit, Margiela's pieces dismantle the illusion of a stable and "authentic" past that the theater costumes are meant to represent. The reconstructed theater costumes deny fixed and stable origins. They carnivalize linear history and, in their obvious fakeness and inverted complex time, question a historical past that is stable and unmediated. These clothes show the complex temporalities of dress history where, at closer scrutiny, one finds a palimpsest of historical periods within a single garment.

# Trompe l'oeil collection: Spring/Summer 1996

Denying and subverting notions of authenticity and origin is a recurrent theme in Margiela's work. His Spring/Summer 1996 collection materializes this idea by featuring photographs of garments, often vintage garments, alongside ones from previous collections (Figure 7.3): "Printed on light and fluid fabrics and made up into garments of very simple construction . . . . A photograph of a 1930s heavy man's half belted overcoat is printed on light viscose, 1940's checked skirts to the

**FIGURE 7.3** Printed silk garments. Maison Margiela, Spring/Summer 1996. *Photo*: Francesca Granata, with permission of the ModeMuseum, Antwerp.

knee are shown in silk chiffon. A secondhand army surplus jacket is printed on stretch cotton and a lighter viscose" (La Maison Martin Margiela 1997). Following Steele's and Prown's methods of close looking and examination, I was able to observe through examples of this work in the collection of the ModeMuseum, as well as through a number of photographic documentations, the ways in which these printed garments instill a temporal and material confusion. The viewer is not sure, at least, at first sight, whether they are in fact vintage pieces and/or pieces from Margiela's previous collection, which, in a further twist, were often replicas of vintage pieces to begin with. This material confusion is exemplified in a garment from this collection which was included in the Rotterdam exhibition: "[A] photograph of the original lining of the 1950s cocktail dress the reproduction of which appears in outfit 14 [part of the Autumn/Winter 1995–1996 collection]" (La Maison Martin Margiela 1997). Furthering the sense of confusion, the garments photographed are of a different material than the one on which the photographs are printed. This creates a trompe l'oeil effect that disorients and upsets expectations. Margiela's disorienting garments appear reminiscent of surrealist techniques especially as articulated by Italian fashion designer Elsa Schiaparelli; in 1938, Schiaparelli created her "Tear Dress" in collaboration with Salvador Dalí by using a trompe l'oeil technique similar to Margiela's to give the suggestion of tears in an otherwise "whole" garment (Te Duits 2007). (It is important to note that this trompe l'oeil technique has become more common and technically easier to achieve in the last ten years, thanks to the widespread use and the improvement in the quality of digital printing techniques.)

Additionally, as is underlined by the Maison Martin Margiela press release, and evident in the examples I was able to study, "the colours of old photographs— black and white, sepia and tones of brown—are maintained throughout." These tones are perhaps more obviously visible in the 1950s cocktail dress lining (included in the Rotterdam exhibition) which, in its yellowish color, seems to carry the patina of an heirloom, thus prone to induce nostalgia and offer the illusion of a direct relation to an authentic past. This strategy would seem to align Margiela with much contemporary fashion and fashion merchandising, which employs references to bygone times in order to induce nostalgia and activate an emotive consumption (Appadurai 2005, 75–79). However, what these goods create in actuality is what Arjun Appadurai describes as "imagined nostalgia," a longing for an imagined past, one never necessarily experienced and lost. Referring primarily to fashion advertisements, he writes, "[They] teach consumers to miss things they have never lost. In thus creating experiences of losses that never took place" (Appadurai 2005, 77). To which he adds: "The viewer need only bring the faculty of nostalgia to an image that will supply the memory of a loss he or she never suffered. This relationship might be called armchair nostalgia, nostalgia without lived experience or collective historical memory" (Appadurai 2005, 78).

Yet Margiela denies or at least ironizes these processes of "imagined" nostalgia. He does so by isolating and doubling up various elements which are supposed to induce nostalgia, such as the old clothes and the old photographs, and putting them back together in ways that render obvious their artificiality. By printing artificially aged photographs of old clothes onto new fabric and leaving the processes readable, he questions notions of authenticity and unveils how nostalgia—and particularly nostalgia for consumer goods—can be potentially constructed and fabricated.

According to the theorist Linda Hutcheon (1998), processes of ironizing nostalgia are common to contemporary cultural productions. She qualifies this claim, however, by arguing that irony and nostalgia were, in fact, associated well before the late twentieth century by citing the example of *Don Quixote*, which is, according to Bakhtin, a quintessential carnivalesque novel. Hutcheon makes a distinction between these practices of ironizing nostalgia versus the unironic and potentially conservative invocation of an idealized past, partially in response to Fredric Jameson's pessimistic view of "late capitalist" society. Jameson, in fact, sees all contemporary nostalgic cultural production as a failure to engage with history. He discusses the phenomenon, according to which, style and periodization is used to invoke past as a testament to the fact that contemporary cultural production has done away with real history in lieu of historicism in the negative sense of the term, "In the bad sense of an omnipresent and indiscriminate appetite for dead styles and fashions: indeed for all the styles and fashions of a dead past" (Jameson 1991, 286).

But as many theorists, including Hutcheon, have commented, Jameson's writings on history are themselves nostalgic—namely, for a view of history understood as more coherent and less fragmented which, according to Jameson, allowed for a greater level of political consciousness (Hutcheon 1988). Hutcheon asks whether "Jameson's implicit mythologizing and idealizing of a more stable pre-*late*-capitalist (that is modernist) world is not in itself perhaps part of an aesthetic (or even politics) of nostalgia" (Hutcheon 1998). The way in which Hutcheon's and Jameson's debates are ultimately dependent on two different understandings of history is discussed by Susannah Radstone, in her writing on the representations of history in film. Like Hutcheon, Radstone ultimately suggests the need for a qualification of different types of nostalgia and the way they operate within different cultural output (Radstone 1995, 37).

# Performing garments: Martin Margiela's Rotterdam exhibition

Margiela's ironization of processes of nostalgia became, perhaps, even more evident in the designer's retrospective at the Museum Bojmans Van Beuningen, a museum of art and design in Rotterdam, which was organized by the Maison Martin Margiela itself in 1997. The exhibition was painstakingly documented in the accompanying catalog, which was also authored by the Maison, remaining as the rare documentation of this time-based work (La Maison Martin Margiela 1997; see Evans 1998 for a review of the exhibition). As a result, the catalog became an object of study in its own right and the basis for my analysis of the exhibition—a temporal event that no longer exists. (Its transformation into an artifact is made further evident by its retailing for over a $1000 in the secondhand book market.) In fact, it would be more precise to call the exhibition a performance, as it was composed of an event, which unfolded over time, and where (rather uncharacteristically) the main subjects were garments as opposed to the people wearing them. The Rotterdam retrospective entered the realm of performance art as the garments became performing "subjects"; the clothes came alive or, rather, their organic life and lifespan was made manifest. Pink yeast, red or yellow bacteria, and green mold were applied onto clothes from Margiela's past collection, which had been treated with the growing medium agar. Their application accelerated processes of aging and decomposition, particularly as the clothes were placed "in incubating structures" in the museum's garden. The use of bacteria is also reminiscent of disease and contagion—a reference, however, subverted by the beautiful pattern obtained through their applications. This reference to disease and medicalized spaces constitutes an undercurrent to experimental fashion produced in the late 1980s and 1990s, and can be observed in experimental fashion's challenge to the clean façade of the body and its boundaries, which can, in part, be read as meditating anxieties and obsessions with bodily borders surrounding the AIDS crisis (see Granata 2010).

The application of molds and bacteria allowed for the fabrication of signs of aging and of patina onto the clothes across a relatively short span of time. Once the bacteria had grown on the garments' fabric and achieved the desired effect, the clothes were exhibited on dress forms alongside the perimeter of the museum's garden, presumably to further age. They were visible to the museum goers both from inside the exhibition hall and in rear view from the museum garden in which the visitors could walk (for images, see also Evans 1998). The mannequins were placed on a plinth outside, but facing in as if looking through the glass walls of the exhibition space at the visitors on the empty space inside. This initiated the first of a series of inversions by switching the traditional placement of mannequins vis-à-vis viewers and playing with categories of inside and outside. Thus, what appeared at first sight as a dismal and abandoned site (especially once the garments were taken out of the enclosures and exposed to the elements) was in actuality painstakingly produced and documented in the book accompanying the exhibition. The garments were aged according to a scientific process in a controlled environment so that the process of fabricating imagined histories and a sense of nostalgia was literally deconstructed and put on display.

In the exhibition, one encounters, once again, Margiela's penchant for carnivalizing time and playing with the order of temporalities. He ages garments that had withstood the passage of time and almost overnight tatters them to pieces. Moreover, he does so in the context of the museum, a place traditionally engaged with the conservation rather than the destruction of objects. Margiela inverts the temporality of the retrospective, which is supposed to anoint a designer's or most often an artist's oeuvre into the "eternal" and stable time of the museum. The designer converts the relation of the museum to permanence to transience. As design historian Linda Sandino points out, in her discussion of contemporary art works, by incorporating ephemeral elements, museums are "complicit in the transition of transient to durable," as they are "dedicated to preserve the fiction that works of arts are fixed and immortal." As a result, "transience [which well-describes Margiela's entire retrospective] subverts the presumed timeless significance and value of the museum collection" (Sandino 2004, 289).

The Maison initiated another central inversion during the Rotterdam exhibition, in which its clothes become animated via the application of bacteria, yeast, and mold to the fabric. To this end, Margiela employed a scientific method, which is fully documented in the catalog accompanying the exhibition. The designer's "animated" garments are also intent on fully exploring fashion's potential for problematizing fixed categories of inside/outside, animate/inanimate, body/clothing, and its potential for continual change and transformation. They are not only animated but also generative as is underlined by the Maison's description of the first stage of the exhibition as "the gestation period." Margiela's "fecund" dresses go against the understanding of fashion (and the woman of fashion) as "profoundly inorganic and anti-maternal" (Evans 1998, 91) and reiterate experimental fashion's exploration of the generative potential of the body and of different models of subjectivities and cyclical temporalities, as articulated by Bakhtin and Kristeva.

## Conclusion

As my discussion of the example of Margiela's collections highlights, a range of theories, methods, and sources are needed to analyze contemporary and near contemporary fashion design. Garments, photographs, exhibitions, catalogs, press releases, and lookbooks are all important sources, which often need to be examined together. Likewise a multimethodological approach alongside theoretical frameworks culled from a variety of disciplines is needed to make sense of this work, which exists as a still and moving image, as well as an actual object. It is only through a back and forth between material and visual analysis and theoretical approaches that these fashions can be thoroughly unpacked. My analysis of Margiela's garments and presentations underscores the way in which contemporary fashion mediates and influences theoretical discussions as opposed to being simply a reflection of it. As argued in this chapter, a close analysis of Margiela's work highlights fashion's cyclical nature, and points to the way that history is unstable and constructed. A study of his work suggests new theoretical models for the study of fashion design and its histories, models that are more fluid in their approach to temporalities and provide an understanding of history as inevitably mediated. Thus, my work underscores the need for scholars and students of fashion to allow theory and practice to enter, in a Bakhtinian "spirit," into dialogical exchanges with each other.

## Notes

1 My research project started in 2006 as a dissertation and is in the process of being transformed into a book titled *Experimental Fashion: Performance Art, Carnival and the Grotesque Body.*

2 I have previously unpacked my use of material culture and, more generally, its importance in fashion research in an article in *Fashion Theory*, titled "Fashion Studies In-Between: A Methodological Case Study" (Granata 2012, 67–82).

3 On these debates within art history, see, for instance, responses in relation to the substantial and somewhat radical updating of the canonical survey text from 1962 by H. W. Janson "History of Art," which was recently (in 2006) revised and republished by a number of authors under the title "Janson's History of Art: The Western Tradition." (For a range of responses to the substantial revision, see Kennedy 2006.)

4 The expression "carnivalized time" is surprisingly seldom used within Bakhtinian literature. The few times it surfaces, it is generally synonymous with carnival time: it retains the more expansive meaning of the cyclical and renewable time of carnival festivities. Bakhtin uses the term to refer to time in Dostoyevsky's novel, as pointed out by Richard Peace. 1993. "On Rereading Bakhtin." *Modern Language Review* 88 (1): 137–46. The only other recurrence of the term in the literature can be found in an article on Seneca's *Apocolocyntosis* to refer to the monstrous body of Claudius: see Susanna Morton Braund and Paula James. 1998. "Quasi Homo: Distortion and Contortion in Seneca's Apocolocyntosis." *Arethusa* 31 (3): 285–311.

5 The literature on new history and historiography is, of course, vast, but for an exhaustive summery of these debates, see Keith Jenkins, ed. 1997. *The Postmodern History Reader*. London: Routledge. For a nuanced discussion, see also Peter Burke, ed. 2001. *New Perspectives on Historical Writing*. University Park, PA: The Pennsylvania State University Press.

## References

Appadurai, Arjun. 2005. *Modernity at Large: Cultural Dimensions of Globalization.* Minneapolis: University of Minnesota Press.

Bakhtin, Mikhail M. 1984. *Rabelais and His World.* Translated by Hélène Iswolsky. Bloomington: Indiana University Press.

Burke, Peter, ed. 2001. *New Perspectives on Historical Writing.* University Park: The Pennsylvania State University Press.

Burman Baines, Barbara. 1981. *Fashion Revivals from the Elizabethan Age to the Present Day.* London: B. T. Batsford.

Clark, Judith. 2004. *Spectres: When Fashion Turns Back.* London and Antwerp: Victoria and Albert Publications and ModeMuseum.

Evans, Caroline. 1998. "The Golden Dustman: A Critical Evaluation of the Work of Martin Margiela and a Review of Martin Margiela Exhibition (9/4/1615)." *Fashion Theory* 2 (1): 73–93.

Evans, Caroline. 2003. *Fashion at the Edge: Spectacle, Modernity, and Deathliness.* New Haven, CT: Yale University Press.

Gill, Alison. 1998. "Deconstruction Fashion: The Making of Unfinished, Decomposing, and Re-assembled Clothes." *Fashion Theory* 2 (1): 25–50.

Granata, Francesca. 2010. *The Bakhtinian Grotesque in Fashion at the Turn of the Twenty-First Century.* PhD Thesis. London: University of the Arts.

Granata, Francesca. 2012. "Fashion Studies In-Between: A Methodological Case Study and an Inquiry into the State of Fashion Studies." *Fashion Theory* 16 (1): 67–82.

Hutcheon, Linda. 1988. *A Poetics of Postmodernism: History, Theory, Fiction.* New York: Routledge.

Hutcheon, Linda. 1998. "Irony, Nostalgia and the Postmodern." Online Database. University of Toronto English Language (UTEL) Library. http://www.library.utoronto.ca/utel/criticism/hutchinp.html.

Jameson, Fredric. 1991. *Postmodernism, or, The Cultural Logic of Late Capitalism.* Durham: Duke University Press.

Jenkins, Keith, ed. 1997. *The Postmodern History Reader.* London: Routledge.

Kennedy, Randy. 2006. "Revising Art History's Big Book: Who's In and Who Comes Out." *New York Times*, March 7.

Kristeva, Julia. 2001. "Women's Time." In *Feminism: Critical Concepts in Literary Cultural Studies*, vol. II, edited by Mary Evans, 27–49. London: Routledge.

La Maison Martin Margiela. 1997. *Martin Margiela (9/4/1615).* Rotterdam: Museum Boijmans Van Beuningen.

La Maison Martin Margiela. 1989–2002a. "Press Releases." Paris: La Maison Martin Margiela.

La Maison Martin Margiela. 1989–2002b. "Lookbooks." Paris: La Maison Martin Margiela.

Martin, Richard and Harold Koda. 1993. "Unpublished Checklist for the Exhibition Infra-Apparel." New York: Metropolitan Museum of Art, Costume Institute.

Palmer, Alexandra. 2010. "Looking is Research." Paper presented at the conference Locating Fashion Studies, held at Parsons School of Design/The New School, New York, NY, November 11–12.

Palmer, Alexandra. 2013. "Looking at Fashion: The Material Object as Subject." *The Handbook of Fashion Studies*, edited by Amy de la Haye, Joanne Entwistle, Regina Root, Sandy Black, Helen Thomas, and Agnès Rocamora, 268–300. London: Bloomsbury.

Proctor, Robert. 2006. "The Architect's Intention: Interpreting Post-War Modernism through the Architect Interview." *Journal of Design History* 19 (4): 297–307.

Prown, Jules David. 1980. "Style as Evidence." *Winterthur Portfolio* 15: 197–210.

Prown, Jules David. 1993. "The Truth of Material Culture: History or Fiction?" *History from Things: Essays on Material Culture*, edited by Steven Lubar and David W. Kingery, 1–19. Washington: Smithsonian Institution Press.

Prown, Jules David. 2001. *Art as Evidence: Writings on Art and Material Culture.* New Haven, CT: Yale University Press.

Radstone, Susannah. 1995. "Cinema/Memory/History." *Screen* 36 (1): 34–47.

Sandino, Linda. 2004. "Here Today, Gone Tomorrow: Transient Materiality in Contemporary Cultural Artefacts." *Journal of Design History* 17 (3): 283–93.

Sandino, Linda. 2006. "Oral Histories and Design: Objects and Subjects." *Journal of Design History* 19 (4): 275–82.

Spindler, Amy. 1993. "Coming Apart." *New York Times*, July 25.

Steele, Valerie. 1998. "A Museum of Fashion is More than a Clothes-Bag." *Fashion Theory* 2 (4): 327–35.

Taylor, Lou. 2002. *The Study of Dress History*. Manchester: Manchester University Press.

Taylor, Lou. 2004. *Establishing Dress History*. Manchester: Manchester University Press.

Te Duits, Thimo. 2007. "Shocking: Surrealism and Fashion Now." In *Surreal Things: Surrealism and Design*, edited by Ghislaine Wood, 177–89. London: V&A.

Thompson, Paul. 1988. *The Voice of the Past: Oral History*. Oxford: Oxford University Press.

Vinken, Barbara. 2005. *Fashion Zeitgeist: Trends and Cycles in the Fashion System.* Translated by Mark Hewson. Oxford: Berg.

# 8 MIXING QUALITATIVE AND QUANTITATIVE METHODS IN FASHION STUDIES: PHILOSOPHICAL UNDERPINNINGS AND MULTIPLE MASCULINITIES

## Susan B. Kaiser and Denise Nicole Green

It is common wisdom that it is not a good idea to "mix metaphors." Metaphors shape and frame understandings of the world. They "stand in" for complicated or nuanced ideas that might otherwise be reduced to sound bytes. Contrary to the idea that the process of "mixing metaphors" is problematic, feminist philosopher Marilyn Frye (1996) argues for mixing metaphors wildly, so that no single metaphor can stand in for complex concepts that cannot be captured monolithically. Every metaphor has its limits, she argues, and no single metaphor can represent the extent to which metaphors break down and demand further explanatory power.

The same can be said about research methods: any single method has its limits. The wildly interdisciplinary field of fashion studies requires a mixture of methods. Just as Frye's work mixes metaphors to subvert singular, hegemonic approaches to seeing and being in the world, we hope this chapter opens a space within fashion studies to mix qualitative and quantitative methods. We share information about a collaborative, "mixed-method" project begun in 2005 and funded by the US National Textile Center until 2009 (but which is still ongoing).[1] The project involved working with a variety of graduate students and colleagues to address basic questions about US masculinities in relation to style-fashion-dress.[2] Our goal was to move beyond hegemonic (e.g., white, bourgeois, straight) masculinities, toward the exploration of masculinities across diverse subject positions (e.g., ethnicity, sexuality, age/generation). To do so, we employed a variety of methods: interviews, discourse analysis, ethnography, and a national survey including both quantitative and qualitative approaches.

In this chapter, we use the multiple masculinities project as a case study to interrogate and illustrate diverse philosophical perspectives (positivist, interpretive, critical) that underpin particular methodologies. For example, quantitative methods tend to be aligned with positivist approaches, while methods such as discourse analysis sit well with critical approaches, and qualitative interviews and ethnographic methods tend to be associated with interpretive approaches. However, we also problematize the idea that definite breaks exist among these perspectives. While the positivist, interpretive, and critical philosophical perspectives presented are good to "think with," we advocate for a mixture of methods in fashion studies. Mixing methods loosens each approach from the philosophical assumptions of respective methodologies.

# The philosophy of mixing methods

Recognizing that no single method can tap the complexity of a phenomenon such as fashion—with its transnational flows, ongoing change, diverse webs of meaning, and material consequences for people and the planet—triangulation makes sense as a methodological strategy in fashion studies. The concept of triangulation comes from the field of land surveying. When there is a need to identify a specific point in space, the idea is that measurements need to be taken from at least two different vantage points. The intersection becomes a point of convergence, with some degree of assurance that more than one perspective has been taken into account. In the realm of social science research, triangulation becomes a strategy, as well, for convergence. Researchers can become more confident that they are representing "reality" when they have used more than one method of evaluation, and when two or more methods point to the same representation (Denzin 2006). Triangulation makes effective use of each method and locates common findings, while recognizing limitations of any single method.

Fashion as a subject and object of study demands more than one "truth." In *Doing Research in Fashion and Dress* fashion sociologist Yuniya Kawamura describes the challenges associated with conducting fashion/dress research: the divide that often exists between qualitative and quantitative research, with quantitative scholars having the tendency to "dismiss" qualitative research as "nonscientific or merely philosophical," while qualitative researchers may attack quantitative studies as perpetuating a "positivist" or "outmoded vision of science" that valorizes numbers over meaning (Kawamura 2011, 26). In the 1994 edition of the *Handbook of Qualitative Research*, Denzin and Lincoln describe the difference between qualitative and quantitative research as follows:

> Qualitative researchers use ethnographic prose, historical narratives, first-person accounts, still photographs, life histories, fictionalized facts, and biographical and autobiographical materials, among others. Quantitative researchers use mathematical models, statistical tables, and graphs, and often write about their research in impersonal, third-person prose. (Denzin and Lincoln 1994, 6)

Between the late 1960s and the later decades of the twentieth century, qualitative research gained more stature in the social sciences. Denzin and Lincoln identified what they called the "postmodern turn" in the 1980s, which blurred boundaries between social sciences and humanities and produced experimental modes of scholarship and heightened self-reflexivity. Yet in the 2005 edition of their handbook, they described the "re-emergence" of "scientism" in the United States in the early years of the twenty-first century, promoted by the National Research Council's call for objective, rigorously controlled studies that employed causal models (Denzin and Lincoln 2005, 8). Advanced statistical techniques such as structural equation modeling (SEM), have become fashionable in the context of consumer studies. SEM enables researchers to test relationships between variables through a conceptual model, which may help to predict and understand consumer behavior. In recent years, the International Textile and Apparel Association's *Clothing and Textiles Research Journal*, which also publishes qualitative research, has included many articles using SEM with a focus on causality. Recently published are Han and Chung's (2014) study using SEM to model the "purchase intention" of organic cotton apparel and an article by Myers, Kwon, and Forsythe (2012), which uses SEM to model the influence of brand motivation on "Cause-Related Marketing."

The contemporary, transnational methodological landscape in fashion studies is complicated: just as there has been what might be identified as a "positivist turn"[3] in fashion-marketing-related research in the United States, fashion studies is taking off as an interdisciplinary, largely qualitative field internationally. More generally, a positivist turn is amplified by the availability of and access to "big data," which are even influencing the field of humanities (e.g., digital humanities). "Big data" are mined daily by fashion consulting companies, like StyleSage, who monitor and aggregate data from purchasing, inventory monitoring, and internet trolling. Proliferation of "big data" calls for more interpretive and critical methods—and a mixing of methods—in order to derive meaningful insights, "to connect the dots," and to triangulate.

Mixing methods requires attention to the philosophical traditions and assumptions that underpin methodologies. We argue that these traditions and

## Table 8.1 *Philosophical approaches to fashion scholarship*

|  | Positivist | Interpretive | Critical |
|---|---|---|---|
| Assumptions about reality (ontology) | An objective reality can be discovered | Reality is socially constructed (and hence there are multiple realities to be known) | Reality can/should be critiqued, created, and improved |
| Ideas about knowledge production, or ways of knowing (epistemology) | Researcher frames approach; often deductive (hypothesis derived from existing knowledge base, and then tested) | Researcher seeks knowledge inductively, allowing multiple perspectives to emerge from the process of discovery | Researcher/ designer strives to improve human conditions and shed light on those that have been inequitable in the past |
| Approach to knowledge production (how to learn what to do in terms of methods; meth-odology) | Scientific method used to test hypothesis; often (but not always) yields quantitative data and use of statistical methods | Typically (but not necessarily) involves qualitative methods: ethnographic, interviewing, archival research, etc. | Critical close readings of cultural texts; participatory design; political economic analysis; feminist, queer, or ethnic studies analyses; digital humanities |

assumptions are not pure, self-contained, nor static, but rather that they "leak" into one another and change over time. We present three philosophical approaches— positivist, interpretive, and critical—not as discrete categories but rather as "ideal types," to use sociologist Max Weber's concept (see Kim 2012). An ideal type is an analytical construct that allows a researcher to compare and contrast without reifying the walls between it and another ideal type. Table 8.1 suggests a way of thinking about the philosophical underpinnings of diverse methods, and how to mix them. This is a model adapted from Denzin and Lincoln (1994 and 2005) and, from our experience, has been particularly useful when sharing epistemologies with fashion and cultural studies students.

## Positivist "ideal type"

As suggested in Table 8.1, positivist formulations of knowledge production are based on the (at least implicit) assumption that there is an objective reality (i.e., there are "facts" or data) to be discovered through the use of the scientific method. Such deductive formulation (i.e., top-down logic) relies upon various empirical approaches (e.g., quantitative surveys, experimental laboratory methods) to test hypotheses derived from previous research, with the goal of building on the progress in the research knowledge base (i.e., what is "known"). The process begins with theory, which shapes "educated guesses" for the next steps in knowledge production. Typically, these hypotheses or educated guesses are tested using statistical methods. Generally, but not exclusively, quantitative methods are employed to provide the empirical bases for assertions. The validity of a deduction is supported by principles of statistical probability, methodological control, and some degree of separation between the researcher ("knower") and the phenomena studied ("known").

Positivist approaches to research dominated the social sciences in much of the twentieth century, but various social movements in the 1960s, in combination with more deeply rooted alternative approaches to knowledge production in the social sciences and humanities in the United States, led to a greater appreciation for the ways in which concepts such as gender, race, ethnicity, and sexuality (as well as class and age) shape and mold multiple constructions of reality. In other words, there is more than one way to know or be known.

Limitations of positivist approaches become evident when questions such as the following begin to surface: Who gets represented in the sampling to represent reality? Who is overlooked? How do "race," class, sexuality, age, and other identity issues preclude participation in a global economy and world? How does a researcher construct a narrative to explain quantitative results?

How does the positivist philosophical tradition apply to fashion studies? The answer to this question depends, in part, on the conceptualization of the field and the types of scholarship it includes. There is a large and transnational tradition, for example, of using quantitative approaches to model consumer fashion behavior using (often) advanced statistical methods. For example, who is likely to be a fashion innovator or leader, and how/why do various social-psychological variables shape consumers' tendencies to assume these roles? The *Clothing and Textiles Research Journal* publishes many studies along these lines, although it is also receptive to other philosophical and methodological approaches (e.g., historical, ethnographic, design research). Commonly, positivist fashion research aims to predict and explain consumer behavior, often using quantitative statistical methods.

## Interpretive "ideal type"

Interpretive approaches to inquiry highlight diverse, individual perceptions of reality, recognizing or assuming that there is no single, objective reality. Interpretive philosophical approaches strive to allow knowledge to surface from the "empirical materials" themselves. These materials might include interview transcripts, field notes, visual media, historical archives, actual clothes, photographs of street style or wardrobes, and so on. Working for the most part inductively (i.e., "bottom-up reasoning") and, in many cases using a grounded theory approach, interpretive fashion studies work from specific empirical materials, such as interview transcripts, field notes, archival materials, objects, and images, to formulate new theories or arguments. This approach allows for diverse constructions of reality to be incorporated into interpretations of "what is going on" or, in the case of historical research, what "has gone on" in the world of fashion. Some statistical methods, such as factor analysis and SEM modeling, have some interpretive qualities and may be used in inductive reasoning as they explore relationships among concepts, variables, and other information collected. A factor analysis helps researchers to find, visualize, and potentially model relationships within data. Factor analysis is particularly suited to "big data" and may reveal unexpected relationships among human behaviors.

## Critical "ideal type"

Critical philosophical approaches do not necessarily claim to be "objective" in perspective: Marxist, feminist, critical race, and queer theories highlight the inequalities associated with cultural and political histories, as well as the present, and there is a stated desire to foster social justice across the categories of class, race, gender, sexuality, and other subject positions. Critical perspectives highlight power issues and cut across disciplines. Questions such as the following emerge from a critical perspective in fashion studies: How does "fast fashion" affect the global environment and conditions for garment and retail workers around the world? Who benefits from fast fashion, and who gets hurt? How do diverse subject positions (e.g., gender, sexuality, ethnicity, class) intersect and alter the ways in which, or the extent to which, style-fashion-dress matter in everyday life? Along these lines, masculinities become a fascinating case study from a critical perspective: How and why do power relations within the complex category of masculinity and in interaction with femininity foster multiple approaches to style-fashion-dress?

# Fashioning masculinities: Ontological interpretations and multiple methods

In the remainder of this chapter, we use our multimethod study of US masculine fashions to illustrate interconnections between philosophical underpinnings and methodological approaches, highlighting the productive possibilities of mixing methods. For a variety of reasons, the study of masculine fashions presents some theoretical and methodological dilemmas from a philosophical point of view. Power relations abound within and beyond conceptualizations of masculinity:

- Hegemonic masculinity in the United States has roots in euro-modern philosophy, which has promulgated a kind of separation between the mind and the body (Connell 1995; Craig 2013). To the extent that style-fashion-dress represents a process of "minding appearances" (Kaiser 2001), or bridging mind and body, it presents a philosophical (and hence a methodological) challenge.

- Fashion still has a feminine connotation in contemporary cultural discourse. The fact that it has to be qualified with a gendered adjective (e.g., "men's fashion") suggests there is gender trouble.

- The concept of multiple or plural masculinities (Connell 1995) acknowledges that subject positions such as age/generation, ethnicity, sexuality, class, and place (e.g., rural, suburban, urban; region of the country) intersect and shape diverse constructions of masculinity, many of which are nonhegemonic. Previous qualitative research had reported greater interest in, or receptivity to, style-fashion-dress in the context of nonhegemonic masculinities (Kaiser, Freeman, and Chandler 1993; Rinallo 2007).

The fundamental assumption in our masculinities project is that of plural possibilities—that is, there is more than one masculine "reality"; therefore, we have left the upper-left box pertaining to positivist ontology in Table 8.2 blank. The interpretive ontological perspective meshes with the study's assumption that there are plural or multiple masculinities based not only on variations in style-fashion-dress, but also on the ways in which these variations result from complex intersectionalities with diverse subject positions such as age/generation, class, ethnicity, religion, nationality, place/space, and sexuality. The critical ontology contributes a power-related dimension to the study, highlighting the dynamics among diverse subject positions and how/why hegemonic masculinities may distance themselves from nonhegemonic masculinities, as well as femininities. And, conversely, a critical philosophical perspective leads to questioning how/why style-fashion-dress may be used as sites and practices of resistance to hegemonic masculinities.

One of the most fundamental ontological issues pertains to the relationship between the mind and the body, and the question of who gets to—or has the capacity to—make sense of "reality." In other words, whose minds and bodies become deployed in the process of producing ideas or knowledge? In the positivist model, with the assumption of an objective reality, there was also a Cartesian split between mind and body—in which the "knower" (presumably white, bourgeois male) became separate from the "known" (i.e., one's own body, others, the natural world) (see Grosz 1994; Kaiser 2001; Craig 2013). In this formulation, made evident by critical (e.g., feminist, critical race, Marxist) ontologies, not all minds and bodies were equal in the process of understanding, explaining, or predicting reality. Interpretive and, especially, critical philosophical traditions open up spaces for more voices, bodies, and ways of seeing, being, and becoming in the world. Further, we argue that multiple methods facilitate opportunities for many voices and perspectives in fashion studies research.

A basic disconnect in euro-modern thought frames hegemonic masculinity as being apart from the body and, especially, from any preoccupations with fashion (thinking "too much" about it or spending too much time "minding appearances"). Fashion, in this mindset, is the component in the trio of style-fashion-dress most associated with a variety of other "*f*" words: feminine, fickle, fun, frivolous, flâneur. These connotations with fashion, in addition to the implications of the bodily links to dress (see Eicher 2010 and in this book) and the thought involved in developing a personalized fashion statement (style), suggest the need for hegemonic masculinity to be constructed in such a way that *appearing* to spend *too* much time and mental energy on how to look and change with the times is suspect and stigmatized. And yet, there is likely to be some ambivalence and ambiguity fostered by the contradiction between wanting to look good or successful and not wanting to appear too engaged in thinking about such matters. Hegemonic masculinity is more complicated than it seems.

## Masculinities project

Our multiple-method research project began with a review of earlier research on style-fashion-dress in relation to gender (Kaiser, Freeman, and Chandler 1993), ethnicity (Kaiser et al. 2004), and sexuality (Freitas, Kaiser, and Hammidi 1996), and their intersectionalities (Freitas et al. 1997), and posed new questions. At the University of California, Davis, we began to conduct interviews with male consumers and professionals in the menswear industry. One goal of the project was to examine the degree to which there was correspondence between the production and consumption of menswear.

Our early attempts at soliciting research participants revealed that phrases such as "masculine fashion" or "fashioning masculinities" did not bring much success in response rate. As much as we wanted (and still want) fashion to be a more inclusive concept, we met a lot of resistance: "Why do you want to interview me?" "I don't do fashion." And so on. Our replies frequently went something like: "But you do wear clothes, and we would like to hear your thoughts." At this point, we began to switch the initial language to "clothing" (when talking about their own attire or appearance) or "menswear" (when talking about clothes on the market) in the initial stages of the interview.

The early stages of the research also involved a review of men's magazines that were proliferating at the time, as well as other media related to masculine style-fashion-dress. An overall survey of media representations revealed patterns that we then investigated in more depth. We conducted a critical discourse analysis of articles related to changes in the US National Basketball Association's (NBA's) uniform and off-court dress codes, as a case study of the regulation of players' masculinities in concert with their ethnic, age/generational, and class identities (Kaiser and McCullough 2010). We also analyzed proscriptive ("what not to wear") and prescriptive ("what to wear") articles in GQ, Details, and weekly Fairchild publications on menswear.

Ethnography was another method employed in 2007–8. Ethnography enabled us to focus on a community of men who attended the Burning Man Project, a festal gathering each summer in the desert of Nevada (Green 2008; Green and Kaiser 2011). The festival was a transformative space that enabled men to test out new styles in a public venue and push the boundaries of masculinity (Green and Kaiser 2011). Many of these men were (re)conceptualizing masculine style through experimentation and, to varying degrees, returned to their everyday lives with somewhat transformed styles.

The next stage of the project involved developing a US national survey, which we conducted online in spring 2008. The survey allowed us to fuse qualitative and quantitative approaches to evaluate our preliminary findings. We worked with an online research firm specializing in nationally balanced demographics to solicit participants. We had 1,952 men in the United States respond to the survey. The survey included attitudinal statements derived from the earlier qualitative interviews (i.e., direct or adapted comments), a number of open-ended questions about personal style, suggestions for menswear manufacturers to meet consumers' needs, and identity issues. With respect to the latter, we intentionally allowed respondents to use their own terminology to describe gender, sexuality, and ethnicity. While this made coding and the analysis of the interview material very time consuming, we did not want to impose labels (subject positions) on individuals who did not relate to binary gender or sexual subject positions, for example, or to specific ethnic labels. We also asked respondents to self-classify as rural, suburban, or urban (we also asked for zip code, but were especially interested in their own "place/space" identities). We included an open-ended component to the survey, in which participants responded to a few photographs of men in everyday style and were asked to "describe what you see" (DWYS) in thirty seconds, a method developed by Janet Hethorn at the University of Delaware (see Kaiser, Hethorn, and Freitas 2007). The use of this visual method revealed men's perceptions of other men's fashion. By combining different methods within the survey, we were able to tease apart men's perspectives about how they would like to appear, and their impressions of other men's fashion. Ultimately, these methods were developed from our research questions: How do men think about, interpret, and express fashion and multiple masculinities?

We used both quantitative and qualitative approaches in our initial analysis of the survey. We began by examining the data demographically; we followed up with a factor analysis, which is a statistical procedure that finds relationships, or intercorrelations, among survey responses. This method is particularly well suited to attitudinal, or Likert scale, style questionnaires. Our factor analysis revealed larger patterns within responses and clustered attitudinal statements into "factors," which could then be explored via demographics. We coded open-ended responses in order to distinguish themes. Throughout this process, new questions arose.

Table 8.2 *Fashioning masculinities project at UC Davis*

| | Positivist | Interpretive | Critical |
|---|---|---|---|
| Assumptions about reality (ontology) | | Masculinities as plural realities, intersecting with ethnicity, age, sexuality, etc. | Focus on gendered and other power relations; how hegemonic masculinity is constructed in US culture and how diverse masculinities resist that construction |
| Ideas about knowledge production, or ways of knowing (epistemology) | Some implicit hypotheses regarding masculinities in relation to ethnicity and sexuality, based on earlier research | Open to new understandings of fashioned masculinities, given the dearth of literature in the area; grounded theory approach using both qualitative and quantitative "empirical materials" | Decipher hegemonic masculinity and interrogate intersecting power relations within and across diverse masculinities |
| Approach to knowledge production (how to learn what to do in terms of methods; methodology) | Quantitative and qualitative survey, based on in-depth interviews and critical discourse analysis (1,952 US men) | In-depth interviews before and after the survey in the box to the left; critical discourse analysis in the box to the right | Critical discourse analysis (e.g., men's fashion magazines); visual ethnography |

These questions have been followed up through further qualitative research (primarily interviews; Bernstein and Kaiser 2013) and critical discourse analysis of media (Kaiser and McCullough 2010). In mixing methods, we also mixed philosophical perspectives.

Table 8.2 represents an overview of the overall project that began with qualitative methods and later included quantitative approaches. Hence, the research trajectory has been iterative, melding—and working across—ontologies, epistemologies, and methodologies. In the process, the very boundaries separating the "ideal types" constructed in Table 8.1 become blurred and permeable. There was free movement between inductive and deductive, qualitative and quantitative, theory and practice, and other modes of thinking, studying, and analyzing. Intersections, rather than boundaries, have prevailed.

# Interpreting results from multiple methods in the masculinities project

In this section of the paper, we outline how our research findings intersect with ontological, epistemological, and methodological approaches and are shaped by methods that harken from positivist, critical, and interpretive philosophies.

The first author, in collaboration with many graduate students, has researched the intersections among gender, ethnicity, and sexuality for the past 20 years. Using a combination of critical (e.g., feminist) and interpretive epistemologies, a picture began to emerge from these qualitative studies: it was predominately white, straight men who tended to express the least interest in fashion, although they (as with all men) often had a lot to say about their clothes. With this project's larger focus on masculinities and with the available funding from the National Textile Center, this seemed to be the time to examine, with depth and breadth, the intersectionalities among gender, sexuality, race, ethnicity, and other subject positions. Hence, while there was never a positivist assumption of a single or objective reality about men and fashion, some of the epistemologies commonly (but not necessarily) associated with positivism (e.g., derivation of hypothesis from existing knowledge, quantitative data, statistical methods) became part of the research design, most directly in the form of our survey. Clearly, earlier research contributed to the deduction of "educated guesses" or hypotheses regarding whiteness and heterosexuality as major contributors to hegemonic masculinity. So, our epistemological approach was not strictly interpretive or inductive. Processes of induction and deduction alternated and intermingled. Mixing methods encourages this sort of oscillation.

And, although the project did draw heavily on feminist, queer, critical race, and cultural studies epistemologies, it was not strictly critical in the "ideal type" sense.

Rather, as the project played out, we moved fluidly and iteratively across the three ideal types in Tables 8.1 and 8.2. Despite the large sample size of the survey, the inclusion of quantitative data, and the use of statistical analysis, there was never a positivist insistence on "hard data" to demonstrate the "truth" about masculine fashion, due to the multiple, intersecting subject positions and perceptions of reality (see Denzin and Lincoln 2005).

Examining intersectionalities clearly requires interpretive and critical epistemologies; yet some statistical techniques associated with more positivist epistemologies add to this examination. For example, we did an exploratory factor analysis of the forty-two attitudinal statements included in the survey (Green and Kaiser 2009) as a means to explore latent, yet fundamental, patterns in men's attitudes and relationships to fashion. Exploratory factor analysis is a first step in developing a set of variables: in our case, ways to measure men's attitudes around and engagement with fashion. Often, exploratory factor analysis will result in the identification of variables (Creekmore 1966) and the development of a scale, such as "clothing interest" (Gurel and Gurel 1979), "fashion involvement" (Tigert, Ring and King 1976), or preference for "anti-fashion" (Yu 2011). In our study, interrelationships among certain attitudinal statements emerged and clustered men's responses into three salient, though not mutually exclusive, "factors": men interested in fashion, men wishing to remain unmarked, and men willing to engage in "risky" fashion behavior. Through further analysis we examined interrelationships between factors and explored differences in factor groups based on intersecting subject positions. In another example, we looked for "statistical significance" according to these subject positions, and found some striking ones along the lines of age/generation, ethnicity, sexuality, and place, in ways that reinforced previous and ongoing qualitative research (see Kaiser 2012). Yet, some statistically significant "interaction effects" between subject positions such as sexuality (gay, bisexual, straight) and place (rural, suburban, urban), for example, tell different, unexpected stories: as our survey showed, gay men living in rural areas expressed the highest level of interest in fashion, and bisexual, urban men expressed the highest level of concern with being "unmarked" (or fitting in). The qualitative descriptions of their styles shed meaningful light on these findings, which fueled a new line of qualitative inquiry focused on sexuality and small-town fashion (Bernstein and Kaiser 2013).

Coming into this project, our research group often discussed Peggy Phelan's (1993) elaboration of what it means to be "unmarked," that is, to maintain hegemonic power by avoiding a certain kind of cultural visibility (standing out too much through style-fashion-dress) that "marks" an individual in an objectifying way. The factor analysis revealed a substantial group of men's devotion to appearing "unmarked"—a finding that reinforced discoveries in a discourse analysis of fashion advice to men in newspapers and magazines, conducted by Ryan Looysen (2008), another member of our research team. Hegemonic masculine subjectivity safely resides in this formulation in the space between the two marked spaces of otherness—that is the "danger zones" of caring too little or caring too much about appearance (see Rinallo 2007). The "safety zone" is in-between, moderate, mediated, and unmarked. Protected by the hegemonic mind-body split, there is seemingly little danger of the masculine subject becoming turned into an object/other, according to this ontology. Or is there? Masculinity, after all, is a fragile construction of identity: one that becomes defined hegemonically by that which it is *not* (Freitas et al. 1997). The avoidance of feminine symbols, for example, becomes a strategy to remain in the "safe zone" of hegemonic masculinity. The cultural discourse on metrosexuality bridges sexuality and place. Coined as a term by journalist Mark Simpson 20 years ago, the concept makes an explicit link between urban masculinity and ambiguous sexuality. A metrosexual, in cultural discourse, is a man who leans toward the direction of "marking" himself as "caring too much" about his style-fashion-dress (Simpson 2014).

Building on Looysen's (2008) aforementioned research, critical discourse analysis was the method employed to analyze metrosexuality as a cultural construction: one that was not neutral, but rather that points to the cultural anxieties and ambivalences associated with masculinity. As one example, we analyzed an industry-sponsored website we found while working on putting together our interview and survey protocols. The website was entitled "Say no to metro" and was dedicated to assuring consumers that their masculinity was safe if they wore the company's pants. This "just say no" (perhaps at least partially tongue in cheek) approach to masculinity harkens back to the hegemonic ontology of remaining "unmarked" (and straight?) and as defining masculinity by what it is *not*. This approach to masculinity has more than a 200-year euro-modern history (see Breward 1999), but it is only one trajectory of masculinity.

As part of our multimethod approach, we derived attitudinal statements from cultural discourses, as well as interviews with men in the early years of this project. For example, we asked approximately fifty middle-aged men, of various ethnic, and mostly middle-class, backgrounds, what kind of new directions they would like to see in the menswear industry. Frequently, across ethnicities, the suggestions they had for clothing manufacturers pointed to the need to navigate issues of age and fashion carefully and strategically. Following are some sample quotes from these interviews:

Make clothes that are in between what the young people wear and the old styles. . . . Have advertising that depicts men in that age bracket. (57, white from the United States)

More emphasis on comfort and style rather than trying to sell sexuality. I think men my age would be more inclined to purchase a broader variety of clothes if there were more ad campaigns showing men my age in the clothes. (50, Middle Eastern American)

I would say try not to have young models. Try to actually have models that wear that style of clothing. (52, Mexican American)

Needs to be professional but not a 3-piece suit, needs character that's more interesting than simply "urban" materials. (52, white)[4]

In addition to wanting to be represented age-wise, the respondents frequently pointed to the importance of negotiating carefully between looking good and up-to-date, but not standing out too much by trying too hard to look young or to be trendy or brand-conscious.

In the survey, attitudinal statements (with which the respondents could agree or disagree on a five-point scale) were analyzed statistically to see the extent to which they correlated with one another, and through an exploratory factor analysis, we identified some groups that could be used for further analysis to evaluate differences and similarities among the respondents. The names of the factors were inductively derived, based on the themes identified in the statements. Following are the top two factors and the attitudinal statements most closely associated with them:

*Factor One: Interest in style-fashion-dress*
"I like to feel attractive in my clothing."
"I like shopping for clothes."
"There should be more fashion advertisements in non-fashion magazines."
"I wish there were more choices in menswear."
"I talk about clothes with my friends."

*Factor Two: Desire to be "unmarked"*
"I do not want my clothes to attract attention to me."
"I do not think about how my masculinity is perceived based on how I dress."
"I prefer clothes that are easy to mix and match."[5]

As Figures 8.1 and 8.2 illustrate, the majority of the men ranked "medium" on each factor; most chose the "in between" option. Nearly one quarter ranked "low" on the "interest" factor, whereas a much smaller minority ranked "low" on the "unmarked" factor. About 20 percent ranked "high" on the "interest" factor, whereas about one third ranked "high" on the "unmarked" factor.

Further statistical analysis sought to look at variations among the men according to subject positions. The respondents varied significantly as a function of age/generation, ethnicity, place, and sexuality in their responses to the first factor. The men who identified as gay expressed the most interest in style-fashion-dress, followed by bisexual and then straight men. Urban men expressed the most interest, followed by suburban and then rural men. African American men expressed the most interest, and white men the least. The younger the men, the higher the degree of interest they expressed in style-fashion-dress.

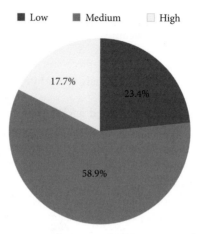

**FIGURE 8.1** High, medium, and low scores on Factor 1, "interest" in style-fashion-dress.

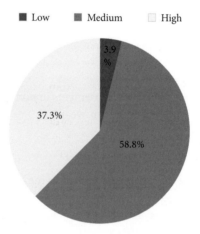

**FIGURE 8.2** High, medium, and low scores on Factor 2, desire to be "unmarked."

Figure 8.3 graphically depicts a trend across six age groups: the younger the man, the more likely it is for him to score high on factor one, "interest in style-fashion-dress." Interest appears to diminish with older men, as illustrated by the low scoring men. Of course, since this is a snapshot survey, it is impossible to know how much of the difference can be attributed to the aging process per se, and how much is based on shifting cultural attitudes toward men's style-fashion-dress over time. When we reach the limitation of one method, another method dovetails and therefore enables researchers to continue a line of inquiry. In our research, we augmented our survey findings with information from qualitative interviews and the cultural discourse analysis. For example, from an industry perspective, there is a desire to capture new, younger markets while also navigating the brand

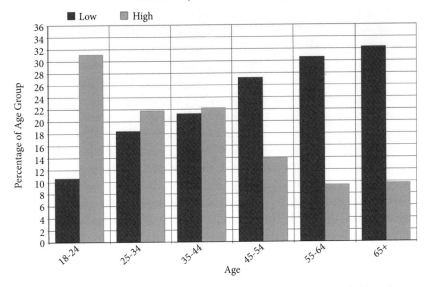

FIGURE 8.3 Age/generational variations in Factor 1, "interest" in style-fashion-dress.

loyalty built up in middle-aged and older customers. There is some evidence of generational challenges. Since the 1980s, menswear companies have marketed aggressively to younger male consumers, yet they do not want to alienate their older and more established market bases, who have helped to build their businesses. One menswear company executive summed up this challenge cogently:

> When we do our advertising, we will still check it against the older consumer to make sure we're not turning him off, but develop our strategy more so that it gets the younger consumer. It's really both; we don't want to do anything that would turn him off from the brand.

Another (of many) qualitative examples of the generation gap between younger and older adult males emerges from a critical analysis of the cultural discourse surrounding the NBA's 2005 dress codes for players on and off the court. The intersectionalities across subject positions were all over the place in the online discourse of sports journalists and followers. The age difference between the NBA Commissioner David Stern (and most box ticket holders) and the players was a factor, but undoubtedly age intersected in complicated ways with issues of race and ethnicity, class, and other subject positions (Kaiser and McCullough 2010). Navigating popular culture in ways that engages a younger audience or fan base and does not "turn off" older and wealthier consumers becomes a challenge that, in this case, was addressed through the regulation of styles popularized by young African American players, who had adopted personal styles adapted from hip-hop culture (e.g., longer shorts, chain necklaces, braided hairstyles).

Yet questions still remain about age and generational subject positions (*when* individuals are not only in their minds and bodies, but also in their locations in time and fashion history). Ultimately, methods that embrace intersectionalities across time are needed: longitudinal studies of cultural discourse, preferably combined with individuals' orientations toward style-fashion-dress.

Within and beyond age/generational considerations in the study of multiple masculinities, questions of intersectionalities prevail. The theme (in both the qualitative and quantitative data) was to strike a balance to be "somewhere in between" perceived extremes (summed up quantitatively in Figure 8.1). Bridging methods resulted in quantitative and qualitative data, all supporting the theme of mediating between "this" and "that," avoiding going "too far" in the direction of fashion, and striking a middle ground in responses to questions. The theme of striking a balance to be "somewhere in between" with respect to the somewhat contradictory world of men's fashion carried through, as well, in the visual ethnography methodology. The second author's ethnographic research at the Burning Man Festival in Nevada employed a range of methods, including in-depth interviews at and after Burning Man, wardrobe studies and closet interviews[6] (see also Woodward 2007 and in this book; Green, Lewis, and Jirousek 2013), observations, documentary ethnography, and film production. In addition to her MS thesis, she produced a documentary film, titled *Somewhere in Between* (Green 2008), to capture the idea of being in an ambiguous place/space and to be navigating gender and sexual boundaries in an experimental way through style-fashion-dress.

This ethnographic documentary project also fed into the development of the survey questionnaire. Insights from interviews played a large role in deciding to make subject positions such as gender and sexuality open-ended on the survey.[7] Even in the case of gender (which the research firm targeting the demographic mix had already narrowed to "men"), there was space for ambiguity, and we were happy that we had allowed this space for gender identity to emerge from the respondents' own words.

# Ontological, epistemological, and methodological intersections/conclusions

The process of mixing methods is a time-consuming, and perhaps messy, practice. Qualitative data, in general, introduce "noise" to what might otherwise be a deceptively clear or singular view of reality. Working qualitative data into a large quantitative survey (and as the foundation for the development of this same survey) sheds light on the quantitative findings; however, it took a great deal of time and energy to code and interpret the qualitative data, to compare what different methods were telling us, and to meld multiple projects over time. It would have been very difficult to mix methods in this way without the funding by the National Textile Center. In retrospect, perhaps we could have developed more efficient strategies for incorporating qualitative data into the quantitative survey, but if we were to do this again, we would still mix the two methods.

The process of navigating and negotiating movements across the three ideal types of philosophical approaches (positivist, interpretive, critical) was perhaps the most instructive part of the multiple masculinities project. Reflecting back, the boundaries between one ideal type and another were very fluid, and in the everyday practice of mixing quantitative and qualitative methods, we do not believe there was a conscious concern about thinking deductively versus inductively. Rather, it was a very iterative process. In many ways, an interpretive, grounded theory approach became a space in between: a way of melding quantitative data with a critical perspective, but not only inductively.

The field of fashion studies inhabits the intersection of many disciplines: anthropology, sociology, social psychology, ecology, economics, fiber/polymer/ nano science, history, psychology, art/design, cultural studies, and many more. It is also an area of study fraught with contradictions, complex power relations, and senses of scale (local and global, individual and collective, etc.). Any research project within the realm of fashion studies will benefit from a multimethod approach. This requires a certain amount of openness and willingness on the part of fashion studies scholars to push our own disciplinary boundaries and assumptions. As a field, we must continue to reach out to scholars in our field and beyond who may offer fresh perspectives from different backgrounds. Collaboration is key, as it is unreasonable to expect that any one of us is simultaneously an expert ethnographer, statistician, fiber chemist, documentary filmmaker, and so on. Certainly we should endeavor to learn different means of gathering information (resulting in different kinds of data). Most importantly, we must acknowledge both limitations and potential of respective methods and what these methods might achieve in conversation with one another.

The masculinities project was one of collaboration and cross-disciplinary fertilization. Qualitative methods—for example, ethnography, discourse analysis, interviews—fueled a quantitative survey (with qualitative dimensions). The complexity of multiple masculinities through style-fashion-dress cries for multimethod practices and extended analysis and interpretation. Our investigation into diverse masculine appearance styles across (and informed by) intersecting subject positions is but one example of how the messy process of mixing methods produces fruitful and nuanced, albeit complicated, findings. This research project is part of a continual quest to make fashion studies a more inclusive field of theories, practices, and identities.

# Notes

1   Our research was part of a larger national, multiyear, and multimethod project on masculinities—involving five US universities (Auburn University; University of California, Davis; University of Delaware; Berry College; Cornell University). We are

indebted to the faculty and numerous graduate students and other colleagues who have collaborated with us in various ways on this project over the last decade.

2  The concept of style-fashion-dress highlights the ontological parts and wholes associated with the three terms. It highlights the interplay among the terms and acknowledges the limits of each (Tulloch 2010; Kaiser 2012). It is especially useful in an analysis of multiple masculinities, due to the challenges associated with terminology (e.g., resistance of some men in the study to the word "fashion").

3  In 2009, the Philosophical Mission Committee of the International Textiles and Apparel Association (ITAA) sponsored a special topic session on "Mixing methods, missing methods" at the annual meeting in Bellevue, Washington. Part of the discussion revolved around a recent "positivist turn" in dominant research models in the organization and the journal (*Clothing and Textiles Research Journal*).

4  These quotes are derived from a series of electronic interviews; the respondents were university students' fathers or other male family members or friends in their 40s or 50s, primarily in California. The interviews were conducted in April of 2007.

5  These attitudinal statements were part of the larger online survey, conducted over a three-day period, May 29, 2008 through May 31, 2008. We provided these statements to the respondents, and they replied quantitatively (on a one- to five-point scale) on the basis of their level of agreement with each statement.

6  Not unlike photo elicitation, closet interviews are a qualitative interview method developed by Green (see Green, Lewis, and Jirousek 2013). This method relies on the assumption that clothing objects and associated material adornments hold meaning and memory and serve as mnemonic devices (Freitas et al. 1997). The research participant goes through their closet and discusses items of significance, resulting in a kind of oral history of the closet (and, by direct association, the closet's curator). The "wardrobe ethnography" discussed by Woodward in this book, is a similar methodology.

7  For many years, research teams working with Kaiser had insisted on making racial and ethnic subject positions open-ended, drawing on critical and interpretive ontologies and epistemologies, so as to leave space for respondents to articulate their own identities.

# References

Bernstein, Sara T., and Susan B. Kaiser. 2013. "Fashion Out of Place: Experiencing Fashion in a Small American Town." *Critical Studies in Fashion and Beauty* 4 (1–2): 43–70.

Breward, Christopher. 1999. *The Hidden Consumer: Masculinities, Fashion and City Life, 1860-1914*. Manchester, UK: Manchester University Press.

Connell, R. W. 1995. *Masculinities*. Cambridge, UK: Polity Press.

Craig, Maxine. 2013. *Sorry I Don't Dance: Why Men Refuse to Move*. Oxford, UK: Oxford University Press.

Creekmore, Anna M. 1966. *Methods of Measuring Clothing Variables*. Lansing, MI: Michigan State University Agricultural Experiment Station.

Denzin, Norman K. 2006. *Sociological Methods: A Sourcebook*. New Brunswick, NJ: Aldine Transaction Publishers.

Denzin, Norman K., and Yvonna S. Lincoln. 1994. "Introduction: Entering the Field of Qualitative Research." In *Handbook of Qualitative Research*, edited by Norman K. Denzin and Yvonna S. Lincoln, 1–17. Thousand Oaks, CA: Sage Publications, Inc.

Denzin, Norman K., and Yvonna S. Lincoln. 2005. "Introduction: The Discipline and Practice of Qualitative Research." In *Handbook of Qualitative Research*, edited by Norman K. Denzin and Yvonna S. Lincoln, 1–32. Thousand Oaks, CA: Sage Publications, Inc.

Eicher, Joanne B. 2010. "Introduction to Global Perspectives." In *Encyclopedia of World Dress and Fashion. Volume 10. Global Perspectives*, edited by Joanne B. Eicher, 3–10. Oxford: Oxford University Press.

Freitas, Anthony J., Susan B. Kaiser, and Tania Hammidi. 1996. "Communities, Commodities, Cultural Space, and Style." In *Gays, Lesbians, and Consumer Behavior: Theory, Practice, and Research Issues in Marketing*, edited by Daniel L. Wardlow, 83–107. New York: The Haworth Press.

Freitas, Anthony J., Susan B. Kaiser, Joan Chandler, Carol Hall, Jung-Won Kim, and Tania Hammidi. 1997. "Appearance Management as Border Construction: Least Favorite Clothing, Group Distancing, and Identity . . . Not!" *Sociological Inquiry* 67 (3): 323–35.

Frye, Marilyn. 1996. "The Possibility of Feminist Theory." In *Women, Knowledge, and Reality: Explorations in Feminist Philosophy*, edited by Ann Garry and Marilyn Pearsall, 34–47. New York and London: Routledge.

Green, Denise N. 2008. *Somewhere in Between* (29-minute documentary film). http://www.imdb.com/video/wab/vi3219849753.

Green, Denise N., and Susan B. Kaiser. 2009. "Men's Reflection on Appearance Styles and Masculinity." Annual Proceedings of the International Textile and Apparel Association #66, Social-Psychology Track: 10–12.

Green, Denise N., and Susan B. Kaiser. 2011. "From Ephemeral to Everyday Costuming: Negotiations in Masculine Identities at the Burning Man Project." *Dress* 37: 1–22.

Green, Denise N., Van Dyk Lewis, and Charlotte Jirousek. 2013. "Fashion Cultures in a Small Town: An Analysis of Fashion- and Place-Making." *Critical Studies in Fashion and Beauty* 4 (1): 71–106.

Grosz, Elizabeth. 1994. *Volatile Bodies: Toward a Corporeal Feminism*. Sydney, Australia: Allen & Unwin.

Gurel, Lois M. and Lee Gurel. 1979. "Clothing Interest: Conceptualization and Measurement." *Home Economics Research Journal* 7 (5): 274–82.

Han, Tae-Im and Jae-Eun Chung. 2014. "Korean Consumers; Motivations and Perceived Risks Toward the Purchase of Organic Cotton Apparel." *Clothing and Textiles Research Journal* 32 (4): 235–50.

Kaiser, Susan B. 2001. "Minding Appearances: Style, Truth, and Subjectivity." In *Body Dressing*, edited by Joanne Entwistle and Elizabeth Wilson, 79–102. Oxford: Berg.

Kaiser, Susan B. 2012. *Fashion and Cultural Studies*. London: Berg.

Kaiser, Susan B., and Sarah Rebolloso McCullough. 2010. "Entangling the Fashion Subject through the African Diaspora." *Fashion Theory* 14 (3): 361–86.

Kaiser, Susan B., Carla Freeman, and Joan L. Chandler. 1993. "Favorite Clothes and Gendered Subjectivities: Multiple Readings." *Studies in Symbolic Interaction* 15: 27–50.

Kaiser, Susan B., Janet Hethorn, and Anthony Freitas. 2007. "Masculinities in Motion: Beyond the Fashion-versus-Uniformity Binary." In *Uniform in Bewegung. Zum Prozess der Uniformierung von Körper und Kleidung*, edited by Gabriele Mentges, Dagmar Neuland-Kitzerow, and Birgit Richard, 189–206. Münster: Waxmann.

Kaiser, Susan B., Leslie Rabine, Carol Hall, and Karyl Ketchum. 2004. "Beyond Binaries: Respecting the Improvisation in African-American Style." In *Black Style*, edited by Carol Tulloch, 48–67. London: Victoria and Albert Museum.

Kawamura, Yuniya. 2011. *Doing Research in Fashion and Dress: An Introduction to Qualitative Methods*. Oxford and New York: Berg.

Kim, Sung Ho. 2012. "Max Weber." *Stanford Encyclopedia of Philosophy*, accessed November 17, 2014, http://plato.stanford.edu/entries/weber/#IdeTyp.

Looysen, Ryan. 2008. *Unmarked Men: Anxiously Navigating Hegemonic Masculinities*. MS Thesis, Davis: University of California.

Myers, Beth, Wi-suk Kwon, and Sandra Forsythe. 2012. "Creating Effective Cause-Related Marketing Campaigns: The Role of Cause-Brand Fit, Campaign News Source, and Perceived Motivations." *Clothing and Textiles Research Journal* 30 (3): 167–82.

Phelan, Peggy. 1993. *Unmarked: The Politics of Performance*. London: Routledge.

Rinallo, Diego. 2007. "Metro/Fashion/Tribes of Men: Negotiating the Boundaries of Men's Legitimate Consumption." In *Consumer Tribes*, edited by Bernard Cova, Robert Kozinets, and Avi Shankar, 76–92. London: Butterworth-Heinneman.

Simpson, Mark. 2014. *Here Come the Mirror Men: Why the Future is Metrosexual [1994]*, accessed August 17, 2014, http://www.marksimpson.com/here-come-the-mirror-men/.

Tigert, Douglas J., Laurence J. Ring, and Charles W. King. 1976. "Fashion Involvement and Buying Behavior: A Methodological Study." *Advances in Consumer Research* 3: 46–52.

Tulloch, Carol. 2010. "Style-Fashion-Dress: From Black to Post-black." *Fashion Theory* 14 (3): 361–86.

Yu, Hong. 2011. "Profiling Chinese Fashion Shoppers in Bejing: Mall Activities, Shopping Outcome, and Demographics." *Journal of Global Fashion Marketing: Bridging Fashion and Marketing* 2 (1): 11–19.

# 9 ACTION! OR, EXPLORING DIFFRACTIVE METHODS FOR FASHION RESEARCH

## Otto von Busch

In the design and scholarship of fashion we deal with objects, processes, and values that are often contradictory and in conflict. An item of dress, for example, a military jacket worn on the street, may simultaneously signal obedience or rebellion, patriotism or militarism, elegance or poverty, all depending on the wearer, viewer, time, and context. As fashion theorist Susan Kaiser argues, fashion exists in a certain time and space, where "the process of deciphering and expressing a sense of *who* we are (becoming) happens in tandem with deciphering and expressing *when* and *where* we are" (Kaiser 2012, 1). In order to tackle these complex lines of interpretation and negotiation, Kaiser proposes that studying fashion is a both/ and, rather than either/or, activity: "Fashion thrives on contradiction (conflicting truth claims) and ambivalence (conflicting emotions): both/and ways of knowing and feeling" (Kaiser 2012, 2).

These conflicts and contradictions are not merely happening on the surface of things, but as most of us know, fashion can affect us on a deeper level. While it allows for a multiplicity of meanings and interpretations, fashion cuts through emotional and social life: it frames and defines, includes and excludes, produces losers and winners, affects self-esteem and social standing. Cultural studies scholar Raymond Williams makes the meaning of commodities explicit stating that "you do not only buy an object; you buy social respect, discrimination, health, beauty, success, power to control the environment" (Williams 1980, 188). If fashion is considered a form of social play (Kaiser 2012, 42), it is a violent playground, where we play for real. We play for power.

Further, employing a perspective of political realism reveals that at its core, fashion is a conflict. As a fashion design and theory educator, I am interested in expanding the roles of designers and researchers by using design agency to manifest conflicting issues in fashion. Sparked by the political rhetoric surrounding fashion—specifically the idea of a "democratization of fashion" circulating in marketing and media around the rise of fashion blogs and fast fashion to celebrate an apparent, new accessibility of fashion "for all"—I offer in this chapter a discussion of political theories and methodological practices that can be used to examine fashion as a site of conflict.

One way to open this site for examination is to use Donna Haraway's method of diffraction, as it can offer a much richer perspective than mere "reflection." Whereas reflection only displaces the same, diffraction bends and impedes perspectives from multiple angles, forcing contextual and situated considerations into the act of observation. Drawing on examples from my own teaching and practice at Konstfack University of Arts, the Museum of Contemporary Craft, and Parsons School of Design, The New School, I discuss how the use of practice-based interventions, diffraction, and provotypes can be tools to actualize new capacities in the field of fashion and to build platforms for discussion and for experiencing its contradictions and interferences.

## The realpolitik of fashion

Fashion has been historically conceived as a metaphor for modernity and as a sign of "civilization" and social progress (see Simmel 2004). A similar stance is taken by American scientist Herbert Simon, who argues that design devises courses of action aimed at changing existing situations into *preferred* ones (Simon 1996). Framing design as an experiment into what *ought to be*, it draws a plan for future ideal situations, improvements, and betterments. Such a position resonates well with an "idealist" perspective in political science. According to the idealists, politics is an art of the possible, where human agency is seen in a hopeful manner, where we can shape situations with our own ideas and often with lofty ambitions. This approach echoes throughout history in abstract concepts such as "liberty, equality, brotherhood" or today's "human rights." These concepts are utilized in the context of fashion marketing, when fast fashion is promoted as a form of "democratic" fashion or a fashion "made for all," as the UNIQLO ads spell out. Even if such "democratization" is critiqued on grounds of ecological, social, or economic sustainability (cf. Thomas 2007; Siegle 2011), the solution from design is normally to draw new plans for yet another hopeful situation of *what ought to be*, for example, various forms of eco-fashion (cf. Fletcher 2008; Brown 2010).

The new wave of "eco-design" is a noble endeavor that needs praise and support, for it rings with an optimism and belief in human betterment. For the idealist, human societies can come to cooperate with the help of reason. Politics is a field of visionary imagination and negotiations toward a better and more harmonious world, with rational dialogues between ideologies and values. The idealists emphasize that universal principles can be understood and translated into norms, manifested in institutions such as the United Nations and ideals such as a belief in the incorruptibility of international law and tribunals. In the eyes of an idealist, war and violence are simply a breakdown of rational and nonviolent means of communication (cf. Guzzini 1998, 17ff).

The main opposing stance to the idealist is that of the "realist," and this perspective is less optimistic. Stemming from the works of political thinkers such as Machiavelli and Hobbes, rather than tainting the view with how a *thing ought to be,* the realist wants to assess a situation *as it is,* without overt emotional involvement or hope, and to see man as practical and pragmatic, fighting for survival and power (cf. Morgenthau 1948/2006). For realists, humans and societies are driven by desire and fear more than by reason, and thus when it comes to politics man is not to be seen as seeking harmony, but instead as seeking power. Power needs not be attained by force, but a realist may leave all options open to attain his or her goals, or in the words popularized by Malcolm X, "by any means necessary" (X 1992).

In the world of realist politics, or what German chancellor Otto von Bismarck called realpolitik, interhuman relations are based primarily on the execution of power with the aim of domination, rather than by explicit ideological notions or moral or ethical premises. As in the writings of Hobbes, Bismarck's realpolitik is a perspective and a mode of action in a world where man is by nature hostile and cruel, rather than cooperative and kind, and where there is no progress, no idealistic, harmonious, or peaceful future. As Robert Berki (1981) argues, realism presupposes reality and the constraints of necessity, whereas idealism puts the emphasis on human freedom's transgression of such boundaries through imagination and reason. But as political philosopher Raymond Geuss emphasizes, "Politics is a matter of human, not merely mechanical, interaction between individuals, institutions, or groups," and these humans are "weak, easily distracted, deeply conflicted, and confused" (Geuss 2008, 1f).

As Bourdieu famously argues, new styles and distinctions continually emerge to upset the dominant order, but also these new expressions have their elites and their inner social hierarchies, essentially reproducing the same process of conflict (Bourdieu 1984). If we don a realist perspective, fashion is not primarily a means to achieve peaceful human togetherness. Human agents do not choose fashion based on reason, or for communication toward a state of social harmony. Instead, a realpolitik of fashion would prioritize the perspective of dress as a tool for social domination. Georg Simmel came close to this perspective, as he emphasized conflict as one of the main driving forces in the formation and expression of social groups (Simmel 1971), but a realist perspective may further highlight the hostilities and social asymmetries that the fashion system creates. The realpolitik of fashion is a weaponized social arena: it is a tool for the bouncer to deny someone entry to a club, or the bully's excuse to debase a victim. It may be a phenomenon driven by desire and pleasure, but even more a realm ruled by fear and anxiety. From a realist perspective, fashion, *as it really is,* is a weapon in nature's beauty contest, in a world that is cold, cruel, and violent.

## Fashion paradoxes

Returning to Kaiser's initial suggestion, to see fashion as a both/and rather than either/or activity opens the subject of fashion to a complex field of forces, which may be contradictory and paradoxical. It is our perspective and priorities that may tilt the subject in one way or another. Even if we do not agree that fashion is predominantly a violent practice, we could don the realist perspective that the ambiguities of fashion are a fertile ground for antagonism and conflict. Not only is this a conflict between political perspectives, as between the realist and idealist camps, of fashion as a lustful play of communication or a violent game of domination, but the conflict also exists within humans, as Geuss suggests above. Conflict is the basis for inter-human relations, and as Plato argues in his *Republic*, it is a conflict harbored both in the divided minds of individuals as well as a conflict in the divided polity or city (Hampshire 2000, 3).

But with this conflict, fashion exposes a set of paradoxes: contradictory situations that may still be true. One such example is that fashion is a phenomenon that is celebrating difference, while it is based on imitation and conformity (cf. Simmel 1971). To flourish, fashion needs autonomous individuals with the possibility of some form of social or symbolic mobility, yet it enacts this freedom through copying others. The paradox may be articulated as "the more free we are, the more we imitate each other."

Another conflict or paradox of the way in which fashion simultaneously attracts and repels, reproduces and destroys: it is simultaneously inclusive and exclusive. This happens both at a level of desire production, through sexual attraction and selection, and it also happens at the social price of banishment, ostracism, and violent selection. Not too unlike the peacock with its tail: the tail is both a signal of attraction, but it also has a natural price as being a cumbersome appendix in flight from predators. It may even be this conflict of evolutionary traits, between sexual and natural selection, that is the foundation of aesthetic practices, as Elizabeth Grosz (2008) has highlighted: so that the more engaged we are in the aesthetic struggle of fashion, the more we become victims of its principles of selection.

The contradiction and paradoxes above expose some of the underlying conflicts in fashion. In accordance with Kaiser, these forces of the social may not best be exposed as either/or dichotomies, but rather within a framework of both/

and. Acknowledging the complex field of fashion as a series of social, cultural, and situated practices, my own practice has been concerned with the aim of producing agency and constructive proposals for fashion designers, including: how to draw trajectories of action through the conflicts mentioned and how new practices for designers may best be articulated. Without creating new either/or dichotomies, my aim has been to create richer environments for these adversary situations with the aim to "hear both sides": that is to let pro/con meet, and make the conflict visible for discussions, negotiations, and new paths of action. The aim has been to find room for new practices to emerge from what could be a disempowering situation of cynical doubt.

# Design diffractions

A perspective that allows for conflicts to thrive can be inspired by Donna Haraway's discussion on reflection versus "diffraction" as modes of inquiry. As Haraway suggests: "Reflexivity has been much recommended as a critical practice, but my suspicion is that reflexivity, like reflection, only displaces the same elsewhere, setting up the worries about copy and original and the search for the authentic and really real" (Haraway 1997, 16). To Haraway, reflexivity reproduces a situation that automatically seeks *one* dominant perspective, even if it is through a mirroring or critical examination. This reflection or displacement of the same hides the interests and position of the viewer behind a veil of objectivity, similar to the graphic perspective drawn from one fixed point on a picture plane.

Instead, to allow for more nuanced and situated knowledges to appear, Haraway suggests a research practice that is "diffractive." Using an optical frame of reference, Haraway's "diffraction" emphasizes interference between waves—or waves transforming and refracting—when meeting obstacles. This emphasis on recognizing conflict is put in order to "get more promising interference patterns on the recording films of our lives and bodies. Diffraction is an optical metaphor for the effort to make a difference in the world" (Haraway 1997, 16). Diffraction offers a way of looking for patterns of difference, and does not try to unify them into one conclusive format or harmony, and could thus be a helpful approach to complex fields, which include both/and perspectives and contradictions. By allowing subjective standpoints to emerge, it offers us a way of putting an emphasis on practice, on process, on ways to do things, rather than in finding a conclusive meaning: it is the interference and conflicts that are the forces under observation.

While retaining a place for vision, diffraction is more about registering movement (as when light passes through the slits of a prism and then diffracted rays are registered on something like a screen). Diffraction is about registering histories of movement in a field of moving forces, such that the movement of dynamism of forces (contexts and processes) can be reoriented or redirected, that is, disturbed and changed (Ticineto Clough and Schneider 2001, 342f). As noted above, a perspective of diffraction allows several tropes or conflicts to exist simultaneously, and lets them intersect so as to create new intensities, and even new possibilities for design. The aim is not to critically debunk other perspectives, but to try to redirect processes into fields of action, into design interventions. This is when criticism by diffraction becomes more desirable, if not necessary; when intervention becomes essential, sometimes to stop, but more often to interrupt, redirect, or reorient the process of technological elaboration (Ticineto Clough and Schneider 2001, 343).

It could be argued that design as a field of action is always dealing with diffraction in various forms and under different disguises, as designers are often dealing with contradictory interests, between briefs, stakeholders, negotiations, and undesirable compromises. But most often such processes are still unified into reconciliation, trade-off, or a final settlement in order to bring the process forward. But another way to engage with inherent conflicts and interference is to manifest it, that is, to make it apparent and situated, through design methods, into the very paradox it is.

## Manifesting diffractions and provotypes

In order to make the conflicts and diffractions of perspectives more tangible, one way to proceed is to manifest them as experiences and render them into physical demonstrations and environments for negotiation.

As Paul Feyerabend expounds in his book, *The Conquest of Abundance* (1999), the scientific method is a filter that reduces the intake of stimuli and casts data into cognitive dummies and concepts on which we try to agree the best we can, while still preserving as much of the rich experience of reality as possible. To Feyerabend, science works with a double action in order to manifest reality; on the one hand, scientific research tries to address the abundance of reality by cutting it down with tools of reduction, and on the other hand, it produces tools and concepts with which to reassemble the world into an understandable model.

A key method for science, Feyerabend notices, is to create isolated events, which help to identify unique forces at work. By producing experiments, "Scientists . . . are sculptors of reality" with the purpose to "create semantic conditions" for testable effects (Feyerabend 1999, 144). As Feyerabend demonstrates, these semantic conditions have altered throughout history and between various disciplines, and art and design has usually been among the main contributors in this endeavor, and likewise, the reliability of our human senses has been valued differently as scientific instruments throughout time. For example, during Byzantine times: "The Eucharist was a true image (of Christ) in this sense; a painted picture was either mockery or an idol" (Feyerabend 1999, 92). In Byzantine times, the semantic conditions of taste were thus considered a more truthful model of reality than the picture. However, the emergence of the one-point linear perspective, an alliance between geometry and painting, reversed this authenticity of the senses. As the painted picture allied with mathematical modeling, and the "rigorously specified conditions" aided by special sight devices, and systematized into linear images, the sense of taste seemed less accurate (Feyerabend 1999, 95ff).

Following Feyerabend's and Haraway's discussions, the semantic conditions of manifesting diffraction would have a certain purpose, to highlight interference, conflict, and objections, and make it sensible so we can engage with the conflict with more senses than pure abstract modeling by reason. The diffractive experiment should thus be as much an intervention into our physical world as into the world of concepts.

A classic way for designers to create systematized and testable conditions of an idea is to make a prototype. However, as noticed earlier, such an endeavor would consist of a rough compromise between forces, perhaps too easily overriding the inherent conflicts. A useful concept here can instead be the "provotype" sketched out by interaction design researcher Preben Mogensen (Mogensen 1992). To Mogensen, interaction is primarily an experience, and must be approached as an imaginative act. He thus proposes a method of "provocation through concrete experience" as a way to "devise qualitatively new systems" (Mogensen 1992, 31). The provotype acts with a double agency: it engages the future through concrete experience, but it simultaneously raises the perspective of what is possible beyond the habitual reference of the actual. It is thus as much a real experience as an imaginative and stimulating action. The aim of the provotype is to break the everyday operations and taken-for-grantedness of our interactions. For a diffractive research practice, the role of the provotype is to raise conflicting interests, contradictions, and ambiguities to the surface and manifest it in a richer environment, where participants can be engaged in the experience of the contradiction. The specific quality of design is its ability to render imagination visible, to make abstract ideas become models that amateurs and citizens can also engage with and perceive as real and as potential futures. As argued by design theorist John Wood, the aim of such design work is to evince what was before unthinkable or uncertain and diffuse, into something more high-definition: the possible imaginable, "thinkable," and discussable (Wood 2007).

# Two cases of conflict

In order to give some examples of how I use diffraction and provotypes in my research and teaching practice, I will show two projects by which I aim to highlight two mentioned dynamics of fashion: first, the *Fashion Safehouse*, concerning the issue of freedom versus imitation, or autonomy and heteronomy, and second, *The Current State of Fashion*, dealing with the issue of inclusion versus exclusion.

Based on the first chapter of Henry David Thoreau's book *Walden* (1854/1992), the *Fashion Safehouse* centered on the paradox of autonomy in fashion, the question of how to be "oneself" with tools and signifiers that are inherently produced outside oneself and part of a very limited economy, where its entire value system is based on exclusivity. Drawing from Thoreau's discussion about dress in his book and his famous building of the Walden cabin, the *Fashion Safehouse* was a project aiming to manifest Thoreau's discussions on autonomy, yet also interfere with his text through various forms of making fashion; craft, design, media production, and dissemination.

The safehouse itself is a building, a simple plywood construction built in the size of Thoreau's cabin, but situated indoors. Developed with students as a small classroom in a design school setting, it is meant to be a site for refuge as well as a site for a critical pedagogy. As a fashion sanctuary, it is a place both for contemplation and independence, for inner struggle and outer struggle, and in this way mirrors some of the motivations behind Thoreau's building of the cabin at Walden Pond. Like Thoreau's cabin, it is a site for asking critical questions about society, values, and resistance and a focal point for the question of how to frame a position of autonomy in relation to surrounding society and politics.

An iconic text on self-reliance and the fostering of autonomy, Thoreau also discusses fashion by pointing out how dependent and controlled we are by the opinions of others. As the author notices, clothes and fashion play an important role in our society, producing a lot of anxiety, and they may even act as a cover for conscience: "No man ever stood the lower in my estimation for having a patch in his clothes; yet I am sure that there is greater anxiety, commonly, to have fashionable, or at least clean and unpatched clothes, than to have a sound conscience" (Thoreau 1854/1992, 14). However, as Thoreau points out, the object of the fashion industry "is not that mankind may be well and honestly clad but, unquestionably, that the corporations may be enriched" (19). Thoreau, partisans, resistance fighters, escaping slaves, all seek shelter in order to break free from domination and test the boundaries of autonomy. For people engaged in fashion, autonomy is a fundamental paradox, as fashion is a phenomenon that rests equally on creativity, collaboration, conformity, and coercion, thus the "problem of participation" is an issue at the foundation of any position in fashion. The safehouse is the site for hands-on and practical examination of this core issue: In the practices of fashion, what is the relationship between the individual and community, how does this relationship manifest in collaborations, and ultimately, how can we create our own community "scenes" of fashion?

The safehouse project has so far taken two incarnations; one was a workshop for craft and curatorial students at Konstfack University College of Arts, Crafts and Design in Stockholm in March 2014, during which the students built the safehouse and used it for three days as a classroom (Figure 9.1). A central part of the workshop was a series of skill sharing exercises where each participant taught one skill to the others, employing the skills to equip and furnish the safehouse. The skills ranged from building simple flowerpots from milk cartons to more advanced versions of spinning thread from wool, using a variety of kitchen machines. Each of the skill sharing exercises also manifested a part of Thoreau's discussions of self-sufficiency and autonomy, and by using craft and co-teaching as alternative modes to consumption, they also became a topic for discussions on Thoreau's perspective on individual agency, political responsibility, and civil disobedience, something we connected to the "dictates" of fashion and potential violence of social competition.

The second incarnation of the project was at the *Fashioning Cascadia* exhibition at the Museum of Contemporary Craft in Portland/Oregon in June 2014. As I highlight in the initial project description and catalog of the exhibit:

> The establishment of safe spaces is the foundation of a pro-active resistance: a safe place to start building alternatives to the dominant logic and regime of violence. The safehouse is a temporary base with one's back covered, a platform for discussion, a boot camp for training and a node in a network of wider social mobilization. A *Fashion Safehouse* is not a place beyond fashion, but a place where it is collectively and collaboratively disarmed and displaced with a sincere attention to the human capabilities and values of the participants. It is a place from where to build an own stance: a resistance. (von Busch 2014)

The safehouse does not explicitly define what kind of "fashion" it aims to displace, but instead leaves it to be defined during the workshop, depending on the urgencies,

**FIGURE 9.1** *Fashion Safehouse* at Konstfack, Stockholm (2014). *Photo:* Otto von Busch.

anxieties, and fears raised by the participants. Particularly the aspect of fear and resistance that I encountered in the writing of philosopher Paul Virilio, who mentions how a safehouse is the basis to challenge a culture of fear. In his book, *The Administration of Fear* (2012), Virilio sees a safehouse as a secure platform from which to build critical thinking, judgment, and responsibility, and a point of departure for action. Virilio draws parallels to his own experiences growing up in occupied France during the Second World War and expounds that resistance must "first [take] refuge at the heart of the micro-collectivity of the family, then the building or the town" in order to get out of the authoritarian administration of fear (Virilio 2012, 20).

In Portland, the group of participants built the physical safehouse during the first day of the workshop as they had in Stockholm. But the four-day workshop program was also engaging local artists and designers, who came to show and discuss their practice in relation to the theme of autonomy. The process of the project included several techniques for autonomy as well, where the first day was dedicated to tools and materials and the toolbox as a point of departure for action. The second day concerned symbolic techniques and the production of insignia, such as a flag or logotype. The third was a day for the production of tactical media and local distribution of printed matter, flyers, propaganda, and a collaborative zine reinterpreting Thoreau's *Walden* as a text on fashion resistance. The fourth and final day was a sum-up and documentation day which also included some of the skill sharing exercises concerned with migrant practices, such as folding a piece of fabric into a backpack, preparing the participants for their coming nomadic resistance practices. The safehouse was later in the exhibition used as a site of residency for four other fiber and fashion artists, Stephanie Syjuco, Cassie Rigdway, Adrienne Antonson, and Drew Cameron.

Thus all steps in the project pointed toward the paradox of autonomy and fashion, mixed with hands-on practices and the cultivation of capabilities and skill sets that are at a tangent with the issue discussed. Mixing discussions with hands-on craft was also important in order to highlight how fear and anxiety is not primarily overcome or understood by a change of perception, but by practical training where the participants shared their skills, approaching the topics of discussion in different ways; sewing garments, making pamphlets and insignia, equipping and building on the house as it grew to mark the exercises and processes of making. Training thus took the center stage of the project, using craft and hands-on making to manifest the ongoing discussions. The aim was thus not about raising awareness, as the emphasis was on fashion as a realist political practice, driven by passions and fears. Thus, as I supported our shared and mutual learning experience, cognitive training became more important to us than finding arguments to reason. The issue was not primarily to think or understand fashion, as much as to do and be with fashion, that is, to deal with our passions and fears.

The second project, *The Current State of Fashion*, was an attempt to manifest the mechanisms of inclusion and exclusion in fashion through the means of a realist politics, perhaps in its most explicit form: a state. The state was enacted at Parsons School of Design, The New School in New York City, one of the centers of the exclusive fashion mythology. Emerging from a play of words, the double meaning of a "state," the project aimed to transpose political theory to fashion in order to put the spotlight on the realpolitik and mechanisms of violence in the glamorous incarnations of fashion. Such violence may take the form of the cultural violence of movies and popular narratives in the style of the ugly duckling, which are used to legitimize the exclusion of the ugly and poor, to the direct micro-aggressions of bouncers at a nightclub using dress code, such as a comment on someone's shoes, to make sure they are excluded from the chosen ones who have access.

Thus the project took the shape of a fictional national state, a state obsessed with the definition with citizenship, of who is "in" and who is "out," or what political philosopher Carl Schmitt (1932/1996) would have defined as the distinction between "friend" and "enemy." The project concentrated on the question of what if fashion was a state. What kind of state would it be? It would probably not be a liberal democracy. It would be something more sinister, more controlling, something more elitist: a state of exclusion.

Highlighting this violent perspective, *The Current State of Fashion* would thus be a state without dictator, but with a population all too eager to follow every command and demarcation. A population that happily embraces the superiority that consumerism evokes and turns in aggression on each other through acts of judgments, micro-aggression, micro-violence, bullying, and passionate micro-fascism. A state in which the poor and ugly have no place, a totalitarian state hidden under the consumer paradigm of "free choice," a mythical superpower with a political mannerism in the footsteps of what political philosopher Sheldon Wolin calls "Inverted Totalitarianism" (Wolin 2008). Following the trope of realpolitik, as Schmitt argues, "All genuine political theories presuppose man to be evil, i.e., by no means an unproblematic but a dangerous and dynamic being."(1996: 61). As highlighted in the beginning, it is the dynamics of fashion that can bring out the dangerous side in man.

The main question of the project was to highlight this obsession with demarcation and its violent undercurrents, to extrapolate this tendency in fashion using the framework of the national state as a model. At Parsons, the first step of this process was to fabricate the physical manifestation of the state in everyday life: the passport and visa application form.

I produced props for a state: insignia, passports, stamps and embossers, visa application forms, and tourist information pamphlets, and the small embassy itself with flag, typewriter, and photo booth for passport photos to be taken (Figures 9.2 and 9.3). During New York Fashion Week, in fall 2012, I set up the small embassy at the entrance of the Parsons building for students and staff to apply for the visa.

**FIGURE 9.2** Embassy props for *The Current State of Fashion* (2012). *Photo:* Otto von Busch.

**FIGURE 9.3** Temporary embassy at Parsons School of Design, The New School, New York (2012). *Photo:* Otto von Busch.

They had to fill in rigorous questions, paraphrasing the US visa form, to enter a world of fashion. While they waited, I created a passport for those accepted, but the passport was only valid for one season, so they would have to come back very soon in order to reapply to be included. Every new fashion has to be the *current* state of fashion. Like the ephemeral legitimacy promoted through the fashion system, last season's acceptance is no longer valid.

The following year I kept working on the format of the state and released a political tract of the state, under then nom de guerre of Ralf Wronsov (2014).

I extrapolated the state into a full-fledged totalitarian state reserved for the rich and beautiful. In one of the chapters of the tract, Wronsov expressed the implications of realism on fashion:

> There is thus no virtue of "good" in fashion. In fashion, as in life, might is right. Power and authority, executed by force or threat, legitimized by popularity, is the rule of law. This is our law; the rule of tooth and claw. The beautiful people lead, the ugly follow. The favoured and powerful punish the weak. (Wronsov 2014, 25)

Wronsov further interprets German philosopher Peter Sloterdijk's book *Rage and Time* (2010) to actually be about fashion, "the rage":

> Throwing out Judeo-Christian moral theorists brought in even more miserable submission to the neurosis of Narcissus and Oedipus, simply for the sake of sanctifying self-admiring academics a place where they safely could mix work and pleasure. It is time to stifle this pitiful failure of thought and bring back a discourse of heroism, power, agency and domination into the realm of enclothed social engagement. (Wronsov 2014, 27)

Along the way, the tract comes to define fashion as an arena for violent struggle for power, with the "fashion system" only serving to legitimize a cruel regime of exclusion and elitism at the heart of liberal democracies that otherwise claim to be celebrating idealist concepts such as "freedom" and "equality." Building on the fiercest aspects of political realism and social Darwinism, such as the lawful rule of the strong and the ideas of Nietzsche's *Ubermensch* (1892/1961), the tract emphasized the legitimization of aesthetic violence against the unworthy ugly, the "victims," those poor souls who are not dignified enough to be superior, to be truly in control of the political concept of the fashionable based on Schmitt's distinction between friend and enemy, or "in" and "out."

Using a nom de guerre as an artistic gesture helped to extrapolate the mechanisms that I had been most uncomfortable taking on in fashion, such as the elitism and inherent cruelty embedded in aesthetic judgments, where the demarcation of "in" and "out" also reflects the social status of included and excluded. The extrapolation also opened a free zone to play with the consequences of a realist perspective of fashion, how it caresses the few while it torments the many. If Zygmunt Bauman is right when he claims that to consume "means to invest in one's own social membership, which in a society of consumers translates as 'saleability': obtaining qualities for which there is already a market demand" (Bauman 2007, 56), then the game of fashion is rigged from the start. The "democratization" of fashion is the perceived equality between lions and lambs, and where we "vote with our dollars," as if we all had equal access to dollars, beauty, and fashion.

In most of my earlier research on fashion I have taken a deliberate constructive tone, aiming to "hack" fashion into a more participatory and liberating practice, and in many ways been dodging many of the systemic problems of fashion (cf. von Busch 2008). But the *Safehouse* and *State* allowed me to approach fashion from new angles, yet not fall into a cynical stance. Through its manifestation as a state, fashion could be discussed with other conceptual tools and forces at play that were normally not employed in fashion theory, and perhaps also open new paths for mitigating the problematic issues. *The Current State of Fashion* thus became a playground for switching perspectives, to seek confrontations in a diffractive manner and take on some of the more problematic sides of fashion that even I had tried to look away from in my own earlier engagements with fashion. Allowing some of the troubling elements of fashion diffract with political theory, state elitism, aristocracy, and social Darwinism opened new vistas for thought and discussions, and by making the full props of a state it became more than a conceptual model: the realism of fashion politics took real tangible shape.

Both the *Safehouse* and the *State* offered participants a tangible representation of the issue discussed, and this not only helped to spark interesting conversations, but also facilitated new perspectives to emerge. Having to apply for a visa to *The Current State of Fashion* opened a lot of questions concerning the mechanisms of exclusion shared between national states and fashion: the treatment by officers at the borders or guards in exclusive shops—who gets checked and blends in, is there a cost of blending in, is it possible for all to blend in? Holding the passport in hand acted as a provocation of further ideas by participants, on counterfeits, trafficking, and the asymmetric warfare of fashion.

## What kind of action

Fashion is a conflict in human being's souls as well as in the social settings of the public realm, and our clothes are the conflict-ridden interface between the two. Many opposing forces meet in fashion, not least freedom and imitation, as well as inclusion and exclusion, which were primarily explored in the cases above. Folding in on each other, mixing with issues of ethnicity, labor, environment, they form the foundation of fashion as a social experience, yet with a diffractive perspective they can be freshly approached as new forms of sense-making in the process of engagement.

While this proposed diffractive and tangible method may be similar to "critical design" (Dunne 1999) and "adversarial design" (DiSalvo 2012), as both these initiatives highlight critical engagement and disagreement, the emphasis above is on the manifestation of conflicting views and paradoxes in ways that also provoke answers. The diffraction aims to highlight relationships of both/and, and highlight the conflicts of pro/con, yet do this in a manner that promotes agency and engagement, negotiate and address an issue, rather than just raise awareness. With the *Safehouse* and *State*, participants were drawn into embodied scenarios, tangible and rich in experience, which also opened new hands-on skills for engagement, or call for other diplomatic strategies to challenge an inherent elitism within the experience of fashion. The provotype aspect in both cases thus takes primarily an instrumental perspective on design rather than the pointing gesture of art.

Other action-oriented traditions of research, which are close to the design practice, such as action research (Lewin 1946) or participatory action research (PAR), are "a form of radical pedagogy" (Carroll 2004, 276), and thus share overlapping concerns. Compared to their iterative processes and thorough engagements to change the subjects involved in the research, the design cases mentioned do not primarily aim to improve conditions through iterative cycles, or develop more accurate methods toward "best practice." The action involved in the manifestations described is highlighting the real politics and paradoxes of fashion, rendering them sensible and discussable, and in both cases, inhabitable as embodied experiences, such as the embassies and safehouses. By their very physical manifestation the conflicts become more apparent, so that the participants can dwell in the space of conflict, and in the end perhaps untangle some of the complex forces at play.

One could see the manifestations, the *Safehouse* and the *State*, as devices for creating "semantic conditions" to unravel conflicts and controversies in order to make them into sensory experiences, imaginable, and discussable parallel to Feyerabend's ideas of scientific models. They are "sculptures of reality," but of realities seldom discussed in fashion, which otherwise remain abstract, distant, and perhaps too ambiguous or complex. Becoming tangible and inhabitable, the issues they bring up come to engage more of our senses and levels of imagination and understanding.

The aim of action is to continuously engage with the real forces at work in fashion, beyond the imaginative models of reason, to instead cut through our habitual thinking with metaphors and manifestations that can shift our perspectives. But action, as a form of performance is best created with props, with richer manifestations of the theme. As in the examples of *The Current State of Fashion* and the *Fashion Safehouse*, the environments of action allow greater interfaces with some of the core contradictions around fashion, issues that hopefully will never be finally solved. Their tug o' war is what makes fashion such a powerful phenomenon in the first place.

# References

Bauman, Zygmunt. 2007. *Consuming Life*. Cambridge: Polity.
Berki, Robert. 1981. *On Political Realism*. London: Dent.
Bourdieu, Pierre. 1984. *Distinction: A Social Critique of the Judgement of Taste*. London: Routledge.

Brown, Sass. 2010. *Eco Fashion.* London: Laurence King.

Carroll, William. 2004. *Critical Strategies for Social Research.* Toronto: Canadian Scholars' Press.

DiSalvo, Carl. 2012. *Adversarial Design.* Cambridge, MA: MIT Press.

Dunne, Anthony. 1999. *Hertzian Tales: Electronic Products, Aesthetic Experience and Critical Design.* London: RCA CRD Research Publications.

Feyerabend, Paul. 1999. *Conquest of Abundance: A Tale of Abstraction Versus the Richness of Being.* Chicago: University of Chicago Press.

Fletcher, Kate. 2008. *Sustainable Fashion and Textiles.* London: Earthscan.

Geuss, Raymond. 2008. *Philosophy and Real Politics.* Princeton: Princeton University Press.

Grosz, Elizabeth. 2008. *Chaos, Territory, Art: Deleuze and the Framing of the Earth.* New York: Columbia University Press.

Guzzini, Stafano. 1998. *Realism in International Relations and International Political Economy: The Continuing Story of a Death Foretold.* London: Routledge.

Hampshire, Stewart. 2000. *Justice is Conflict.* Princeton: Princeton University Press.

Haraway, Donna. 1997. *Modest-Witness@Second-Millennium.* New York: Routledge.

Kaiser, Susan B. 2012. *Fashion and Cultural Studies.* London: Bloomsbury.

Lewin, Kurt. 1946. "Action Research and Minority Problems." *Journal of Social Issues* 2: 34–46.

Mogensen, Preben. 1992. "Towards a Prototyping Approach in Systems Development." *Journal of Information Systems* 4: 31–53.

Morgenthau, Hans. 1948/2006. *Politics Among Nations: The Struggle for Power and Peace.* Boston: McGraw-Hill.

Nietzsche, Friedrich. 1892/1961. *Thus Spoke Zarathustra: A Book for Everyone and No One.* London: Penguin.

Schmitt, Carl. 1932/1996. *The Concept of the Political.* Chicago: University of Chicago Press.

Siegle, Lucy. 2011. *To Die For: Is Fashion Wearing Out the World?* London: Fourth Estate.

Simmel, Georg. 1971. *On Individuality and Social Forms: Selected Writings.* Chicago: University of Chicago Press.

Simmel, Georg. 2004. "Fashion." In *The Rise of Fashion*, edited by Daniel Leonhard Purdy, 298–309. Minneapolis and London: University of Minnesota Press.

Simon, Herbert. 1996. *The Sciences of the Artificial.* Cambridge, MA: MIT Press.

Sloterdijk, Peter. 2010. *Rage and Time: A Psychopolitical Investigation.* New York: Columbia University Press.

Thomas, Dana. 2007. *Deluxe: How Luxury Lost its Luster.* New York: Penguin.

Thoreau, Henry David. 1854/1992. *Walden and Resistance to Civil Government.* New York: W. W. Norton.

Ticineto Clough, Patricia and Joseph Schneider. 2001. "Donna J. Haraway." In *Profiles in Contemporary Social Theory*, edited by Anthony Elliott and Bryan Turner, 338–48. London: Sage.

Virilio, Paul. 2012. *The Administration of Fear.* Los Angeles: Semiotext(e).

von Busch, Otto. 2008. *Fashion-able: Hacktivism and Engaged Fashion Design.* Gothenburg: Artmonitor.

von Busch, Otto. 2014. "Fashion Safehouse." In *Fashioning Cascadia,* catalogue from Museum of Contemporary Craft, Portland OR.

Williams, Raymond. 1980. *Problems in Materialism and Culture: Selected Essays.* London: Verso.

Wood, John. 2007. *Design for Micro-Utopias: Making the Unthinkable Possible*. Aldershot: Gower.

Wronsov, Ralf. 2014. *Tractatus Fashionablo-Politicus: The Political Philosophy of the Current State of Fashion*. Gothenburg: Selfpassage.

X, Malcolm. 1992. *By Any Means Necessary: Malcolm X Speeches & Writings*. New York: Pathfinder Press.

# 10 EDITING FASHION STUDIES: REFLECTIONS ON METHODOLOGY AND INTERDISCIPLINARITY IN *THE ENCYCLOPEDIA OF WORLD DRESS AND FASHION*

## Joanne B. Eicher

To this date *The Encyclopedia of World Dress and Fashion* (Eicher 2010) is one of the most comprehensive reference works that represents diverse forms and practices of dress and fashion across geographic boundaries. It is the outcome of a complex international and cross-disciplinary research endeavor of 620 contributors writing 848 articles for its ten volumes, comprising a total of 3.6 million words and 2,000 images. Published both in hard copy and online, the online publication annually adds 100,000 words, making this reference work, at least to a certain extent, a flexible "encyclopedia-in-progress." In its international scope, the publication is closely intertwined with the global growth and interdisciplinary expansion of the study of fashion and dress in recent decades, and as such is informed by the perspectives and methodological approaches of a wide variety of academic fields. In this chapter I chronicle the development of this encyclopedia, elaborate on its organization and methodological approach to dress and fashion, and reflect on the increasingly global and interdisciplinary scope of the field. I will particularly highlight two aspects: the role of terminology, specifically the definition of dress and fashion, and the role of the editors' and writers' varied disciplinary and international backgrounds that were crucial to the approach of this encyclopedia. Before exploring the implications of these two factors, I will first elaborate on the project's history and its connection to my own research interests.

# History of the encyclopedia's development

Encyclopedias are reference works, single or multiple volumes that are comprehensive for the subject or subjects indicated by the title, with articles that summarize and are thought to be authoritative. Some are broad and universal in scope, like the *Encyclopedia Britannica*, the oldest in the English language, first published between 1768 and 1771 and which with its last hard copy printed in 2012 grew to sixty-two volumes (Preece and Goetz 2009), but now is published only online. Other encyclopedias have a narrower topic and focus, like *The Encyclopedia of World Dress and Fashion* with ten volumes. Encyclopedias differ from dictionaries, which define or explain the meaning of words, by providing instead a more factual description and analysis of a selected topic. Encyclopedias are considered as academic treatises, and as such they not only inform but also help to define a field.

In describing the inception of the idea for *The Encyclopedia of World Dress and Fashion*, its organizational development and underlying methodologies, I want to point out and emphasize the role of publishers in initiating projects, because their commissioning editors often surmise and perceive a trend or interest arising among various sections of the public, but their astute roles as a rule remain invisible. This encyclopedia exemplifies how two editors' interests interfaced with mine, illustrating that scholarly pursuits and needs can intertwine with market needs, both developing and shifting ones as well as those well established.

To set the stage for how my own interests meshed with a publisher's interest, I briefly elaborate on my background and interest in fashion. Starting in early childhood, with my mother who sewed and taught me to love fashion, this interest extended through my teenage and college years, and culminated in choosing some university courses related to fashion merchandising, including an internship in a department store during my senior year and a brief sojourn in retailing after graduation. My interest in dress and fashion was then put on hold during my graduate education, for a combined degree in anthropology and sociology at Michigan State University, where I learned both qualitative and quantitative research approaches, including ethnography, oral history, surveys, and questionnaires. I first taught a general social science course at Boston University, collaborating with faculty in economics, psychology, and history as well as in anthropology and sociology.

When I accepted a research and teaching position in the Department of Textiles, Clothing, and Related Arts at Michigan State University,[1] I drew from these resources to focus my research initially on dress practices among teenage girls, followed by coediting *Dress, Adornment, and the Social Order* (Roach and Eicher 1965), and coauthoring the first edition of *The Visible Self* (Roach and Eicher 1973). Both of these books drew from and crossed disciplines in their perspectives on the social roles of dress. Meanwhile, my research turned into conducting fieldwork on dress and textiles in Nigeria during a three-year residence. After moving to the University of Minnesota, in the Department of Textiles and Clothing (later Design, Housing, and Apparel), my opportunities increased for expanded fieldwork in West Africa and forays to India to conduct research on the India to Africa textile trade. In addition, serving at the University of Minnesota as director of the Goldstein Museum of Design[2] brought me face-to-face with viewing and exhibiting material culture within a museum setting. Through membership and participation in a wide range of professional organizations, I crossed disciplinary boundaries, read widely, and traversed beyond the social sciences to appreciate and work with historians, art historians, economists, home economists, and textile and apparel scholars, who shared my interests in dress and fashion. Related to this interdisciplinary work, my collaboration with Berg Publishers began in the early 1990s, with my coedited book *Dress and Gender* (1992), and with my appointment as editor for the *Dress, Body, Culture* book series, which launched in 1997.[3]

Over the forty years of my career, I had thought about the need for a comprehensive, bibliographic resource about dress and fashion that extended across space and time. Such an opportunity happened when Valerie Steele, editor in chief of a three-volume project for Scribner's, asked me to join her on the *Encyclopedia of Clothing and Fashion* (Steele 2005) as one of three associate editors. I saw my role as providing a cultural dimension, particularly in regard to the non-Western world. Midway into this project the reference director from another publisher, Sylvia Miller, contacted me. Miller had played a critical role in publishing Scribner's ten-volume *Encyclopedia of World Music* (Netti et al. 1998). She proposed mounting a parallel encyclopedia project, geographically organized for world costume and adornment, based on the results of her having held a number of focus groups made up of librarians from colleges, universities, public libraries, and high schools. They knew the Scribner music set and were unusually unanimous in their enthusiasm for a geographically organized work that would not privilege the West. I persuaded her that rather than using "costume" a larger, more encompassing concept of "dress" existed. She agreed to use the term, resulting in the title *Encyclopedia of World Dress and Adornment*. The opportunity to work on a ten-volume work that spanned cultures across the world appealed to me, and I felt that this work would complement Steele's A–Z encyclopedia. Such a scheme acknowledged that the history and cultural significance of dress stretched across the world and back in time 5,000 years, to Egypt, India, and China, with the latter two often overlooked or omitted in English sources; Egypt has been a special case as its history is usually included as part of the Mediterranean world linked to Europe. By using a geographic focus for nine volumes and having a tenth on global perspectives we avoided highlighting the West, a focus commonly found in most histories and cultural analyses of dress and fashion published in English. We implicitly agreed that the project would draw contributions from many disciplinary and international perspectives to enable us to engage with the wide variety and global scope of dress and fashion.

Miller asked me to be the editor in chief, and our collaboration launched a project that culminated in publication seven years after her initial phone call. The first step was developing a proposal involving almost a year of emails and drafts, ending with ten peer reviews from academic and library professionals across a variety of disciplines, followed by my rejoinder to their comments, and finally, the acceptance after approval by her review board. My next step was to contact potential volume editors. Within four months, six volumes had editors, allowing four of us to meet in New York City with our publisher's editor and her staff. In the overall selection of volume editors, I worked from my network of colleagues—and a snowball system of their suggestions. The editors' backgrounds underpin the varied methodologies inherent in the project. I contacted scholars who were experts both for a geographic area and for fashion, dress, or textiles research and publishing. The goal was to bring together a group of editors, and authors, who would represent multidisciplinary and international perspectives from across the globe.

I initially headed *Volume One: Africa*, but later asked Doran Ross, director emeritus of the Fowler Museum, University of California, Los Angeles, an American art historian with extensive fieldwork and publications on Africa and a supplementary interest in Latin America, to join me. (I also edited *Volume Ten: Global Perspectives*). Margot Blum Schevill, an American anthropologist with expertise in Guatemala headed *Volume Two: Latin America and the Caribbean*. Phyllis Tortora, an American dress historian with many published works, including *Survey of the History of Western Dress* (Tortora and Marcketti 2015) spearheaded *Volume Three: The United States and Canada*. Jasleen Dhamija from India and expert on Indian handloom and handcraft industries and United Nations consultant in Iran, West, Central, and Southeast Asia and Africa, served as editor for *Volume Four: South and Southeast Asia*. Gillian Vogelsang-Eastwood, a British ethnographer who heads the Textile Research Center in Leiden in The Netherlands and is affiliated with the National Museum of Ethnology in Leiden, is the editor for *Volume Five: Central and Southwest Asia*. John Vollmer, American art historian and museum consultant on East Asia, particularly China, provided editorship for *Volume Six: East Asia*. Margaret Maynard, an Australian dress scholar at Queensland University, organized *Volume Seven: Australia, New Zealand and the Pacific Islands*. Lise Skov, a Danish cultural sociologist at the Copenhagen Business School, became editor for *Volume Eight: West Europe*. With expertise on East Europe and its relationship to Western fashion, Djurdja Bartlett, research fellow at the London College of Fashion, is editor for *Volume Nine: East*

*Europe.* Thus, nine volumes had each a specific geographic focus with the tenth spanning the globe, which focused on fashions crossing geographic boundaries. The editors' backgrounds spanned anthropology, art history, ethnography, history, sociology, fashion studies, and dress history. They were aware of the multidisciplinary aspects of dress and fashion studies and reached beyond their own disciplines for authors. Yet their areas of expertise, fieldwork specialty, or location could also influence the content of their volumes. For example, John Styles noted in his *Fashion Theory* review of *Volume Eight* (2012), how Lise Skov used her links to the Nordic countries to complement the usual prominence given to France, England, or Italy (Styles 2010, 68).

Additional scholars provided assistance with four volumes. Two consulting editors, Blenda Feminias and Lynn Meisch, both American anthropologists and Latin American specialists, supported Margot Schevill for *Volume Two.* In *Volume Three,* Phyllis Tortora relied on Joseph Horse Capture, museum curator and member of the A'aninin Indian tribe of Montana as consultant for North American Indian entries. For *Volume Eight,* Lise Skov drew on the expertise of Valerie Cumming, UK dress scholar and museum specialist. For *Volume Ten,* Phyllis Tortora served as the assistant editor.

In our early New York City meeting, we organized a general program of work and a schedule. The primary articles were to be 4,000–10,000 words in length with additions, where appropriate, of a "snapshot" to offer elaboration through a special case study. We agreed to include as many authors directly from the varied geographic areas where possible, a factor leading to considering bi- or multilingual authors. Because the encyclopedia was to be published in English and the project had no funds for translation, authors who did not write comfortably in English found their own translators. I am delighted with the fact that scholars from more than eighty countries are represented in the encyclopedia.

# Notes on the encyclopedia's organization

With general decisions in place, each editor drafted a table of contents for approval by the publisher's editor and me, after which volume editors began contacting potential contributors, experts for topics identified as key for their volume. As usual for encyclopedias, authors would be expected to draw from already completed and published research, but in several cases, editors decided that a topic was crucial and requested colleagues to conduct new research. No template existed across volumes for a table of contents, and two examples shall follow as illustration: each geographic volume was organized by country, but general topics preceded geographical listings yet varied by volume. For the volume on Africa, the introductory topics included archeology, colonial history and dress, African fashion and fashion designers, as well as body and beauty, followed by countries organized regionally—North Africa, West Africa, etc. But this was not the format used for other volumes. For the volume on East Europe, Bartlett (2010) appreciated the rich diversity of regional dress practices and commissioned separate articles for each country, with her volume having the largest number of articles. Due to this regional emphasis, Bartlett noted that there was less scholarship devoted to dress more obviously influenced by transnational flows of "fashion." Her introduction illustrates the complications of the use of terminologies, such as "dress" or "fashion," and how varied understandings of these concepts are at work across time and place.

Progress in developing the project halted suddenly when the publisher abruptly cancelled the editors' contracts and mine, abandoning the project. (I later learned that the publisher had decided to pull back on publishing reference works after Miller departed for personal reasons, when our project had barely begun.) Dismayed, but not easily daunted, I pursued other avenues for publication, one contact being Kathryn Earle, managing director of Berg, who had already spawned my *Dress, Body, Culture* book series. She understood the importance of the encyclopedia and came forward to take up the contract, another example of the impact and importance of publishers in foreseeing a need. She asked that the title be changed to *Encyclopedia of World Dress and Fashion*, dropping adornment, which is included in the word "dress," and highlighting the growing interest and increased academic acceptance of the word "fashion." Berg carried through successfully with Earle, enlarging its scope by conceptualizing a larger, online project—the *Berg Fashion Library* (*www.bergfashionlibrary.com*) that would incorporate the encyclopedia and add several other dimensions with photographic archives from museums, links to related journals, and e-books. At this point in time, 2005, the media fervor for fashion had not yet burgeoned as fully as happened in the years following and continuing to the time of writing this chapter, as two librarians elaborate in "Style and Substance: Fashion in Twenty-First Century Research Libraries" (King and Clement 2012). This larger project expanded Earle's vision for Berg as a major player as a "dress press" in publishing academic works on dress and fashion, which she began with launching both the *Dress, Body, Culture* series and the journal *Fashion Theory* in 1997, as well as the journals *Textile* in 2003 and *Fashion Practice* in 2009. Bloomsbury took over Berg in 2012 and continues to expand publishing fashion books, including other reference works, such as *The Handbook of Fashion Studies* (Black et al. 2013).

With the entry of Berg into the project, however, a major shift in the program of work arose with the stipulation that all ten volumes be published simultaneously as opposed to the first publisher's plan of producing two volumes a year for five years. In retrospect, this strategic decision, along with launching the *Berg Fashion Library* (BFL) simultaneously, provided a larger and more immediate impact on fashion studies than the strung out publication schedule would have allowed. The shift in plan challenged all editors and contributors to meet deadlines, which we did successfully. Underlying the collaborative research and organizational undertaking was a wide-framed, encompassing definition of dress that could work across place, time, and discipline.

## Defining dress: The impact of terminology on methodology

Using a specified definition of dress encouraged methodological interdisciplinarity, by searching for authors to move beyond an emphasis on apparel to all aspects of dressing the body that includes all five senses, and an allied emphasis on fashion for all geographic areas. The latter point encouraged editors and authors to document that fashion as a phenomenon is not exclusive to the Western world. As the base for the encyclopedia, as authors were selected, their attention was turned to the definition of dress as:

> a coded sensory system of non-verbal communication that aids human interaction in space and time. The codes of dress include visual as well as other sensory modifications (taste, smell, sound, and feel) and supplements (garments, jewelry, and accessories) to the body which set off either or both cognitive and affective processes that result in recognition or lack of recognition by the viewer. As a system, dressing the body by modifications and supplements may facilitate or hinder consequent verbal or other communication. (Eicher 1995, 1)

Stated simply as "body modifications and body supplements," this definition of dress allows a scope going beyond "clothing" or "costume," which refers obviously to garments and accompanying accessories like shoes, purses, jewelry, and umbrellas. Furthermore, I see the word "dress" as a larger, less culturally charged term and concept than fashion, considering that the word "fashion" has historically also been used to support narratives of Western modernity and "progress," that also served in the construction of a "traditional other." I use Herbert Blumer's definition of fashion: "A pattern of change in which certain social forms enjoy temporary acceptance and respectability only to be replaced by others" (Blumer 1968). Blumer pointed out, writing at a time when the word "fashion" was definitely out of fashion in the academic world in contrast to its acceptance today, that fashions exist in many areas of life—such as food habits, automobiles, interior design, and in dressing the body. My own point of view for a long time had been that human beings are basically creative and that fashion, that is, change in ways of dressing the body, was as possible in cultures beyond the West as in the West. Generally, due to limited documentation or discourse, assumptions have been made that "fashion" has not existed in non-Western cultures (Eicher 2001). What is seen or understood as fashion depends on space and time, and so is pinpointing that change in dress is fashion.

"Getting dressed" involves many human actions of cleansing, scenting, smoothing, and coloring skin and combing or styling hair that are common, daily activities of life across the world, all or any of which can go in and out of fashion, and they can do so at a varied pace. Using the word "dress" allows setting a focus on its varied forms and practices in everyday life and contexts around the world, leaving "costume" to focus on what is designed and worn for performance, theater, dance, and masquerade. Although "costume" has been favored as a term in some museums for collections and exhibits, many have adopted the words "dress" and "fashion," especially in the United Kingdom and Europe. Equally, various programs of study in academic and design institutions internationally have dropped the word "costume" and adopted "fashion" for their programs of study. This, however, is a more recent shift, as many university programs in the past have avoided the word. This tendency was influenced by fashion being thought of as shallow and superficial, a point to which Blumer refers, arguing that awareness of fashion indicates awareness of current trends in daily life. Valerie Steele similarly analyzed how dismissive of the word many academics have been, when she wrote her essay on "The F Word" in 1991.

The definition of dress as body modifications and body supplements encompasses more than garments and emphasizes a totality of activities involved in dressing the body, relating to all the senses, products, and artifacts, and of course, fashion involved in accepting products and practices. Coiffure, cosmetics, accessories, and scent can be as critical as apparel in constituting personal, social, and cultural identity. By understanding that dress is more than garments and inclusive of ways in which we, as human beings, add to our bodies for varied reasons, from communication purposes to protective ones, we immediately begin to draw from many disciplines and their methodologies—the resources of archeology, anatomy, anthropology, art and design, art history and history, cultural studies, economics, folklore, home economics and human ecology, physiology, psychology, sociology, textile science, and theater. This becomes apparent when viewing the classification system for types of dress and their properties in Table 10.1 (Roach-Higgins and Eicher 1992).

Critical to understanding the definition of dress underlying this classification is that when we dress our bodies, we become involved in a series of processes that allow us to communicate to others something about us or our sense of self. The popularity of some of these processes and products that we use to dress our bodies can become wider fashions of dress in points of time, not just with regard to the apparel and accessories donned, but also with regard to the various ways we practice hygiene and adorn various parts of our bodies when we bathe or shower, comb and style our hair, apply scent, etc. Scrutinizing the table delineating the various aspects involved in the definition of dress, as well as possible fashions arising from types of dress makes clear how many different disciplines can be involved in regard to methodologies of related research.

Table 10.1 *Classification system for types of dress and their properties*

| Types of dress[a] | Color | Volume and proportion | Shape and structure | Surface design | Texture | Odor and scent | Sound | Taste |
|---|---|---|---|---|---|---|---|---|
| BODY MODIFICATIONS | | | | | | | | |
| Transformations of | | | | | | | | |
| *Hair* | | | | | | | | |
| *Skin* | | | | | | | | |
| *Nails* | | | | | | | | |
| *Muscular/skeletal system* | | | | | | | | |
| *Eyes* | | | | | | | | |
| *Teeth* | | | | | | | | |
| *Breath* | | | | | | | | |
| BODY SUPPLEMENTS | | | | | | | | |
| Enclosures | | | | | | | | |
| *Wrapped* | | | | | | | | |
| *Suspended* | | | | | | | | |
| *Preshaped* | | | | | | | | |
| *Combination-type* | | | | | | | | |
| Attachments to body | | | | | | | | |
| *Inserted* | | | | | | | | |
| *Clipped or pressure-fastened* | | | | | | | | |
| *Adhered* | | | | | | | | |
| Attachments to body enclosures | | | | | | | | |
| *Inserted* | | | | | | | | |
| *Clipped or pressure-fastened* | | | | | | | | |
| *Adhered* | | | | | | | | |
| Handheld objects | | | | | | | | |
| *By self* | | | | | | | | |
| *By others* | | | | | | | | |

[a]Both body modifications and body supplements can be further classified according to
(a) general body locus (e.g., head, neck, trunk, arms, legs) or
(b) more specific locus (e.g., lips, nose, eyelids or lashes, ears, hands, ankles, feet, breasts, genitals).
*Source:* Adapted from Roach-Higgins and Eicher (1992).

# Interdisciplinary and global scope

One challenge involved in using the above definition of dress and classification system across a wide variety of disciplines is that different disciplines have different methodologies and terminologies embedded in their approaches. Getting scholars to communicate with each other and understand another's methodological approach takes patience at times. Historians and art historians, for example, may not be as interested in or able to analyze the construction of a garment or textile fiber content as a textile and dress scholar can. The volume editors understood the challenge of seeking potential contributions from a variety of disciplinary perspectives and arose to meet it. In the following paragraphs, I present a few examples from across the ten volumes to show the range of disciplines and contributions that enabled the breadth of fields covered in the encyclopedia.

The article "Research Approaches" in *Volume Ten* specifically addresses methodology, indicating that the methodological aspects of studying fashion "bring together different conceptual frameworks and disciplinary approaches" (Skov and Melchior 2010, 11–16). The authors Lise Skov and Marie Riegels Melchior provide an assessment for embarking on or considering the ways to conduct research and critical discourse. They cover terminology and analytical frameworks, such as the study of the impact of class, gender, or language and interdisciplinary and transnational developments in the field from 1985 to 2010. A major thrust involves identifying the four main and distinctive approaches that help to organize the wide range of research methods used: object-based, culture-based, practice-based, and production-based.

Across volumes, the editors and I, with backgrounds in anthropology, history, art history, dress, fashion, museum studies, sociology, and textiles, drew from our networks of colleagues to provide an additional array of methodological approaches and disciplines, such as economics, geography, folklore, journalism, and theater. The selected examples given below illustrate some of the disciplines and methodologies that inform the encyclopedia's wide range of article types and topics. Only through the inclusion and mixture of different perspectives from article to article throughout the encyclopedia, can readers gain a richer experience in learning about dress and fashion, than if the encyclopedia had recruited scholars from a single discipline (such as textile analysis, dress history, or economics).

In *Volume One: Africa*, American geographer Philip Porter, with more than fifty years of fieldwork in Africa, wrote "Climatic Zones and Cultural Regions" (Porter 2010, 10–16) for Part One: "Overview of Dress and Fashion." His framework for regional and country specific articles provides an overall perspective about clothing and the environmental aspects of rainfall, as well as the variation in temperature according to latitude and elevation. As a cultural geographer, Porter cautions that "clothing is worn for many reasons other than to cover one's body and protect it from the elements." His analysis encompasses subtopics of regional distinctiveness, ideas of authenticity and identity, clothing and creditability, the indigenous textile industry, cosmetics and masks, and the role of European clothing.

The historian and native of Jamaica, Steeve Buckridge, who authored *The Language of Dress: Resistance and Accommodation in Jamaica, 1760–1890* (2004), wrote two articles for *Volume Two: Latin America and the Caribbean* (Buckridge 2010): "Overview of the Caribbean" (247–50) and "Jamaica: Nineteenth Century to Present" (264–69). In his first entry, Buckridge observes: "In spite of a shared history and similar patterns of development, the Caribbean is profoundly one of the most complex and culturally diverse regions on the globe," providing both historical and contemporary discussion of the diversity into the categories of secular and nonsecular. He then briefly surveys select dress customs across the islands, with notice given to carnival costume and headwraps. In the same volume, dress and theater scholar Jose Blanco F. presented the "Overview of Central America" (Blanco F. 2010, 149–57) noting the variety of pre-Hispanic ethnic backgrounds and the heavy impact of European influence on dress from the Conquest period onward. He summarized how traditions are kept alive through *Carnaval* celebrations, folkloric dances, and folklore revival programs.

*Volume Three: United States and Canada* covers only two countries, however, each has a vast geographic area and great ethnic diversity. The dress scholar, Gwendolyn O'Neal, argued in this volume that African American dress practices "differ from those of the dominant culture (being) both complex and diverse and are rooted in a cultural aesthetic that can be called neither African nor American." She highlights as examples the styles in church dress and dressing the head, which she analyzes as forms of a particular "African American aesthetic of dress—a blending of material culture, a manifestation of the fashioning of an identity under the pressure of double consciousness" (O'Neil 2010, 536–45). O'Neil points out four aesthetic elements that she sees as particularly distinctive in the context of African American style practices, including an affinity for high-affect colors, individual expression, improvisation and the use of "exotic" patterns, and a tendency to "dress up." To understand the complexity of fashion, research across and within many cultural groups, including migrant, ethnic, or religious communities, is critical because dress and fashion in specific cultural groups can have their own "rules," challenges, and expectations that can differ markedly from what is perceived or promoted in the so-called mainstream.

An art historical perspective is represented in *Volume Four: South and Southeast Asia*, by the distinguished Indian scholar, B. N. Goswamy in "The Sash, Patka, or Kamarband" (Goswamy 2010, 147–51). He provides complex details about a single garment: a long textile strip wrapped around the waist that has many manifestations linked to a long history found in Indian and South Asian sculpture and paintings from early Sanskrit times through the Mughal period into the twenty-first century. In *Volume Five: Central and Southwest Asia*, Turkish scholar Sumru Belgar Krody, an archeologist and senior curator in the Textile Museum, Washington, DC, wrote "Turkish Embroidery" (Krody 2010, 121–25). Emphasizing the role of gender, she reported that by studying embroidery, women's significant contributions to the Ottoman economy can be recognized. She detailed techniques and changes in Ottoman urban embroidery traditions throughout the centuries and at different periods, including the influence of artistic ideas from Europe. In *Volume Six: East Asia*, the cultural historian Elizabeth Semmelhack, senior curator at the Bata Shoe Museum, Toronto, Canada, analyzed "Footwear" for China, Tibet and Mongolia, Korea, and Japan and provided a snapshot on "Footbinding" (Semmelhack 2010, 99–105). Asian footwear types, she indicated, are diverse and relate to geography as well as to historical and cultural developments, "but frequently issues of ethnic identity overrode all other considerations" (Semmelhack 2010, 99). Earliest evidence of footwear points to a skeleton found 42,000–39,000 years ago in a cave near Beijing. She described boots, shoes, sandals, and slippers of many types and shapes made from leather, cotton, silk, fiber, and even wood. In addition to place, class distinctions, occupations, and sexuality link to choices of footwear across Asia, just as elsewhere in the world.

The background of an artist and scholar trained in Koori oral history and art connecting to her Australian Aboriginal heritage, Fabri Blacklock, wrote a snapshot on "Aboriginal Skin Cloaks" (2010, 35) in *Volume Seven: Australia, New Zealand, and the Pacific*. As an article of dress for both men and women and fashioned in different styles, the animal skin cloaks could be worn ceremonially, as rugs for keeping warm or as burial shrouds. She addressed several reasons for the scarcity of extant examples, one being the impact of European clothing that discouraged making them further.

The British business anthropologist Brian Moeran focused his article in *Volume Eight: West Europe* on another aspect of dress, "Fragrances and Perfume" (Moeran 2010, 426–30). The sense of smell is important in the act of dress, and he included a fascinating history of the development of perfume that relates to "hygiene, the body, appearance, dress, and social status," adding a snapshot on Chanel No. 5, a favorite scent of many women the world over since its introduction in 1921.

*Volume Nine: East Europe*, includes a perspective from museum curator Julia Demidenko, deputy director for research at The State Museum of the History of St. Petersburg in two snapshots, "Soviet Underwear" and "Fashion Contest in the Soviet Union" (Demidenko 2010, 366–70). In the essay on underwear, she notes "both its manufacturing and consumption—were determined not only by fashion but also, to a great extent, by the ideology and political goals of the state and its economic priorities at different stages," providing readers provocative ideas to consider that are not usually attached to undergarments.

Another entry in *Volume Ten* by dress historians Nan Mutnick and Phyllis Tortora (2010, 319–34) highlights the need for interdisciplinarity, along with the historical and global scope of dress in an "Appendix: Timeline" illustrating a richly layered history by listing items and practices from prehistory to 2010.

Their chronology clearly indicates that research cannot be carried out from one perspective alone. They trawled through exhaustive sets of sources by using the definition of dress for both processes and products. Intriguing examples begin with citing bivalve shell beads in use during the Paleolithic Period in Morocco, (ca. 80,000 BCE). Some examples that may surprise readers regarding dates are copper shaving razors in India and Egypt (ca. 4,000 BCE), materials for nail varnish and lacquer found in China (ca. 3,000 BCE), corsets stiffened with copper ribs for men and women in Crete (ca. 2,100 BCE), and false teeth from ivory and bone in Italy (ca. 700 BCE). Moving into the Common Era (CE), I picked up curious examples idiosyncratically: a textile band used to support women's breasts in Rome (first century BCE), a pressing iron invented in China, (ca. 400 CE), a folding fan invented in Japan, (ca. 670 CE), buttonholes for clothing, (Europe ca. 1200 CE), first portable timepiece invented (Germany, 1504), bifocal invented by Benjamin Franklin (United States, 1784), a safety pin patented (United Kingdom, 1849), an athletic supporter for men (United States, 1920), the Wonderbra (United States, 1994), and solar-powered jackets to charge small electronic items (Italy, 2007).

## Conclusion

For me, the largest contribution that the encyclopedia makes to the field of fashion and dress research or scholarship is to help establish a solid, global base for fashion studies. The number and diversity of authors, who work in a range of disciplinary fields and international locations are moved by and aspire to describe and attempt to define a field. The willingness of these diverse researchers to participate in this project demonstrates how the approach to dress and by implication, fashion, used for the encyclopedia can work as an important and attractive framework through which scholars believed they could legitimately participate. Together their work has led to an interdisciplinary and international accomplishment, honored with the American Library Association's 2011 Dartmouth Medal (established in 1974), awarded for "a reference work of outstanding quality and significance."

Although the United States, the United Kingdom, and Australia have the largest number of authors (223, 63, and 50 respectively), these numbers primarily represent authors' institutional affiliation, not their country of origin. Important to recognize, however, is that thirty-one countries have one author each, ranging from Austria and Benin to the United Arab Emirates and Venezuela. Twenty-five countries can claim two or three authors, ranging from Belgium and Chile to Uganda and Ukraine. More needs to be done to advance the possibilities for exchange and collaboration on a global scale.

My final comments relate to the impact of technology on developing the encyclopedia and implications for its future. In the twenty-first century the encyclopedia is embedded electronically through a library subscription to a larger entity, the BFL. As of 2014, the online portal includes about eighty e-books from Berg, along with abstracts of journal articles from *Fashion Theory*, *Fashion Practice*, and *Textile*, a timeline, and a topical classification system. Kathryn Earle devised www.bergfashionlibrary.com as a searchable online system to encompass the field of dress and fashion. Her inspiration resulted from her prior work in the Modern Language Association as a bibliographer. Most likely the print copy will remain as a first and only edition, whereas the online version will allow new developments and ways of use over time. Oxford University Press, the distributor for the encyclopedia to the United States and Canada and globally for the BFL, has instituted a system of providing lesson plans related to their stable of published encyclopedias and urged us to follow suit with *The Encyclopedia of World Dress and Fashion*. We have begun this process and will continue to do so with as many topics possible: such as time periods within fashion history, street dress across the world, or other global topics of dress in relation to varied identity positions such as gender, ethnicity, nationality, and dress technologies. The online portal for the research and analysis of dress and fashion enables new ways of thinking about organizing courses and syllabi, and provides a dynamic approach to reach potential tens of thousands of users by encouraging interactivity.

Other developments are in store for fashion studies from the BFL site as it initiates a contribution of bibliography articles related to a specific discipline or topic for scholars and students who want to learn about an unfamiliar area. The first is "The Social Psychology of Dress" (Johnson and Lennon 2014). Other entries are: "The Aesthetics of Dress" (DeLong 2014), "The Anthropology of Dress and Fashion" (Hansen 2014), and "The History of Dress and Fashion" (Paoletti 2014). In light of the interdisciplinary scope of fashion studies, which can often feel overwhelming for students, it remains important to provide introductions to major ideas and concepts by highlighting the significant literature from which they emerge.

Other recent themes arising for the encyclopedia and BFL site relate to further exploration of fashion practices among varied cultural groups around the world. For example, modesty arises as a fashion issue for Muslim and Mormon women and girls, who develop distinct practices that often require complex negotiations and adaptations of the clothing styles offered in the mass market. Another focus is on developing entries that explore and document celebratory fashions for special occasions, such as the quinceañera, or varied cultural forms of wedding attire. More interest is also developing with regard to color preferences and choices, as well as interest in pursuing the senses of touch, smell, and hearing as they relate to dress practices.

These and new additions to the encyclopedia over time exemplify how the study of dress and fashion draws from methodologies across many disciplines, demonstrating how fashion studies, including developing ideas for research and teaching, is a collective, interdisciplinary endeavor. By using an open definition of dress that spans and invites participation across disciplines and locales, this encyclopedia project has made a firm beginning in encouraging fashion studies scholars to look and collaborate with others beyond their own disciplines, and encourages students to do so as well. Dress and fashion relate to everyday lives across the world and has extraordinary potential to draw attention to the many important issues that relate to the dressing of bodies and the fashioning of personal and sociocultural identities.

# Notes

1  Later the department name was changed to Human Environment and Design and the college name from Home Economics to Human Ecology.

2  The Goldstein Museum of Design (GMD) was initially named the Goldstein Gallery, when it was formed in 1976 as part of the Department of Design and continued when the Design and the Textiles and Clothing departments combined to become the Department of Design, Housing, and Apparel (DHA) in the College of Human Ecology in 1983. It became GMD when the College of Design was formed in 2006 with three units, DHA and the Departments of Architecture and Landscape Architecture.

3  As of 2015, the *Dress, Body, Culture* series has published over sixty titles. Additionally, a new Bloomsbury series, *Dress and Fashion Research* was started as an outlet for in-depth, specialized monographs on overlooked and new research approaches, with the first two titles published in 2014.

# References

Barnes, Ruth and Joanne B. Eicher, eds. 1992. *Dress and Gender: Making and Meaning in Cultural Context*. Oxford: Berg.

Bartlett, Djurdja. 2010. "Preface to East Europe, Russia, and the Caucasus." In *Encyclopedia of World Dress and Fashion, Volume 7*, edited by Djurdja Bartlett, xvii–xviii. New York: Oxford University Press.

Black, Sandy, Amy de la Haye, Agnes Rocamora, Regina Root, and Helen Thomas. 2013. *The Handbook of Fashion Studies*. London: Bloomsbury. doi: http://dx.doi.org.ezp1.lib.umn.edu/10.2752/BEWDF/EDch7006.

Blanco F., Jose. 2010. "Overview of Central America." In *Encyclopedia of World Dress and Fashion. Volume 2*, edited by Margot Schevill, 149–57. New York: Oxford University Press. doi: http://dx.doi.org.ezp1.lib.umn.edu/10.2752/BEWDF/EDch2021a.

Blumer, Herbert. 1968. "Fashion." In *The International Encyclopedia of Social Sciences, V*, edited by William Darity, 142. New York: Macmillan.

Buckridge, Steeve. 2010. "Overview of the Caribbean" and "Jamaica Nineteenth Century to Present." In *Encyclopedia of World Dress and Fashion, Volume 2*, edited by Margot Schevill, 247–50, 264–69. New York: Oxford University Press. doi: http://dx.doi.org.ezp1.lib.umn.edu/10.2752/BEWDF/EDch2040.

DeLong, Marilyn. 2014. "The Aesthetics of Dress." In *Berg Fashion Library.com.* doi: http://www.bergfashionlibrary.com.ezp1.lib.umn.edu/page/Aesthetics$0020of$0020Dress/aesthetics-of-dress.

Demidenko, Julia. 2010. "Soviet Underwear" and "Fashion Contest in the Soviet Union." In *Encyclopedia of World Dress and Fashion, Volume 9*, edited by Djurdja Bartlett, 366–68, 369–70. New York: Oxford University Press. doi: http://dx.doi.org.ezp1.lib.umn.edu/10.2752/BEWDF/EDch9069.

Eicher, Joanne B. ed. 1995. *Dress and Ethnicity: Change Across Space and Time.* Oxford: Berg Publishers.

Eicher, Joanne B. 2001. "Fashion of Dress." In *National Geographic Fashion*, edited by C. Newman, 17–23. Washington, DC: National Geography Society.

Eicher, Joanne B., ed. 2010. *Encyclopedia of World Dress and Fashion, Volumes 1–10.* New York: Oxford University Press.

Goswamy, B. N. 2010. "The Sash, Patka, or Kamarband." In *Encyclopedia of World Dress and Fashion, Volume 4*, edited by Jasleen Dhamija, 147–51. New York: Oxford University Press. doi: http://dx.doi.org.ezp1.lib.umn.edu/10.2752/BEWDF/EDch4019.

Hansen, Karen Tranberg. 2014. "The Anthropology of Dress and Fashion." In *Berg Fashion Library.com.* doi: http://www.bergfashionlibrary.com.ezp1.lib.umn.edu/page/Anthropology$0020of$0020Dress$0020and$0020Fashion/anthropology-of-dress-and-fashion.

Johnson, K. P., and Sharon Lennon. 2014. "The Social Psychology of Dress: A Bibliographic Guide." In *Berg Fashion Library.com*, accessed September 30, 2014, http://www.bergfashionlibrary.com/page/The%20Social%20Psychology%20of%20Dress.

King, Lindsay M., and Russell T. Clement. 2012. "Style and Substance: Fashion in Twenty-First Century Research Libraries." *Art Documentation: Journal of the Art Libraries Society of North America* 31 (1): 93–107.

Krody, Sumru Belgar. 2010. "Turkish Embroidery." In *Encyclopedia of World Dress and Fashion, Volume 5*, edited by Gillian Vogelsang-Eastwood, 121–25. New York: Oxford University Press. doi: http://dx.doi.org.ezp1.lib.umn.edu/10.2752/BEWDF/EDch5021.

Moeran, Brian. 2010. "Fragrances and Perfume." In *Encyclopedia of World Dress and Fashion, Volume 8*, edited by Lise Skov, 426–30. New York: Oxford University Press. doi: http://dx.doi.org.ezp1.lib.umn.edu/10.2752/BEWDF/EDch8070.

Mutnick, Nan and Phyllis Tortora. 2010. "Appendix: Timeline." In *Encyclopedia of World Dress and Fashion, Volume 10*, edited by Joanne B. Eicher, 319–34. New York: Oxford University Press. doi: http://dx.doi.org.ezp1.lib.umn.edu/10.2752/BEWDF/EDch10044.

Netti, Bruno, Ruth Stone, James Porter, and Timothy Rice, eds. 1998. *Garland Encyclopedia of World Music.* New York: Garland Publishers.

O'Neal, Gwendolyn. 2010. "African American." In *Encyclopedia of World Dress and Fashion, Volume 3*, edited by Phyllis Tortora, 536–45. New York: Oxford University Press. doi: http://dx.doi.org.ezp1.lib.umn.edu/10.2752/BEWDF/EDch3075.

Paoletti, Jo B. 2014. "Fashion, Dress, and Gender." In *Berg Fashion Library.com.* doi: http://www.bergfashionlibrary.com.ezp1.lib.umn.edu/page/Fashion$0020Dress$0020and$0020Gender/fashion-dress-and-gender.

Porter, Philip. 2010. "Climatic Zones and Cultural Regions." In *Encyclopedia of World Dress and Fashion, Volume 1*, edited by Joanne B. Eicher and Doran Ross, 10–16. New York: Oxford University Press. doi: http://dx.doi.org.ezp1.lib.umn.edu/10.2752/BEWDF/EDch1003.

Preece, Warren E., and Philip W. Goetz. 2009. *Encyclopedia Britannica.* 15th edn. Chicago: Encyclopedia Britannica, Inc.

Roach-Higgins, Mary Ellen and Joanne B. Eicher. 1965. *Dress, Adornment and the Social Order*. New York: John Wiley and Sons.

Roach-Higgins, Mary Ellen and Joanne B. Eicher. 1973. *The Visible Self: Perspectives on Dress*. Englewood Cliffs, NJ: Prentice-Hall.

Roach-Higgins, Mary Ellen and Joanne B. Eicher. 1992. "Dress and Identity." In *Clothing and Textiles Research Journal* 10 (4): 1–8.

Semmelhack, Elizabeth. 2010. "Footwear" and "Footbinding." In *Encyclopedia of World Dress and Fashion, Volume 6*, edited by John Vollmer, 99–105. New York: Oxford University Press. doi: http://dx.doi.org.ezp1.lib.umn.edu/10.2752/BEWDF/EDch6018.

Skov, Lise and Marie Riegels Melchior. 2010. "Research Approaches." In *Encyclopedia of World Dress and Fashion, Volume 10*, edited by Joanne B. Eicher, 11–16. New York: Oxford University Press. doi: http://dx.doi.org.ezp1.lib.umn.edu/10.2752/BEWDF/EDch10003.

Steele, Valerie. 1991. "The F Word." In *Lingua Franca: Journal of Academic Life* 1: 4.

Steele, Valerie, ed. 2005. *Encyclopedia of Clothing and Fashion*. Detroit: Thomson/Gale.

Styles, John. 2012. "Volume 8: West Europe." Special Supplement Berg Encyclopedia of World Dress and Fashion. *Fashion Theory*, edited by Peter McNeil, vol. 16, *Supplement*, S57–S62.

Tortora, Phyllis and Sara Marcketti. 2015. *Survey of the History of Western Dress*. New York: Fairchild Publications.

# INDEX